Leadership
FOR
DUMMIES®

by Dr John Marrin

WILEY

A John Wiley and Sons, Ltd, Publication

Leadership For Dummies®

Published by
John Wiley & Sons, Ltd
The Atrium
Southern Gate
Chichester
West Sussex
PO19 8SQ
England

Email (for orders and customer service enquires): cs-books@wiley.co.uk

Visit our Home Page on www.wileyeurope.com

British Library Cataloguing in Publication Data: A catalogue record for this book is available from the British Library.

ISBN: 978-0-470-97211-3 (paperback), 978-0-470-97435-3 (ebook), 978-0-470-97300-4 (ebook), 978-0-470-97301-1 (ebook)

Printed and bound in Great Britain by Bell and Bain Ltd

10 9 8 7 6 5 4 3 2 1

About the Author

Dr John Marrin is an expert on how leaders of organisations totally engage their directors, managers and employees to enhance their commitment and achieve higher levels of individual, team and business performance. He is a leadership coach and organisation development specialist to a wide range of clients including large multinationals, privately owned businesses and public sector organisations. While working primarily with organisations throughout the United Kingdom, John is also experienced in supporting clients in Europe and South America.

John is intensely enthusiastic about engaging people to work better together through enhancing mutual understanding and establishing shared commitment and accountability for achieving success: he redefined the meaning and practice of engaging through his DPhil. John is a Chartered Fellow of the Chartered Institute of Personnel and Development, and holds a Master of Arts in Management Learning from Lancaster University.

John is founder of Marwel & Co. which specialises in leadership development and employee engagement. To find out more about the services of Marwel & Co., visit his website: www.marwel-co.com. John's email address is jmarrin@marwel-co.com.

Dedication

I dedicate this book to my wife Linda, and my sons, Paul and David, who have given me the inspiration, encouragement and support to clarify and fulfil my vocation.

Author's Acknowledgements

My special thanks go to my wife and sons for putting up with seeing much less of me during the process of writing this book, and to my wider family and friends for their tolerance. You have all been much neglected, but not forgotten, for many months. I also want to acknowledge my parents, John and Vera, for encouraging me and instilling values that I continue to cherish.

Thanks to the team at Wiley, especially David Palmer for inviting me to write this book, to Rachael Chilvers for guiding and supporting me throughout the process, and to Andy Finch for helping me to clarify my thinking.

I thank my clients and colleagues for the opportunities to work and learn with you, and for the experiences that have eventually been distilled into the contents of this book.

Publisher's Acknowledgements

We're proud of this book; please send us your comments through our Dummies online registration form located at www.dummies.com/register/.

Some of the people who helped bring this book to market include the following:

Acquisitions, Editorial and Media Development

Project Editor: Rachael Chilvers

Development Editor: Andy Finch

Commissioning Editor: David Palmer

Technical Editor: Richard Pettinger, Business Management lecturer, UCL

Proofreader: Kim Vernon

Assistant Editor: Ben Kemble

Production Manager: Daniel Mersey

Cover Photo: © Steve Hamblin / Alamy

Cartoons: Ed McLachlan

Composition Services

Project Coordinator: Kristie Rees

Layout and Graphics: Andrea Hornberger, Corrie Socolovitch

Proofreader: Laura Albert

Indexer: Claudia Bourbeau

Publishing and Editorial for Consumer Dummies

Diane Graves Steele, Vice President and Publisher, Consumer Dummies

Kristin Ferguson-Wagstaffe, Product Development Director, Consumer Dummies

Ensley Eikenburg, Associate Publisher, Travel

Kelly Regan, Editorial Director, Travel

Publishing for Technology Dummies

Andy Cummings, Vice President and Publisher, Dummies Technology/General User

Composition Services

Debbie Stailey, Director of Composition Services

Contents at a Glance

Table of Contents

Chapter 3: Leadership and Management: Two Sides of the Same Coin 41

Part II: Leading Yourself.. 59

Chapter 4: Leading 'Inside Out': Knowing Yourself to Become a Better Leader 61

Introduction

●●●

*L*eadership is something that you recognise when you see it and notice when you don't see it, and yet most people find it hard to articulate what leadership really *is*. I've written this book because I want to remove the mystique of leadership and enable you to ground leadership in your everyday work practice.

Every chapter in this book is designed to help you to understand different aspects of leadership and how to lead in different contexts and situations. The information you find within the covers of this book is grounded in the real world. This information is primarily distilled from my working with thousands of leaders in many different types of organisations, including owner-managed and public limited companies, public sector organisations and charities. I coached and mentored leaders, built high-performing work teams, worked through difficult leadership dilemmas and facilitated senior management teams to transform their organisations.

About This Book

Reading this book enables you to discover how to work on becoming the great leader you aspire to be (who aspires to be an average leader?). If you're new to the world of leadership, you can find all you need to succeed in your new position. If you're an experienced leader, I challenge you to turn the kaleidoscope, and look at your leadership philosophy and practice from a new perspective to identify what's working for you – and the people you lead – and what's not.

You can make the fastest progress in enhancing your leadership skills by putting what you learn into practice, and then reflecting on and learning more from your experiences.

Leadership in a work setting is all about engaging people and gaining their commitment to making a highly valued contribution to improving the performance and success of their organisation, and enable them to gain a real sense of fulfilment through doing so. Among the topics covered in this book are:

- ✔ How leading and managing people are different.
- ✔ How to gain the commitment of people who work for and with you.
- ✔ Why you have to start with leading yourself.

✔ How to succeed in leading people through change.

✔ How to increase your influence in your organisation.

✔ How to challenge people whose behaviour or performance doesn't meet your standards.

✔ How to lead different types of teams.

✔ How to build a great senior leadership team.

I do my best to explain these things, and much more, clearly and concisely. Now that you have an insight into the content of this book, I hope you're raring to go!

Conventions Used in This Book

To help you navigate through this book, I've set up a few conventions:

✔ *Italic* is used for emphasis and to highlight new words or terms that I define.

✔ **Boldfaced** text is used to highlight important text in lists.

✔ Monofont is used for web and email addresses.

Also, I use the term *organisation* quite loosely. I define an *organisation* as a group of people who have formally come together to achieve objectives. Many different types of organisations exist, including small owner-managed businesses, global public limited companies, charities, public sector organisations and so on. I use the term *organisation* (or sometimes *company*) to refer to the business, charity or whatever that you work for.

What You're Not to Read

I've written this book so that you can easily access and understand what you want to find out about leadership in a work context. I've made it easy for you to identify material that you don't absolutely have to read. This information is interesting stuff, and you can benefit from it, but it isn't essential for you to know:

✔ **Text in sidebars:** The sidebars are shaded boxes that share interesting stories about real life examples to illustrate points made elsewhere in the text, but you can skip them if you wish.

✔ **The stuff on the copyright page:** You'll find nothing here of value unless you're looking for legal notices and reprint information! If you are, then this is the place to look.

Foolish Assumptions

I wrote this book assuming some things about you:

- ✔ You're enthusiastic about developing your leadership ability.
- ✔ You want to improve your own and others' performance.
- ✔ You've some experience of leadership through coming into contact with good or bad leaders, or through the position you currently hold in your organisation or positions you've held in the past.
- ✔ You want to know what works. While you want to understand key concepts about leadership, you're more interested in a pragmatic and practical approach to becoming the leader you aspire to be.
- ✔ You like discovering *why* as well as *what*. That is, you want to know *why* people typically do what they do at work rather than just knowing *what* they do.
- ✔ You want to make a positive difference and contribution to the organisation you work for and the people you work with.

How This Book Is Organised

I've organised this book into six parts to make the material easier to understand and access by keeping related material together. Each part is broken down into chapters, and the table of contents gives you details on each chapter.

Part 1: Introducing Leadership

In this part, I provide an overview of leadership and explain the words and phrases you typically encounter in talking and reading about leadership. You discover how to come up with a definition of leadership that really works for you, and start to identify your own leadership strengths and development needs. You also find the key differences between leading and managing people in this part.

Part 11: Leading Yourself

This part focuses on you. I introduce you to the notion of being an authentic leader, and explain why working on leading yourself is critical to becoming the leader you aspire to be. You find out how to identify the values that are really important to you and how these may impact on how you lead people.

You discover how to learn more about leadership from reflecting on your experiences, and how to handle the dilemmas you may experience in stepping up to a leadership position.

Part III: Leading Others

To be a successful leader, others have to choose to follow you. I explain how you can really engage people so that they give you their commitment: they put all the effort, knowledge, expertise, and skills they have into doing a great job rather than just being compliant. You find out about leadership styles and how to choose the most appropriate style for different situations. I emphasise why you have to consciously set the standards that you expect people to work to, and you discover how to effectively challenge people who don't meet your standards.

Part IV: Leading People Through Change

In this part, I explain why many people don't like change, and you find out how to be a change agent. I introduce you to approaches to implementing change in teams and organisations that enable people to embrace change. You also find techniques for embedding new ways of working, and how to prevent people from slipping back into old habits.

Part V: Leading Different Types of Team

This part is where you find out about different types of teams that you may have to lead, and the challenges that you may experience. You discover the characteristics that separate great teams from good ones, and how you can build a high-performing team. I provide tips on how to create a senior leadership team that's a great role model for everyone in the organisation.

Part VI: The Part of Tens

When you're looking for a quick reminder of good leadership practice or a bit of inspiration, you can find it here. This part directs you to ten tips on taking the lead, leading yourself and leading people.

Icons Used in This Book

The icons in this book point out particular kinds of information that you may find useful. Here's an explanation of what each icon stands for:

Take particular notice of the text next to this icon because it provides advice on how to become an exceptional leader.

This icon is a friendly reminder of important points to take note of.

This icon highlights practical advice that you can use to lead people in a wide range of work situations.

This icon highlights real-life stories about leadership that I hope you find inspiring or useful.

Discover exercises to help you to explore leadership next to this icon.

Watch out! If you don't heed the advice next to this icon, you may end up facing a worse situation.

Where to Go from Here

You don't have to read this book from cover to cover as you can get most benefit from it by going though it in the order and at a pace that's right for you. I organise the contents of this book to enable *you* to take the lead. You can take a structured, sequential approach or read the chapters in any order; immediately diving into a section to find out what you need to know to deal with a situation or problem you're experiencing.

Use the table of contents to see what you're attracted to first. For example, if you want to improve your understanding of leadership, go to Chapter 2. Or if you'd like to hone your skills in encouraging people to work to your standards turn to Chapter 11.

Regardless of how you work your way through *Leadership For Dummies*, I'm sure that you'll become the great leader you aspire to be. I'm enthusiastic about helping people to become great leaders so if you've any specific questions or comments, please feel free to visit my website at `www.marwel-co.com`.

Here's to your ongoing success!

Part I
Introducing Leadership

'So you think you were born to be
a leader, Mauleverer?'

In this part . . .

The chapters in this part help you to acquire an understanding of leadership and start to lay the foundations for you becoming the great leader you aspire to be. I introduce you to common language used in practising leadership and in management literature, and guide you to see the key differences between leading and managing. You can use these chapters to work on clarifying your expectations of yourself and others as leaders.

Chapter 1

Taking the Lead

*L*eadership is common sense; but unfortunately not always common practice. With the right information gleaned from my experience of working closely with thousands of managers, and some practice and thought on your part, leading can become as natural as riding a bike (even if you do experience a few wobbles along the way)!

If you couple your common sense to this book's numerous tips, prompts, guidelines, memory joggers and even (dare I say it) pearls of wisdom, you can become the great leader you aspire to be. You can literally get your ducks in a row – just like on the front cover – reflected by your staff wanting to follow you without you having to look behind to check whether they're still there. Carry out the exercises and implement the advice throughout the book, and you can turn effective leadership into your personal common practice.

In this chapter, I describe the importance of leaders, how and why you should step up to become a leader and how to lead different teams and implement workplace change successfully.

Appreciating Why the Work of Leaders Isn't Easy

Why is effective leadership not more often put into practice? Well, too many managers don't demonstrate great leadership because they don't think enough about the situation that they and their people are in: they rush in and get things wrong or fail to act when people are looking for leadership. You've probably all too often experienced situations in which you get too much, too little or the wrong type of leadership.

Leaders can have too much or too little presence!

In defence of leaders, although leadership is common sense, leading people isn't easy. People are complex and have different needs, motives, abilities and expectations. Human flexibility and adaptability are great strengths, but people can also be unpredictable and changeable: their moods may alter, reflecting whether they're happy, sad, enthusiastic, angry or depressed. People's emotional states affect their approach to work and their performance at work.

Part of your role as a leader is to get the best from people who work for and with you; you have to consider all these issues in deciding how best to lead individuals and teams.

Leaders also have to champion and look after the needs of their organisation whether it's a business, charity, public sector service or whatever. You have to enthuse about and promote the purpose and objectives of your organisation, department and/or team (depending on your position), the products or services you and your team provide, reconcile differences in priorities between your team and other teams, and so on.

Bearing these challenges in mind, leadership is difficult!

You may not know how to handle the leadership dilemmas that these and many other challenges throw up for you, and that's probably why you bought this book! In this chapter, you find out more about the challenges and opportunities of being a leader – and discover insights into how to address the problems. I also provide directions to other relevant chapters that allow you to explore leadership in depth.

Looking for Leadership . . . and Leaders

Life in general, and especially in the workplace, seems to be becoming more uncertain and complex for most people. The old adage of 'a job for life' no longer applies to most people as private and public-sector organisations change, downsize and merge.

In such uncertain times people look for leadership and leaders, but don't always find what they need. This section helps you to discover more about the typical situations being experienced by thousands if not millions of workers every day, and why people are looking for leadership and leaders.

Cooking the stew rather than being in one!

Many people become anxious or agitated when they experience workplace complexity and uncertainty: they are, as we say, 'in a bit of a stew'. People can be mixed up, het up, cut up, or shut up when they're in a stew! Here are some of the more common work situations in which people experience getting in a stew, and how being in a stew affects them:

✔ **Too much work to do:** Such as when a company's sales order book is bursting at the seams. The pressure to satisfy customer demand pushes capacity, systems and people to their limits causing mistakes and problems.

✔ **Too little work to do:** Such as when a company's sales order book is getting empty. When people have too little work to do over long periods, they start worrying about when the next big order is coming.

✔ **Too few people to do the work:** Such as when a company is growing quickly and can't recruit the right people or following people being made redundant due to the company cutting costs. When people have too much work to do over long periods of time they struggle to cope, become exhausted or even 'burn out'.

✔ **Too many people to do the work:** Such as following a merger between two companies. People are concerned or worried about their job security and meeting their personal financial commitments.

✔ **Too many system or structural changes:** Such as people suffering from initiative overload and becoming confused about what they should be doing and how they should be working.

✔ **Too few system or process changes:** Such as people struggling to complete their work due to outdated and archaic systems not providing them with the right information at the right time to do their job well.

People look for leadership and leaders in these situations because they're searching for how to get out of the stew: they want to exert influence (to 'cook the stew' if you like, rather than drown in it) by contributing to overcoming the problems and difficulties. After all, they know about their own problems; they may even be experts in how to solve them!

I encourage you to demonstrate appropriate leadership in these situations whether doing so is your job or not. When people are looking for leaders, step forward and show leadership even when you're just one of the people experiencing the situation.

Find out more about stepping forward and demonstrating leadership in the later section 'Filling the vacuum with the right fluff (stuff)', and discover the purpose and meaning of leadership in Chapter 2.

Experiencing leadership . . . or perhaps not!

You know that feeling when you desperately need a taxi to get you to an important appointment or to get you home, and yet you can't find one? Well, you can experience the same frustration when you need a leader!

I suggest that when people want to see great leadership in turbulent times – such as during the current economic problems – they tend to get more management instead.

Please don't misunderstand me: I'm not saying that management itself is bad, because both effective leadership and management are necessary to run an organisation well; but too much management and not enough leadership isn't only bad, it can be a catastrophe! Jump into Chapter 3 to discover the most important aspects of and differences between leading and managing people.

One of the consequences of the economic downturn for many companies is that profits fall due to a drop in orders and margins are squeezed as competition for potential work increases. Faced with this situation, senior managers typically act to control expenditure more tightly by restricting decisions to spend money. They fail, however, to realise the following:

- ✔ Their greater emphasis on managing costs may undermine some of the values or principles on which they're running the company.
- ✔ Management of the company may increase at the expense of leadership!

Read the later sidebar 'Looking after the pennies rather than the pounds' for a typical example of over-managing and under-leading a company.

Looking after the pennies rather than the pounds

The directors of a manufacturing firm had to make difficult decisions when the company experienced a big downturn in the market. As orders dried up and expenditure was running too high for the level of sales, decisions were made to reduce costs by making employees redundant and introducing tighter controls on expenditure.

The directors informed all managers that all decisions involving more than a few pounds

expenditure had to be agreed with the relevant director before the decision could be taken and actioned. As a result, almost all decisions involving overtime, overseas travel and so on had to be referred up to director level.

Many managers thought that directors were 'penny pinching' but, worse still, interpreted the actions of the directors to mean that they, the managers, couldn't be trusted to make the right decision on expenditure. Managers also thought that their credibility with their staff was undermined because they were unable to make decisions quickly due to having to involve their director in making decisions.

In the months before this situation, the directors had been emphasising that they wanted to empower managers and expected them to show more leadership of their teams. Managers interpreted directors' actions on managing expenditure more tightly as disempowering rather than empowering them. At a time when managers looked for leadership from directors through directors trusting them to look after the interests of the business, all they got was more management. 'Look after the pennies (yourself) rather than trust other leaders to look after the pounds' was perceived to be the new motto of directors!

Seeing Yourself as a Leader

Like everyone you work with, you have the potential to be a great leader by having a positive influence on the way people around you think, feel and act. I'm sure that you've already demonstrated leadership ability if you take time to think about it. Complete the following exercise and recognise that you've already been a leader.

Take a few minutes to think about and write brief notes on one or more of the following scenarios in a notebook. These scenarios may have occurred in any aspect of your life: at home, education, work and so on:

- ✔ I was really enthusiastic about something, and someone caught or was infected by my enthusiasm.

- ✔ I stood up for something or someone I believed in when it or the person was being wrongly criticised.

- ✔ I did something that I knew was right to do when I doubted my ability to do it.

- ✔ I helped someone to understand the difference between right and wrong.

- ✔ I influenced someone to raise his standards.

- ✔ I challenged someone who was behaving in an unacceptable way to change his behaviour.

Realising that you've already taken the lead in situations in the past helps you to be confident to step up and take the lead again.

Filling the vacuum with the right fluff (stuff)

Have you noticed that a vacuum forms when a manager doesn't demonstrate leadership? You may think that this question is peculiar because a vacuum is full of nothing, and how do you notice nothing forming?! Well, unlike toothache, you do notice some things when they're absent:

- ✔ Your team has no direction.
- ✔ Your team lacks energy and commitment, and people are apathetic.
- ✔ Decisions aren't made and problems don't get solved.
- ✔ High standards don't exist.
- ✔ Things generally don't get better.

When the above situations occur, you may catch your colleagues looking around for someone to do something: people are waiting to be led!

Step forward and fill the vacuum – instead of wasting your time looking for leadership – by doing the following:

- ✔ Reflect on past occasions when you demonstrated leadership; you took the lead then and you can do so now!
- ✔ Listen to your colleagues' moans and groans; they give you a clue to what they think needs to be done, but don't let any negativity dampen your enthusiasm and commitment to improving the situation.
- ✔ Approach your manager about what you think needs to be done; if you're not sure, use your common sense! Work with your manager rather than undermine him.
- ✔ Stay upbeat and positive because your enthusiasm rubs off on colleagues who then want to support you to improve things.

Check out Chapter 4 to find out how to develop your self-confidence to fill leadership vacuums.

Transforming starts with you

Many years – or was it eons? – ago, I used to think that developing leaders primarily involved focusing leaders on how to get the best from their followers. All leaders needed to learn, I thought, was how to get followers to follow them!

Leading people starts with leading yourself; you have to look inwards at yourself before you look outwards towards the people you work with.

The main reason for my change in viewpoint and practice is that I believe that, like every leader, you need really to know and understand yourself. For example, you need to identify:

- ✔ The values that are important to you, because these influence the standards you set for yourself and other people.

- ✔ Your motives, assumptions and mindset, and appreciate how they affect the way you think, feel and act.

- ✔ How your behaviour is likely to impact on others and how they interact with you as their leader.

Don't worry that you're not yet the finished (leadership) article: all leaders are a 'work in progress' because they never stop encountering new situations, dilemmas and challenges.

Take a look at the later section 'Knowing what you're about' to find out what 'understanding yourself' means in practice, or dive into Chapters 4 and 5 if you can't wait to start working on yourself to become the leader you aspire to be.

Rising to all leadership occasions

Although the first occasion in which you need to rise to being a leader is your first appointment to a leadership position, more opportunities exist for you to rise to the occasion than you may imagine – so you've no excuse for not becoming a great leader! (If you're a new leader and in a hurry to discover how to survive being thrown in the deep end, avoid being seen as an 'imposter', succeed in leading your friends and much, much more, read Chapter 6 now.)

These occasions enable you to practise, fine-tune and hone your skills in leading people. Opportunities are lurking around every corner: for example, in team meetings, project meetings, performance and work reviews, reporting procedures, visits to customers and suppliers, informal conversations in corridors and chats with colleagues down the pub.

You have opportunities to show leadership when you're dissatisfied with the standard of work, or with colleagues' performance or behaviour such as their timekeeping or behaviour in meetings.

I take a look here specifically at meetings, to help you spot opportunities for taking the lead. You've probably sat in meetings in which:

- ✔ The meeting started late due to people waiting for someone to arrive.
- ✔ The conversation drifted off the subject.
- ✔ Subjects or issues were discussed but no decisions were made.
- ✔ Decisions were made but it wasn't clear who would take action.
- ✔ Deadlines weren't set for actions to be taken.
- ✔ People weren't held accountable for taking actions that had been agreed at previous meetings.

No doubt you've also heard colleagues (outside of the meeting) moaning to each other about how badly a meeting was run, even though they didn't raise the point in the meeting.

Every meeting in which you experience one or more of the above instances is an opportunity to show leadership by positively influencing the way your work colleagues think, feel and act in the meeting.

Take the lead in encouraging your colleagues to examine and improve the effectiveness of meetings by doing one or more of the following:

- ✔ Always demonstrating good practice in meetings.
- ✔ Pointing out – constructively – when any of the items in the previous list occur and, if necessary, how the instance influences the effectiveness of the meeting.
- ✔ Inviting colleagues at the start of the meeting to share their expectations regarding how they want to work together for the meeting to be productive.
- ✔ Asking colleagues to review how effective the meeting was with regard to achieving the purpose or objectives of the meeting.

Give yourself permission to take the lead and seize the moment to practise honing your leadership skills. Always act with integrity by showing that you have a genuine interest in your colleagues and are working with them to bring about changes for everyone's benefit, to avoid them thinking that you're just promoting yourself or acting in your own self-interest.

Seizing opportunities also enables you to expand your sphere of influence in your organisation. You find out more about how to expand your sphere of influence in Chapter 7.

Leading People and Teams

Loads of people look to you for leadership: everyone who reports to you, your boss, your customers (inside or outside your organisation), members of your project team if you have one and so on. For you to cope with the different expectations, and perhaps demands, of all these people and demonstrate great leadership you have to get a few key things clear. In this section you discover what these are and where you can find more about them in this book to enable you to work on becoming a great leader.

Knowing what you're about

Your boss and your team expect you to know what you're about! If you don't know, your colleagues are going to find out that you don't know sooner or later. You need to be clear about the following:

- **Your team's purpose and direction:** To avoid being seen as a 'wanderer' who's unsure about where you're taking the team.

- **What you expect your team to achieve:** To avoid being seen as an unfocused 'squanderer' who wastes your own and others' time on the wrong priorities.

- **The values that are important to you:** To avoid being seen as a 'ponderer' who's indecisive about the standards you expect from people.

I mention in the earlier section 'Transforming starts with you' that leading people starts with leading yourself, but what does this mean in practice?

Leading yourself means finding out about yourself and then putting your increased self-knowledge to good use.

One of the dangers of not being aware of your own tendencies and biases is that you can end up adopting inappropriate approaches to leading people based upon whether you do or don't believe that people are generally trustworthy.

When you believe that people are generally trustworthy, you expect them to be reliable and do a good job. You're therefore likely to give people a lot of autonomy over how they do their work, and adopt a light-handed approach to monitoring them and their work. In comparison, when you believe people to be generally untrustworthy, you closely monitor and check up on them, and even question them more thoroughly about how they're spending their time.

The two different views about people's trustworthiness reflect two different approaches to leadership: each approach has a significantly different impact on how people work for their leader depending upon whether people like to be micro-managed or not! Be aware of your own tendencies and preferences, and their implications on your approach to leading people. Choose the appropriate approach based on your assessment of each situation including whether or not your staff have the skills and commitment to work autonomously.

Increase your self-knowledge by clarifying your values and questioning your beliefs, assumptions and so on, and use your increased knowledge to gain valuable insights into any potential implications for how you lead people. Go to Chapter 5 to discover how to clarify your values and question your assumptions, and dip into Chapter 4 to discover how developing your skills in reflecting can help you to increase your self-awareness and self-knowledge.

Work through Chapter 7 to clarify the purpose of your job and your team, the objectives you want to achieve and tips for how to be a high performer through achieving your objectives.

Increasing your self-knowledge enables you to be authentic: the people who work with and for you respect you when they perceive you as being genuine, especially when you act with integrity and have a genuine interest in them.

Engaging people in work and change

You may be satisfied if your team comply with what you want them to do, but I challenge whether you're setting your sights high enough if your aim is only for people to be compliant. People who are committed do more: they, as Americans tend to say, 'go the extra mile'!

If you're fortunate enough to have bags of charisma and staff are throwing themselves at your feet wanting to please you, you're already experiencing colleagues 'going the extra mile'! If you don't have to climb over bodies all the time, you may still gain the commitment of, at least, some people by enthusing or inspiring them.

Everyone knows that you can catch (and transmit) bugs and germs off (and to) other people: I propose that you can also catch and transmit energy or enthusiasm. Have you ever been in a group of lethargic or negative people and felt your energy draining from you, or been in the company of someone who was enthusiastic and bubbly and felt enthused or uplifted? Then you've experienced people being infected by other people's energy.

As well as being enthused or inspired by relating to a positive enthusiastic person, people can also become enthused about an idea, purpose, objective or task that resonates with them. Such items can become so meaningful, important and worthwhile that people commit to them.

Gain the commitment of every member of your team to do the team's work and achieve its objectives by doing the following:

- ✔ Inspiring them by being positive and enthusiastic so that your enthusiasm rubs off on team members.

- ✔ Advocating the importance of your team's work – its purpose – and the objectives that your team have to achieve to contribute to your organisation's success.

- ✔ Engaging team members in meaningful conversations so that everyone is involved in enhancing each other's understanding and commitment to work better together towards achieving their objectives.

Discover the power of engaging leadership in Chapter 8, and how to become an engaging leader in Chapter 9.

One of the biggest challenges as a leader is leading people through an organisational change such as a restructure, change in systems and so on. This is because most people don't like, and react badly to, change especially if they feel that changes in the workplace are being imposed on them . . . and they may then take out their frustrations and anger on you! You may think that this reaction is unfair, especially when you have to implement changes with which you disagree!

If you want to improve your staff's behaviour or performance, and sustain that improvement, you need to be skilled in engaging people in order to gain their commitment to workplace change. If you get only their compliance, their performance may eventually deteriorate. Chapter 11 explains how to lead and coach people to achieve and sustain peak levels of performance. In addition, you can discover the need to develop a range of different leadership styles and how to modify your style to encourage people to change in different situations in Chapter 10.

Strive to have a big positive influence on the people you lead during periods of change because people are always looking to you, watching you and how you react to change. Dive into Chapter 12 to uncover how to be a 'change agent' rather than a victim of change.

If you're about to implement a change into your workplace or are currently consumed by problems with introducing changes, turn to Chapters 13 and 14 for guidance. I provide lots of tips on how to lead and implement change successfully, and how to be successful in sustaining such changes.

Leading all types of teams

Success in all organisations depends on teamwork because almost all work is now done in teams. (You can test this notion yourself by thinking about whether achieving success in your job is solely dependent on you and what you do.) Not only have teams proliferated in organisations over the last few decades, but they've also evolved into many different types – project, permanent, temporary and virtual teams – with each type posing different challenges, opportunities and problems for you as a team leader.

For example, project team leaders have the particular challenges of leading team members who belong to more than one team and so have multiple commitments. You discover how to handle this and other challenges in leading project teams in Chapter 16.

A project team can also be a virtual team with members rarely if ever meeting in person because they're scattered over large geographical areas, perhaps over different continents. Chapter 17 describes some of the typical hurdles facing you when leading a virtual team and provides tips on how to handle these challenges.

Whatever the nature of your team, make sure that you build it around the key characteristics shared by all great teams (dip into Chapter 15 to discover these attributes). Enjoy the wide range of roles you have to play – even if you find them challenging – in ensuring that your team is a high-performing one, for example:

- **Advocate:** Promoting your team's purpose and objectives to people within and outside your team, as well as enthusiastically promoting your company and its services or products to your customers.
- **Standard bearer:** Upholding and reinforcing your team's values and standards of behaviour and performance.
- **Cheerleader:** Encouraging and supporting your team to do well, and recognising success.
- **Facilitator:** Engaging team members in meaningful conversations to enhance understanding, make decisions, build commitment and solve problems.
- **'Agony aunt':** Acting as confidant to help individual team members with personal issues.

You can encourage team members to share responsibility and accountability for the team's success by involving them in assessing their team's effectiveness, and continually improving how well team members work together and how the team performs. Chapter 15 shows you how to conduct team self-assessments and engage team members in striving continually to improve performance.

Excelling in leading your senior leadership team

How you lead your senior team is crucial to how your whole organisation works (as well as to the performance of the senior team itself) because your senior leadership team is a role model for the entire organisation: middle managers are looking to and taking a lead from directors, and junior managers are looking to and taking a lead from middle managers.

As leader, you're the living, breathing, walking example of how you want your employees to be! You're constantly leading by example: promoting what you stand for, believe in and expect from others through your everyday actions and behaviours such as:

✔ What you pay attention to, for example, standards of behaviour, performance measures and key performance indicators.

✔ How you react or don't react to problems, failures and breaches of standards.

✔ How you allocate rewards, who you promote and why.

People are looking to you and taking more notice of what you do than what you say! Demonstrate excellence to promote excellence.

Encourage your senior leaders to take collective responsibility for the success of the organisation as well as the success of their own departments, especially if you notice that they have a parochial view of success (a 'silo' mentality). Chapter 18 describes helping senior managers out of this problem.

The highest performing (senior leadership) teams in my experience also encourage and value diversity: different perspectives, ways of thinking, ideas and so on. Team members have found out how to engage each other effectively to overcome the difficulties that may be experienced when confident, often strong, characters in the team have different views and opinions.

These members recognise that becoming skilled in engaging each other improves decision-making, problem-solving, commitment to act and accountability in their team. You can discover how to enhance your own and your senior leaders' skills in effectively engaging each other in Chapters 9 and 18.

Chapter 2

Pinning Down the Meaning of Leadership

. . . .

In This Chapter

▶ Understanding the differences between leadership, leading and being a leader

▶ Exploring leadership concepts

▶ Knowing what it takes to be an engaging leader

▶ Deciding what leadership means for you

. . . .

*Y*ou may find that the more you try to capture what leadership means, the more that meaning seems to slip through your grasp. So many people are writing so much about leadership that you may become confused when searching for a description of leadership that you can understand and put to use successfully.

Don't worry. In this chapter I guide you through the language of leadership and explain the differences between leadership, leading and being a leader. You also discover a few popular concepts of leadership, as I lead you (no pun intended!) through the fog of leadership writing so that you can pin down a meaning that works for you.

The main reason for pinning down the meaning of leadership in this way is so that you understand what's expected of you as a leader – that is, what you expect of yourself and what others may expect of you – and then put this knowledge and understanding into practice. Then you can work progressively on becoming the great leader that you aspire to be.

Spotting the Differences between Leadership, Leading and Leader

When I last searched for the meaning of leadership on the Internet by typing 'What is leadership?' into the search engine, I was presented with almost four million results! The huge amount of writing on leadership reflects the incredible interest in this topic and the lack of any universal agreement on what leadership means and what great leadership looks like.

My own experience of working with leaders reflects this wide range of views on leadership. When asked to describe what leadership means to them, all the managing directors and chief executives I've worked with give their own unique description of leadership, in which they emphasise the aspects of leadership that are important to them.

In this section I guide you through the haze that is the numerous descriptions of leadership and clarify the differences between leadership, leading and being a leader.

Leadership is a process

Leadership is a process: not only a process that goes on *between* you (the leader) and the people who report to you (your staff), but also one that *includes* you and them in the sense that you all influence, and are influenced by, the process.

How you and your staff think, feel and act affects, and is affected by, your experiences of each other. Therefore, those you lead aren't passive in this process.

This description recognises that leadership is a dynamic, complex process that's also ongoing: the way that you and your followers affect each other is influenced by your previous experiences of, for example, working together as well as by your current experiences of working with each other.

So does leadership simply describe the spontaneous exchanges – the actions and reactions – that occur between a leader and followers? The answer is, of course, no! To explore the concept of leadership further, I now consider the view that a leader is (surprisingly!) someone who's in the lead.

Traditionally, a leader is recognised as someone who's at the front or ahead of a group. Being ahead in a work context can mean, for instance, being ahead of others in thinking about an issue, such as for the leader to have thought through and understood the goals and objectives that have to be achieved by the group (team, department or organisation) for that group to be successful. A group must know what's expected of them if they're to have any chance of succeeding.

Leaders also have to be able to bring members of the group with them. Leadership, therefore, in a work context is a process in which you as the leader involve members of your group in working towards the goals and objectives that you require them to achieve.

I believe, however, that this description of leadership is inadequate, because it implies that followers simply expect and are expected to carry out the work that their leader requires them to do to achieve the team's goals and objectives. In my experience, most people want to contribute to decisions that shape and help achieve their team's goals and objectives, and propose and take action that enables the group to succeed. I suggest, therefore, that leadership is a process in which you as the leader totally engage the people who report to you in their work so that they become committed and contribute fully to achieving the goals, objectives and tasks that have to be completed to enable the group to succeed.

This description also provides an insight into the purpose of leadership, which is to positively influence the way that people think, feel and act.

In a work context, the purpose of leadership is to influence positively how people think, feel and act so that they become committed to making a valuable contribution to achieving the objectives of their work team, department and organisation.

I encourage you to examine one of your experiences of leadership to appreciate how leadership is a process that affects those involved in it.

Take a few minutes to reflect on your experience of working with or being in the presence of someone you really admire as a leader. Use the prompts in Table 2-1 to make a few notes to describe briefly one recollection that you have of leadership.

This exercise helps you to discover how a leader and follower(s) have a positive effect on each other.

Table 2-1	Reflections on a Leadership Experience
The situation:	
What the leader did:	
The effect that this action had on my thinking, feelings and/or behaviour:	
How I responded:	
How I perceive my response affected the leader:	
How the leader subsequently treated me:	

Leading is an activity

Leading people is what leaders do! Leading is an activity or rather a wide range of activities that leaders perform. Leading isn't necessarily being busy: it isn't doing all or even most of the work, although leaders do have to do their fair share of the work. You have to 'pull your weight' to avoid losing credibility with your staff or engendering the sense that they're 'carrying you'!

As a leader you don't have to come up personally with the solutions to all the problems you and your team experience, but you're responsible for ensuring that decisions are made and that action is taken to solve problems. In leading your team, you need to involve them in contributing to the team's objectives by, for example, contributing to decision-making and taking action to implement those decisions.

I rush them in and I rush them out

I was asked to help a blue-chip company discover why their appraisal process wasn't working. The Human Resources Manager was concerned because the company used the appraisal process to demonstrate and reinforce to employees how important employees were to the company. The appraisal meetings were the only formal meetings where line managers had an in-depth conversation with every person who reported to them about their individual strengths and development needs, aspirations in the company and other issues important to each individual.

My approach to conducting the research involved examining the documentation and completed forms, but mainly talking to managers and employees about their experiences of the appraisal system. I was talking to a Production Manager at 5:45 a.m. one Friday (the only time he had free) when he said: 'I rush them in and I rush them out!' while he was describing how he managed the appraisal meetings. When I asked

him to explain, he said that he had to appraise over 40 people who reported to him within a two-week period, *and* keep five production lines running! He could only spend ten minutes on each appraisal meeting.

When I talked to some of the people who reported to the Production Manager, they described the appraisal process as a waste of time because he had already 'made up his mind' about each person and filled most of the form in before meeting each individual. A typical response was 'You're just told what he thinks!' I pointed out that every person has the right to add comments at the end of their appraisal form. A common reply was 'What's the point? Nothing will change.'

Employees' experiences of how their manger was using the appraisal process completely undermined the fundamental aim of the process, which was to enable people to feel valued. The credibility of the manager was also undermined!

When you lead people, be aware that you're also being seen to be a leader: your presence and what you pay attention to creates an effect or has an impact on people. Your staff note what you take notice of and what you ignore. For example, if you tell your staff that the quality of work they produce is important, but you then don't highlight their mistakes and errors to them (even if you're correcting the mistakes yourself), your staff are going to take less care in doing their work.

You're always being watched as a leader: and your team are taking more notice of what you do than what you say. Your actions are more important than your words, and for this reason you have to set the standard regarding all aspects of work. For example, if you emphasise to your staff that being on time for meetings is important, but you occasionally turn up late, don't be surprised when they start to think that being late for meetings is okay. Remember, you have to demonstrate the standards you expect of others.

Refer to the sidebar 'I rush them in and I rush them out' for an example of how the actions of one manager were more important to the people who reported to him than what he told them.

Being a leader can be a role and/or position

More leadership positions in organisations now include the term 'leader' in their job title. For example, you may have come across Team Leader or Customer Services Leader in your own organisation or in your dealings with people in other organisations. Senior Management Teams in many organisations are also changing their name to Senior Leadership Team to reinforce the importance of being a leader at the top of and within their organisation. This use of the term 'leader' in job titles emphasises the importance of leading people to the job holder and their staff.

You may think that having the term 'leader' in your job title entitles you to the right to lead people: surely your organisation must give you the authority to lead if you're expected to lead your staff! Even if the term 'leader' isn't mentioned in your job title, you may still be expected to lead staff because everyone in a management position is expected to lead the people who work for them.

This viewpoint is important because whether you think that you have the right to lead or not can affect how you lead. If you believe that your organisation gives you the right or authority to lead, you may adopt an approach to leading typified by you making decisions, giving instructions and expecting your team to carry them out. Alternatively, you may think that you have to earn the right to lead – that only the people who you're leading can give you this right – and adopt a more inclusive approach to leading your team.

My view is that a leader does have the authority associated with the position to request or instruct staff to do tasks that have to be undertaken to achieve the team's objectives (providing, of course, that the tasks comply with health and safety legislation). How a leader speaks to and treats a member of staff may affect whether that person is compliant or committed to doing the task they've been asked to do: to gain a person's commitment a leader has to earn the right to lead by, for example, treating that person with respect. (Dip into Chapter 3 to find more about earning the right to lead people.)

As well as being a position, being a leader is also a role that you can perform in almost any group situation: you don't have to be the appointed leader of the group to have a positive influence on how your colleagues think, feel and act in carrying out the work of the group. You can positively influence how your colleagues work together towards achieving the group's objectives in a number of ways including the following:

- Encouraging colleagues to follow a certain course of action.
- Proposing and promoting good ideas that help the group to solve problems.
- Recognising and praising one of your colleagues for doing a great job.
- Resolving differences that adversely affect how well colleagues work together.
- Volunteering to take the lead in ensuring that certain tasks are done.

Each of these actions is the work of a leader because of the positive effect it has on the group.

I'm sure that you've experienced many occasions when you, and others, have had the opportunity to take on the role of leader. One example is when you become aware that you're dissatisfied with how members of a group work together, and yet nobody steps forward and takes responsibility for improving how the group functions.

A common illustration of people not working well together is badly run meetings. Often, I notice that group members talk about a meeting that was badly organised and run – even to the extent that it was a complete waste of time – afterwards but not during the meeting. When this situation occurs, I suggest that no one is taking on the role of leader: people are simply sharing their disappointment or frustration.

Make sure that you notice when opportunities arise for you to take the lead: you can then seize each one to practise being a leader and develop your leadership ability, as well as enable your colleagues to work together better towards achieving the group's objectives. To help you to spot and seize these opportunities, check out Table 2-2, which provides the following:

- Two examples of opportunities.
- Suggestions on what you can do to take the lead.
- Descriptions of the potential benefits to the group of you taking action.

I leave space in the table for you to add your own opportunities for being a leader, noting the actions to take and subsequent benefits to the group.

Table 2-2	Seizing Opportunities for Taking the Lead	
Description of the Opportunity	*Actions to Take*	*Description of the Potential Benefits to the Group*
People are complaining about a meeting after the meeting.	Guide the group to question constructively the effectiveness of the meeting and agree actions to improve effectiveness at the next meeting.	Concerns about the meeting are aired and explored. Productivity of the meeting is improved.
You and, perhaps, others think that you don't get enough direction from your manager.	Propose priorities to your manager and ask for guidance about whether your proposals are correct.	You and others have a clearer description of work priorities. People spend time on the most valuable work.

Deciphering the Language of Leadership

The preceding section 'Spotting the Differences between Leadership, Leading and Leader' shows that several different concepts of leadership exist. Getting the various terms and ideas clear is necessary to avoid confusion and to help you build your own meaning of leadership. Whereas that section describes the basic terms of 'leadership', 'leading' and 'leader', here you discover more about the language on leadership. In addition, I take the opportunity to present an exercise on one of the core leadership terms: competence.

Diving into the soup of leadership jargon

Do you remember having alphabet soup as a child? You'd stir the soup to mix up the pasta letters and then try to make words out of the ones that rose to the surface. Diving into the mass of text on leadership reminds me of playing with my soup, because I have to strive to make sense of leadership from a combination of everything I've read about leadership and my own experiences.

No doubt your own experiences of leading and being led have shown you that leadership is a complex process. This complexity is also reflected in the numerous descriptions of leadership that exist in management literature. In the following list, I explain some of the more common terms used in writing about leadership that you're likely to encounter:

- **Competences.** Having competence is demonstrating the ability to do something. For you to be competent at something, you have to demonstrate that you can do it well: you have to use that skill in your everyday work. You may have a skill and not be competent because you don't fully utilise the skill! Your organisation may have invested a lot of time and effort in identifying and describing the leadership competences considered to be important in developing leaders in your organisation. One of the main attractions of competences is that they can be described as observable behaviours enabling organisations to describe what they expect their leaders to do. You can use competences to identify your leadership strengths and development needs via self-assessment and feedback from your colleagues. (Jump into the next section 'Sampling leadership competences' to experience using competences to identify your leadership strengths and development needs.)

- **Nature/nurture.** You may hear or be asked the question, 'Are leaders born or made?'. If you believe that people are born to be leaders (nature) rather than the fact that leadership can be developed (nurtured), you may as well put this book down because you're not going to find anything useful in it! I don't think this way, and nothing is going to persuade me otherwise.

- **Qualities/characteristics.** When you think about leaders who were (apparently) born to be leaders, you probably also think about the innate qualities and characteristics they possessed. One example is the 'bulldog' spirit associated with Sir Winston Churchill. You're likely to come across the personal quality of self-confidence when reading about leadership. One definition of *self-confidence* is having a belief in or trusting your own abilities: when you're confident in a situation, you believe you can cope with or handle any issues that arise during the situation.

  Like most ambitious managers, you want to enhance your self-confidence, especially during the early stages of your career. If you do, then, like me, you believe that rather than being an innate quality, self-confidence is something that can be developed.

- **Skills.** No doubt you want to develop your skills in leading people. Being skilled in, for example, influencing people –a skill typically associated with leading people – is having the ability to speak clearly and concisely, listen carefully, construct logical arguments and so on. You can develop your skills in leading people by practising just as you discovered how to ride a bike: by doing it rather than just talking about it. I encourage you to look for and seize opportunities to practise developing your skills in leading people (for more details, take a look at Table 2-2 in the earlier section 'Being a leader can be a role and/or position').

To be a successful leader, you need to continually develop yourself and your staff: your own and their positive qualities, relevant skills and competences. I take a more detailed look at the latter aspect in the next section.

Sampling leadership competences

You found out in the previous section that your organisation may have produced a list of leadership competences. Get hold of the list if one exists and use it to assess your leadership strengths. Complete the next exercise if your organisation hasn't produced such a list.

Table 2-3 illustrates a few examples of leadership competences that relate to being an effective leader. Complete the following exercise to experience how you can use competences to identify your leadership strengths and development needs:

1. Read the first competence and reflect on how you normally behave around the people who report to you at work and the effect you have on them with regard to this competence.

2. Rate yourself against this competence by choosing a number between 1 and 6. If you consider yourself to be highly competent, choose a score 5 or 6; if you think that you're poor with regard to this competence, choose a score 1 or 2. Choose 3 or 4 if you believe you're between these extremes.

3. Repeat steps 1 and 2 for the rest of the competences.

4. Write a few words that describe your leadership strengths and development needs based on your scores and reflections in completing this exercise.

Table 2-3   Assessing Yourself Against Leadership Competences

	Description of Competence	*I Rate Myself As*
1.	I inspire my staff by being enthusiastic and positive.	1 2 3 4 5 6
2.	I act to ensure that everyone fully understands the objectives and targets that we have to achieve.	1 2 3 4 5 6
3.	I encourage my staff to achieve high standards in everything we do.	1 2 3 4 5 6
4.	I gain the commitment of each person by enabling individuals to fulfil their needs by working towards the objectives we have to achieve.	1 2 3 4 5 6

	Description of Competence	I Rate Myself As
5.	I support and develop individuals to help them to fulfil their potential.	1 2 3 4 5 6
6.	I constructively challenge unacceptable behaviour and performance.	1 2 3 4 5 6
7.	I actively seek feedback from my staff about the effect I have on them.	1 2 3 4 5 6
8.	I encourage people to speak their mind and I consider what they say.	1 2 3 4 5 6
9.	I engage people in meaningful conversations to identify and solve problems.	1 2 3 4 5 6
10.	I challenge the status quo with the aim of continually improving the performance of my team.	1 2 3 4 5 6

I describe my main leadership strengths as follows:

I describe my main leadership development needs as follows:

The main advantage of competences – that they describe easily observable behaviours – is also a major limitation. After all, you can't describe every behaviour you expect a leader to demonstrate because the list would be a lot longer than your arm!

The best approach is to identify the few really important competences and then focus development activities on them: that is, the competences that make a significant contribution to improving the performance of leaders and their teams in the organisation.

Don't waste time trying to describe every last aspect of leadership and developing numerous competences within which the most important ones get lost. Instead, invest time in identifying and using the vital leadership competences that are going to make a significant contribution to your own and your staff's performance.

Sampling a Few Tasty Bits of Leadership

In this section you discover my own description of great leadership (focused around engagement) and two other models (active and serving) that resonate with my understanding.

Becoming an engaging leader

For me, leaders have to engage their staff so that they work together for the organisation's success. *Engaging leaders* need to aim to engage their staff to enhance mutual understanding and commitment to work better together towards achieving their objectives.

By being an engaging leader you:

- ✔ Achieve higher levels of performance and productivity for every person who reports to you and your whole team.

- ✔ Build a sense of team spirit that exceeds most people's experience of teamwork.

- ✔ Convey the purpose and direction of your team.

- ✔ Enable all people to find meaning in their work.

- ✔ Gain the commitment of all individuals through genuinely involving them in decisions and activities to achieve objectives.

- ✔ Have a positive influence on the way people who work for and with you think, feel and act.

- ✔ Tap into, and continually develop, the knowledge, skills and expertise of your whole team.

You can discover more on how to become an engaging leader in Part III, especially in Chapters 8 and 9. In addition, Chapters 4 and 5 help you to find out how to work on developing a better understanding of yourself, which assists you in leading others.

Research on employee engagement over recent years reinforces the importance of leaders becoming engaging leaders. This research indicates that all types of organisations are interested in employee engagement because the leaders of organisations recognise that they can increase productivity and gain a competitive advantage by effectively engaging their employees. The research also shows that how employees' line managers treat them has a huge impact on whether employees are really engaged in their work. For example:

✔ Most employees expect their line manager to seek and listen to their ideas and opinions.

✔ Most employees expect their line manager to show an interest in their well-being.

✔ Most employees expect opportunities to develop in their job.

✔ Most employees expect to be kept well informed about what's happening in their organisation.

Work hard at engaging your team to enhance mutual understanding and the commitment to work better together towards achieving objectives.

Being an active leader

Like virtually every leader I know, you're probably stretched in trying to get through your work. Your days are full and you're always on the go, always active! Take a moment to reflect on a typical day in your life as a leader and answer the next two questions:

What do you spend most of your time on during a typical day?

What grabs your attention?

Two main issues are likely to be high on your list:

✔ Getting the work done to achieve the results expected of you and your team.

✔ Handling difficulties and problems that you experience with individual members of your team in trying to get the work done.

You may well notice that these two issues compete for your time. You may feel that just being able to focus on getting the work done would be great, but that you have to spend some of your time dealing with a wide range of issues or problems that involve or are caused by your staff: both individual problems and problems between people.

As a leader, you're expected to achieve results through people, and expected to achieve those results today, tomorrow, next month, next year and onwards. In fact, you're required to do even more than that: you're expected to improve your own performance continuously as well as the performance of people who report to you. To be successful you have to:

- ✔ Focus yourself and others on completing the tasks that lead to achieving your objectives.

- ✔ Motivate and develop the capability of individuals, and resolve any behavioural and/or performance problems with them.

- ✔ Encourage, guide and support people to work together in teams and sort out any interpersonal issues or problems between team members.

And do much, much more besides! These three points describe the three aspects of, or roles in, a leadership model called *action-centred leadership*, as developed and made famous by John Adair. The roles – often described as overlapping and interdependent spheres in the model – are achieving the task, developing the individual, and building and maintaining the team. As a leader you need to focus your attention and effort on performing each of these roles depending on the situation: sometimes you have to focus more on the task, sometimes more on concerns and problems with individuals, and sometimes more on improving teamwork. You have to spend enough time on carrying out all three roles in doing your job.

Many leaders experience problems spending enough time on all three aspects of leadership. Like most of them, you probably think that you have to focus on the tasks that have to be completed first simply because tasks tend to have deadlines. If you do think this way, focusing on hitting work deadlines takes priority over spending time on developing the people who report to you and getting them to work better together in teams simply because the latter two aspects don't tend to have deadlines attached to them.

Try to see these three aspects of leadership as complementary rather than competing: instead of thinking which activity to do first, look for opportunities to do more than one at the same time. For example, when you have a meeting with your team to make decisions and organise how to do certain tasks, also seize the opportunity to spend a few minutes to review how effective the meeting has been: what went well and what can be improved? You develop your team effectively by recognising how the team performed well in the meeting and improve the productivity of the meeting and your team by acting on improvements suggested by team members.

You can do a simple check to see whether completing tasks tends to take priority over developing people. No doubt the organisation you work for has an appraisal process, or something similar, for reviewing the performance and development of employees. Question yourself and the managers you work with about whether:

✔ They hold the appraisal meetings to review their own performance at the appointed time.

✔ They hold the appraisal meetings they're expected to hold with their staff at the appointed time.

If managers hold appraisal meetings later than expected, or not at all, in the organisation you work for then completing work is taking priority over developing people. Don't fall into the trap of overly focusing on deadlines and neglecting the development of your staff.

Leading through serving others

You discover in the earlier section 'Becoming an Engaging Leader' that leaders have to engage their staff in ways that gain their commitment to work together towards achieving their objectives. (Flip to Chapters 8 and 9 for how to engage people effectively to unlock their commitment.) One important issue is that the extent to which you show a genuine interest in people affects their willingness to work for and with you. In my experience, when you demonstrate that you're genuinely interested in others, 99 per cent of them reciprocate and show an interest in helping you to achieve what you want.

A small step further than showing a genuine interest in others is serving others: viewing your leadership role as one of serving the people who report to, and also work with, you. This approach reflects Robert Greenleaf's description of *servant leadership*, in which he explains that leaders need to focus on the needs and concerns of followers, and care for and nurture their staff.

Some managers may think that serving others tips their organisation's hierarchy upside down, as the emphasis shifts to leaders serving the people directly under them instead of simply expecting their staff to do what the leader wants them to do.

But you don't have to give people everything they want to serve them. For example, you don't have to allow a person to go home early when a crucial job must be completed by a deadline. You're not really looking after people's interests by allowing them to leave early if you subsequently fail to complete a job that results in poor customer service or loss of income for your organisation, which then undermines long-term job security.

Showing a genuine interest in someone to the extent of serving them in this context means that you:

✔ Are actively interested in helping them to fulfil their needs, achieve their aspirations and work through their concerns.

✔ Care about their work security and long-term employability.

✔ Display that you're genuinely interested in them as individuals.

✔ Value them for who they are rather than only what they can do for you.

Reflect on occasions when you showed a genuine interest in someone – you may even have felt you were serving them – perhaps when you put yourself out to help a work colleague or someone in your social life:

1. Get a notebook and divide the pages into four columns as shown in Table 2-4.

2. Write a few words that describe the first occasion in the first column.

3. Note the actions through which you helped or served the person in the second column.

4. Describe the outcome in the third column.

5. Note how the person subsequently responded towards you in the last column.

6. When you've completed this exercise and reflected on your experiences, consider what you now think about the relevance and/or importance of leaders serving others.

Table 2-4   Reflections on Showing a Genuine Interest in Someone

Brief Description of Each Scenario	Action to Help or Serve the Person	Description of Outcome	How the Person Responded

Coming Up with a Meaning that Works for You

I explore the more common concepts of leadership in this chapter so that you can understand leadership and come up with your own meaningful description. Getting a clear understanding of the purpose of leadership allows you to:

✔ Use your understanding to guide your actions as a leader.

✔ Convey to others what you're attempting to achieve as a leader.

✔ Explain to others what you expect from your leaders.

You can, of course, choose one of the descriptions I share with you in this chapter or take the most appealing parts and add your own. Alternatively, you can answer the following questions to come up with your own meaning:

✔ What is the purpose of leadership?

✔ What is my approach to leadership?

✔ What does leadership mean to me?

Chapter 3

Leadership and Management: Two Sides of the Same Coin

· ·

In This Chapter

▶ Making sense of your experiences of being led and managed

▶ Getting to grips with changing leadership and management roles

▶ Appreciating the key differences between leading and managing

▶ Earning the right to lead

· ·

Some people strongly argue that 'leadership' and 'management' are different practices, whereas others see them as simply different aspects of the same thing. Although many boffins may think otherwise, this question is far too important to leave to academics – after all, leadership and management are part of everyday life!

So, what do you think? Don't worry if you're unsure about how to answer this question at the moment, after reading the guidance and information I provide in this chapter, your answer will be as clear as the nose on your face. For now, however, take the hint from the chapter title: I see leadership and management as two complementary aspects of the same overall discipline.

In this chapter, I help you sort through the maze of your personal experiences of being led and managed, so that you can distil your thinking and decide on how you view leadership and management. You get to compare your significant experiences with the information I provide and by doing so clarify what leadership and management involves, what you expect of leaders – yourself and those leading you – and the key differences between the two practices.

In addition, you can use the outcomes from the exercises in this chapter to develop your leadership ability when working on Part II, 'Leading Yourself'.

Flipping Through Your Experiences of Leadership and Management

Ever since you were a baby you've been experiencing leadership and management, although you weren't conscious of doing so then! As a small child, no doubt you started to notice aspects of leadership and management as regards how you were brought up – and you won't have enjoyed all of those experiences because, for example, you didn't always get what you wanted. These early insights are significant in developing your personal idea of leaders and managers.

Your parents or guardians were leading and managing you through your childhood and adolescence, and even into your adult life if they're anything like my mother! (She told me, virtually every time we met, that I was working too hard and advised me to slow down.) For example, by instilling certain values in you and getting you to school on time, your parents were leading and managing you.

In this section, I help you to think about your own experiences of being led and managed, so that you clarify your expectations and are able to utilise the insights you gain in working more effectively with your own leaders and the people you lead.

Choosing and working with a new boss

Your experiences of leadership and management that start with your parents continue into your working life. The experiences you have are likely to impact heavily on your ideas of these practices and what makes a good and bad leader or manager.

The chances of you getting a great or an awful boss when you move into a new job in a new organisation are probably 50/50: discovering that you now work for a great boss may as well depend on the flip of a coin. Normally, you find out about the job, and perhaps the company, when you make an initial application for a position: I can't think of any job advertisement or circular that proclaims that 'you'll be working for a great boss' or tells you anything about the person who'll be managing you!

Unlike the applicants on *The Apprentice* TV programme, you don't get much of a chance to see your potential boss in action when you apply for a job. Usually, your exposure to your potential new boss is limited to the following situations:

- Chatting to colleagues you may be working with, if you're lucky! Even if you do get this chance, how likely is it that they're going to tell you what they really think of their boss?

✔ Checking the Internet to see whether you can find any information about your potential boss.

✔ During your job interview, when people are likely to be on their best behaviour!

✔ Having a chat during a tour of the work area.

You always take a risk when accepting a new job, because you've so little information about what your new boss is really like. And yet you can turn this situation to your advantage. I describe in the sidebar 'Making the best of a bad job!' how Jane 'lost', and then turned her loss into a win after sharing the story she told me during a coaching session. You can do the same and turn a loss into a win/win outcome for yourself, your new boss and your staff by taking the initiative to address your reasons for being critical of your boss.

Making the best of a bad job!

Jane is a dynamic person who's incredibly business- and customer-focused – as Head of the Marketing and Sales department she needs to be! Jane was excited about her new job, but several months into it she began having doubts about whether she'd made the right decision. Jane expected her boss to give her a clear direction and demanding sales targets when she joined the company, but nothing was forthcoming and she received no feedback about whether she was doing a good job or not.

Jane also discovered that the members of the team she'd inherited weren't high performers. In fact, she described them as underperforming, lazy, careless and lacking initiative. Jane was starting to think about leaving when I had a coaching session with her as part of a leadership development programme I was leading for her company.

I explored with Jane how her team had been led and managed before she joined the company, and I suggested that the way they were behaving and performing indicated that they'd probably been mismanaged. I also suggested that if they were continuing to exhibit the same behaviour after they'd been working for her for several months, she must have been contributing to the problem through the actions she was taking or wasn't taking.

Jane decided to go through the completed appraisal forms for each member of her team for the period before she joined the company. She discovered that her team had not received any constructive feedback about their performance from their previous manager, and had therefore assumed that they were doing an 'okay' job. When Jane discussed her findings with members of her team and talked to them about their expectations of working for her, she was pleased to discover that they wanted to take on more responsibility and develop their skills to do their job. Yes, they needed coaching and regular constructive feedback, but with this help they started to move in the right direction.

Jane also recognised the importance of taking the initiative in proposing the direction she thinks the department needs to go in, as well as her own stretch targets to her boss. She showed strong leadership by filling the leadership vacuum that existed and turned a loss situation into a win for herself, her boss and her staff.

Avoid biting the hand that feeds you

I was encouraged to find out how to be more diplomatic and shrewd in working with senior managers as part of my own early leadership development. I was, as the organisational psychologist who assessed me explained, in danger of biting the hand that fed me. He meant that, by having a strong sense of right and wrong and being keen to speak my mind, I may run the risk of criticising and antagonising the managers who had a big influence over my career in the company.

I've always been keen to develop new skills and valued having a mentor from whom I could learn at each step along my early career path. I knew that Dave was a great corporate man who worked directly for the Chief Executive,

and that Dave was renowned for being skilled in picking his way through political minefields. I sought and gained a two-year secondment working for Dave.

I found out that logic doesn't always work when trying to influence a senior manger to accept and support your proposal. I also discovered the value of finding out what's important to every senior manager, and being able to couch your proposal or argument in terms that appeal to the interests and priorities of individual senior managers whose support you need to have your proposal accepted and implemented. I learnt a lot from choosing a good boss who I wanted to work with.

When deciding whether to accept a job or not, of course you consider the whole package: responsibilities, pay, type of organisation, opportunities to advance your career and whether you want to work for the person who interviewed you. The last point may not be a high priority for you when making your decision, unless you suspect that your potential boss adopted Homer Simpson as a role model!

Sometimes, though, you may want to consider giving a higher priority to the person you want to work for than just the job itself: perhaps someone you admire and from whom you can learn a lot.

The sidebar 'Avoid biting the hand that feeds you' provides a personal example of what I mean.

Working through your own experiences

In this section and the next one you:

✔ Discover how much of an effect your experiences of leaders and managers have shaped your current thoughts about how you prefer to lead and manage people.

✔ Find out that you can have a significant impact on how people who work for and with you think, feel and act.

✔ Clarify your expectations of leaders and managers by completing a few exercises. You can use the outcomes of these exercises to think more about your strengths and development needs in leading and managing people.

Although I start this chapter by revealing that you've been experiencing leadership and management since you were a baby, I don't ask you to dredge your memories of childhood when working through your experiences. Instead, I want you to reflect on experiences that were significant to you during your formative years and adult life. Clarifying your own current thinking on leadership and management before you explore my description of what leaders and managers are expected to do is important for the following reasons:

✔ Building on your existing knowledge and approach helps you to understand and practise leading and managing people.

✔ Comparing and contrasting your views with my description of what leaders and managers are expected to do enables you to consider the implications of any similarities and differences.

✔ Working through your own experiences enables you to better understand leadership and management as you make sense of your personal experiences.

I suggest that you start to clarify your thinking on leadership and management by identifying any principles or values acquired during your formative years as regards how you were expected to treat people, and then describe how this experience shaped the way you treat people. The following exercise show you how.

1. **Complete Table 3-1 so that you have the information handy for future reference.**

2. **Write each 'principle' or 'value' in the first column.** It can be a phrase or saying that you recall hearing your parent or guardian say many times.

3. **Note in the second column what this item meant to you.**

4. **Write a few words to capture how each principle or value shaped how you treat people or expect to be treated by others.** I give one example to help you get started.

Table 3-1	Principles or Values Acquired through Formative Years Shape how You Treat People	
Principle or Value	*What This Means to You*	*How This Meaning Shaped How You Treat, and Expect to be Treated by, Others*
Look after others and they'll look after you.	Treat people how you like to be treated.	I always strive to treat people with respect.

Your approach to working with people is likely to be significantly influenced by the content of the third column. These notes describe you and how you prefer to work with people: they're part of your 'DNA' regarding your thinking and approach to working with people. Of course, the people you work with have similar or different DNAs based on principles and values they acquire in their formative years and how they interpret them, and these similarities or differences have a big effect on how well you work together.

Just as you can improve by taking the best from the best bosses you've worked for, you also discover how you *don't* want to lead and manage from observing and working with bad bosses.

Now build on these lessons from your formative years and explore your experiences of being managed by great and bad bosses.

1. **Complete Table 3-2 so that you have the information handy for future reference.**

2. **Note the approach or behaviour you admired in the best bosses you've worked for and with in the first column.** Describe the impact or effect their approach or behaviour had on you and how you performed your job in the second column.

3. **Repeat step 2 for your experiences of working for or with bad bosses.** Note the approach or behaviour you didn't admire in the third column and its impact on you in the fourth.

Table 3-2	Summary of Good and Bad Practices I've Noticed in Great and Poor Bosses		
Approach or Behaviour of Great Bosses	*Impact or Effect on How I Performed my Job*	*Approach or Behaviour of Poor Bosses*	*Impact or Effect on How I Performed my Job*
Hannah enthused about the importance of achieving our team's objectives.	I became more committed to achieving my objectives.	James didn't recognise how hard I was working.	I started to question myself about whether working all the extra hours I was doing was worthwhile.

Now reflect on the content of the second and fourth columns in Table 3-2, and think about how significant other people's leadership and management practice have been on you. Also take a few minutes to consider how working for good and bad bosses shaped your own approach to leading and managing people.

Listing your expectations of leaders and managers

Your current understanding and approach to leading and managing people is an amalgam of who you are and the lessons you learn through your own practice as a leader and manager, and how you interpreted your experiences of other leaders and managers. You continue to develop your own approach to leading and managing people throughout your working life.

I encourage you to take the next steps on your journey by further clarifying your understanding of leadership and management by listing your expectations of leaders and managers.

1. **Go through the notes you made in column 3 in Table 3-1 and column 1 in Table 3-2.** Decide whether each point describes what you expect of a leader or manager, or both.

2. **Go through the notes you made about the approach or behaviour of poor bosses in column 3 of Table 3-2, and note the opposite of each approach or behaviour.** Decide whether each point describes what you expect of a leader or manager, or whether you think a point is relevant to leaders and managers, in which case note 'both'.

3. **Complete Table 3-3 by transferring the relevant points from steps 1 and 2 into the relevant column.** Translate each point into an action that describes what you expect a leader or manager, or both, to do.

4. **Add to your lists by noting any further expectations you have of a leader and a manager, assuming that you're working for one.**

Table 3-3	My Expectations of Leaders and Managers	
I Expect Leaders to	*I Expect Both Leaders and Managers to*	*I Expect Managers to*

In the preceding exercises, you're practising the important and often underused skill of *reflecting*, in order to make sense of your experiences. (Chapter 4 has loads more details about this skill and how to enhance your ability to learn more and quicker through reflection.) Seize the opportunity now to assess how good a leader and manager you are against your current expectations by reflecting on whether you do what you expect leaders and managers to do, and whether you do it well. (Refer to the leadership development needs you identified if you completed the exercise on assessing yourself against the leadership competences in Chapter 2.)

My leadership strengths are:

My leadership development needs are:

My management strengths are:

My management development needs are:

If necessary, make additions to this summary after reading the later section 'Pinpointing the Differences between Leading and Managing'.

Use the Leadership Learning Plans in Chapter 4 to plan how you're going to work on your leadership and management development needs.

Understanding Society's Changing Expectations of Leaders

Management and, more recently, leadership have become more important in society ever since people flocked to the towns and cities looking for work during the 18th-century industrial revolution. Labour was cheap in those days, but captains of industry sought better ways of managing people to drive improvements in efficiency and effectiveness to increase profits.

Nowadays, many senior leadership teams use *employee engagement* as a means of gaining the commitment of their employees to contribute to achieving the organisation's objectives. Research into the factors that affect whether employees are engaged shows that the most significant aspect is an employee's line manager. (Dip into Chapter 8 for more on employee engagement, and Chapter 2 for why an employee's line manager has such an impact.)

As a leader and manager, you have the biggest impact in your organisation on whether the people who report to you are fully engaged in their work.

Read the later section on 'Earning the right to lead' for more on how to have the right impact on people for them to want to follow you, and check out Chapter 9 for more on becoming an engaging leader.

Jump! Yes sir, how high?

In the old days, the barons of industry in mining and other sectors ran their businesses more or less how they wanted to run them. The power to make and implement decisions rested with owners and their representatives: their managers.

Whether many people ate properly or not depended on whether they had a job because today's social security system didn't exist. In the mining industry, for example, a house came with the job and if a miner lost his job he also lost his home. Therefore, unsurprisingly, employees were keen to please their boss even if they didn't like the way they were being managed. If a boss said 'jump', meaning 'move now', a typical response may have been 'yes sir, how high'. You didn't normally question or challenge your boss about the work you were being told to do.

Jump! Why should I?

Fortunately, in recent decades things have progressed. Employees have acquired more bargaining power though the formation of trade unions, and more rights through a raft of legislation on health and safety, employment law and human rights. Employees now have rights about how they're treated in the workplace, such as to:

- Be trained and developed to perform the job to the required standard.
- Be treated with respect.
- Know what's expected of them and how well they're doing their job.
- Raise a grievance if they think they're being treated unfairly.
- Work in an environment that's safe and that doesn't damage their health.

As a leader, the people who report to you want to know the reasons for doing the work you expect them to do. Some are sure to ask you about what you're asking them to do, especially if they think the request or instruction is unreasonable. Nowadays, the answer to the injunction to 'jump' becomes, perhaps, 'why?'.

Pinpointing the Differences between Leading and Managing

I've led hundreds of leadership workshops and explored the differences between leading and managing with thousands of practising managers. In this section, I help you discover the key differences between leading and managing based on my experiences of coaching and working with leaders (see Figure 3-1). Numerous activities are associated with leading and managing, but I restrict my descriptions to the items that I consider to be most important.

Figure 3-1: The key differences between leading and managing.

MANAGING

Planning

Organising

Monitoring and controlling

Establishing and using systems and processes

Reviewing progress

LEADING

Setting the direction

Gaining commitment

Enthusing people to raise the bar

Developing the capability of your team

Making change happen for the better

Describing the key differences

In this section, I describe some crucial differences between the activities and associated skills of leading and managing. I list the activities to reflect the general rather than absolute order in which to do them, especially for managing.

Leading involves:

- ✔ **Setting the direction.** Clarify the purpose of your team and how it adds value to your organisation by answering questions such as:

  - Why does this team exist?

  - What objectives are we expected to achieve?

  - How can we achieve these objectives?

  Answering these questions enables you to clarify and set the objectives that have to be achieved for your team to be successful and the main actions to take to achieve the objectives. In practice, many leaders involve members of their team in completing this analysis to enable them to:

  - Create a shared sense of purpose and meaning to doing their work

  - Develop a shared responsibility for the team's success

  - Appreciate the team's and each individual's priorities

- ✔ **Gaining commitment to action.** Members of your team can deliver quite good levels of performance by complying with what you expect of them, but if you really want people to give their best you have to gain their commitment. The difference between people being committed and compliant is ownership: they take ownership for doing the task to the best of their ability rather than just doing it because you want them to. Engage individuals and the whole team through meaningful conversations about the importance of their work and gain their commitment to achieve objectives and deliver results.

- ✔ **Being enthusiastic about 'raising the bar'.** Enthuse about the standards of performance and behaviour you expect from your team. Question and challenge current ways of working and encourage innovation. In my experience, many teams think that they're already performing well and that they can't significantly improve their performance: they can't raise the bar!

Having a clear picture or vision about the future, including how you see the team functioning, and sharing it enthusiastically encourages members of your team to strive to improve the team's performance. Set high standards by acting with integrity and modelling the behaviours you expect from others.

✔ **Developing the capability of your team.** Act as a coach by encouraging people to be and give their best, and provide them with continual feedback. Hold individuals accountable: recognise and praise good practice, and promptly confront unacceptable performance and behaviour. Agree improvements and the support to be provided, and how to measure progress. Focus the whole team on finding better ways of working together to achieve higher levels of performance.

✔ **Making change happen for the better.** Become an active agent, rather than a victim, of change. Leading people involves having a positive impact on how they think, feel and act: and I mean people within your team and people outside of your responsibility over whom you don't have authority. You can have a positive impact on your manager, as well as your work colleagues, in striving to make changes happen that lead to better outcomes for your team, your organisation and you.

Managing involves:

✔ **Planning the work.** Produce detailed plans and schedules for how and when the team's work is to be done, including breaking down major tasks into simple steps and agreeing deadlines.

✔ **Organising people and other resources.** Assign tasks and responsibilities to team members based on their commitment and capability to do the work, and make best use of the knowledge, skills and expertise in your team. Provide the resources necessary to enable people to do their work.

✔ **Monitoring and controlling the work.** Check that the work is being progressed according to plan to achieve the objectives and results your team is expected to deliver.

✔ **Establishing and using systems and processes.** Establish and use systems and procedures, including the use of key performance indicators (KPIs) to ensure that the work is done effectively and efficiently.

✔ **Reviewing progress.** Conduct reviews to identify problems: make decisions to solve problems and take corrective action to get back on track. Use reviews to continue to find more effective and efficient ways of completing projects and tasks.

These two lists indicate that, generally speaking, effective leadership involves taking a fundamental, long-range perspective to work, and enthusing people to excel whereas good management requires you to be hands-on and focused on the day-to-day running of your group or department.

Getting people to follow you

You have the right to manage the people who work for you simply by having the role of being their manager: your job gives you the authority to ask and expect your staff to do whatever is reasonable to get the work done, providing that you're fair and treat people with respect. You've probably experienced occasions when your staff question what you ask them to do, because their interpretation of what's a reasonable request is different from your interpretation. Here are examples of requests that people may consider to be unreasonable:

- ✔ Helping a colleague to complete an urgent task when they're already busy.

- ✔ Staying later than normal at the end of the day to complete a task when they've plans to go out with their friends.

- ✔ Working closely with a colleague whom they don't get on with to complete a task.

Having the right to manage people doesn't mean that all your staff automatically do what you ask them to even when you're being reasonable. At times, you may need to use your authority to ensure that an important task is completed by the required deadline, but the more competent you become in leading people the less you have to use that authority in such situations. (Turn to Chapter 2 to find out how your view about whether you've the *right* to lead people can affect your *approach* to leading people.) Also, you discover how to develop your skills in leading people in Part III.

Earning the right to lead

Some managers are perceived to abuse their authority by the people who report to them. Most people respond positively to being asked to do a task that's reasonable even if it causes them inconvenience, but people don't generally respond well to being told what to do when they think that they're being:

- ✔ Belittled.
- ✔ Made to feel that their needs are ignored.
- ✔ Patronised.
- ✔ Treated disrespectfully.

Avoid treating people in any of these ways because they can perceive you as abusing your authority and they're not then willingly doing what you ask them to do.

You choose to lead, but the people who work for you choose whether they want to follow you in the sense that they choose whether they're going to do only an 'okay' job or a great job for you. People choose whether to put in the extra effort often necessary to do a great job – often referred to as *discretionary effort* because they've the discretion as to whether they apply it. Engaged employees do great work.

Earn the right to lead your staff by fully engaging them:

- ✔ Build confidence through everyone knowing that they can come to you at any time with any problems at all.

- ✔ Inspire them: talk enthusiastically about why and how their work is important, and the consequences of not doing it well.

- ✔ Respect how they're different to you, without lowering any standards regarding work or behaviour.

- ✔ Show a genuine interest in them: their needs, hopes and concerns.

- ✔ Treat them as equals: don't speak down to them.

- ✔ Value them for who they are, as well as for what they can do for you.

- ✔ Work with them rather than doing things to them: ask them for, consider and, if appropriate, use their ideas, views and opinions.

Leading and managing together

I'm sure that your job is demanding and you, like most leaders, find fitting everything into your daily schedule difficult: doing your own work as well as leading and managing the people who report to you. You probably experience dilemmas about whether to focus your attention and time on getting the work done or dealing with staff issues, and whether to spend time managing or investing your time in leading people.

You may end up focusing and spending more time on getting the work done because tasks, unlike staff issues, tend to have deadlines! An example is doing a task yourself rather than delegating it to someone because you think you can complete the task quicker and better than that person, and you don't have time to train someone to do the task before the deadline. Another example is correcting people's mistakes yourself because you think you don't have time to coach them to do the task correctly and hit the deadline.

The reality is that you don't have the luxury of choosing to manage or lead: you need to do both! Yes, you have to deliver results now, but you also have to build commitment and develop the capability of individuals and your team to achieve success in the future: you need to achieve sustainable success.

You have many opportunities to lead and manage people at the same time even though the activities are different (as I describe in the earlier section 'Describing the Key Differences'). For example, during a meeting with your team, you may involve everyone in thinking and deciding how to complete a major task and, in doing so:

- Enhance how people are working together on solving problems.
- Enthuse your staff about the importance of the task.
- Gain their commitment to do a great job.
- Plan how the task can be completed.
- Organise who's going to do each sub-task.
- Reinforce certain standards regarding quality and hitting deadlines.

You need to put more emphasis on managing in some situations and more emphasis on leading people in other situations to achieve success.

Remain conscious at all times of your behaviour and the actions you're taking in leading and managing people, to increase the likelihood of you having the desired effect on your team, and achieving the outcomes you intend.

Although I encourage you to treat every situation as unique, and think about the issues you want to deal with and the outcomes that you want to achieve, you're more likely to adopt the right approach to each situation if you know how to recognise that different situations require a different emphasis on leading and managing in dealing with them:

1. **Divide a piece of paper into three columns as shown in Table 3-4.**

2. **Describe briefly in the first column examples of situations when you need to put more emphasis on *leading*.**

3. **Describe briefly in the second column examples of situations when you need to put more emphasis on *managing*.**

4. **Describe briefly in the last column examples of situations in which you can take opportunities to *lead and manage at the same time*.**

I give a few examples in the first row to help you get started.

Use your analysis to practise quickly recognising when to put more emphasis on leading or managing in different situations, and adopt the right approach to dealing with each situation.

Continue to reflect on your experiences so that you're constantly refining your leadership and management skills, and make sure that you question yourself about whether you adopted the best approach in different situations.

Table 3-4	When to Lead, When to Manage and When to Do Both at the Same Time		
Situations in Which I Need to Put More Emphasis on Leading	*Situations in Which I Need to Put More Emphasis on Managing*	*Situations in Which I Can Seize Opportunities to Lead and Manage*
When I need to enthuse people about changes in how we work.	When a job has to be organised quickly to hit an urgent deadline.	During team meetings to plan major tasks and gain commitment from individuals to take on additional responsibilities.

Part II
Leading Yourself

'Before we start on the leadership
training, I hope you're not feeling too nervous.'

In this part . . .

You start to work on developing your leadership ability by initially focusing on leading yourself, and you find techniques on how to learn more about leadership from your experiences. I invite you to spend time on clarifying the values that are most important to you and how these guide your behaviour in leading people. I introduce you to some dilemmas that you may experience when you step up to a new leadership position and you find out how to handle them.

Chapter 4

Leading 'Inside Out': Knowing Yourself to Become a Better Leader

*Y*ou don't need to turn yourself inside out to become a better leader, but in order to lead others successfully you do need to know yourself: for example, your preferences, strengths, weaknesses, beliefs and values. To put this idea another way: leading outwards starts with looking inwards. Looking inwards allows you to get to know yourself better, because the better you understand what's important to you and how that affects the way you think and behave, the better you understand why you act and react as you do in different situations. You can then use this 'inside' information to consider how you, as a leader, impact on and affect the people who work with you.

In this chapter, you discover a range of techniques to look inside and at yourself, and how you can learn more from your experiences to better understand yourself and use this knowledge to enhance your leadership ability. You build on this work in Chapter 5, where you discover how to clarify what's important to you – your values – and in Chapter 7, where you develop a sense of purpose that's meaningful to you and others.

Leading Others Starts with Leading Yourself

In the helter-skelter of doing your job, you have to spend time on the things that grab your attention: achieving objectives, hitting deadlines, solving problems with jobs and problems with people!

Focusing all your attention on these areas and other issues means that you may give yourself too little or no attention, with the result that you become less aware of your behaviour and the reasons why you behave the way you do.

 Turning the spotlight on yourself helps to accelerate the process of becoming the leader you aspire to be. Doing so enables you to be more conscious of the following aspects of yourself:

✔ Your thoughts and the assumptions you make that affect how you think and interpret information and situations.

✔ Your feelings and how they impact on your attitude, especially towards other people.

✔ Your behaviour and whether it's intentional or automatic: whether you think things through and act accordingly or whether you act automatically without fully considering the potential impact or effect that your behaviour has on others.

Becoming an authentic leader

Many different descriptions of authentic leadership exist in the management literature. (*Authentic Leadership* by Bill George (Jossey-Bass) gives one example.) In this section I describe the most important aspects of authentic leadership and pose questions for you to reflect on how authentic you are. Initially, however, I need to examine the consequences of being perceived as an inauthentic leader.

Do you recognise any of the following situations in which a leader can be perceived as not being authentic? If you do, what effect did the leader have on you and your desire to follow that person?

✔ The leader says, 'It's not me who's asking you to make these changes, I'm just the messenger.'

✔ The leader abdicates responsibility by doing nothing when she can see tension or conflict between members of the team.

✔ The leader praises a member of the team for doing a task badly.

✔ The leader is perceived as having 'slopy shoulders': that is, she avoids taking responsibility for something that goes wrong.

✔ The leader was prepared to criticise some people but not others for the same errors.

✔ The leader wasn't prepared to tackle people who were known to be prickly, temperamental or unpleasant.

If you ever catch yourself doing any of the above behaviour, be aware of the potential consequences that such actions can have for you and your colleagues!

So what are the consequences of you being perceived by your staff or other work colleagues as inauthentic?

Your staff or work colleagues question themselves or doubt whether they should, or worse decide not to, follow you when they perceive you as not being authentic. In practice, they may comply with what you expect of them, but you don't get their full commitment.

Authentic leaders:

✔ **Know themselves.** They invest time questioning and clarifying who they are and what's important to them: that is, their values. Develop your own self-knowledge so that you can be authentic by working through questions such as:

  • What's important to me?

  • What are my values?

  • What makes me happy and what do I get upset about?

✔ **Are genuine.** Total alignment exists between who the leader is and what she does, so that followers see the leader's 'true self'. Authentic leaders also have a genuine, rather than superficial, interest in others: their need to do meaningful work, and their hopes and concerns. Challenge yourself about whether you're always genuine by asking questions such as:

  • Do I always behave in line with my values even though I may choose to modify my behaviour according to the needs of others or the situation? (Refer to the later sidebar 'How should I be?' for an example of how I modified my own behaviour and stayed true to my values.)

  • Do I really value people for who they are as well as what they can do for me?

  • Do I acknowledge my weaknesses as well as my strengths in working with others?

✔ **Are open and honest.** Authentic leaders have the courage of their convictions and say what they think even if that means standing out from the crowd: they tell the truth. They're also open or receptive to others' views and opinions.

Do you ever catch yourself holding back and keeping your views to yourself in meetings, especially if you:

- Disagree with proposed decisions and actions?
- Consider the behaviour of a colleague to be unacceptable?

If you do notice yourself behaving this way, ask yourself the following questions:

- Why am I not expressing my thoughts and opinions?
- What do I think is going to happen to me if I do share my views, and why do I think this way?

Most people are uncomfortable about expressing their views in a meeting if they think they're going to be embarrassed or may embarrass others by stating their opinion. (Refer to Chapter 6 to discover a simple technique to help you to face up to and address difficult situations by becoming more comfortable being uncomfortable.)

Answering the above questions allows you to gain further insights into, and build upon, your leadership and management strengths and development needs (check out Chapter 3 for help with these aspects). Use leadership learning plans as described in the later section 'Achieving more by learning quickly' to plan how you're going to work on your leadership development needs.

How should I be?

As a young superintendent, managing works operators at several treatment works, I had to wrestle with the dilemma of being authentic. A lot of banter or mickey-taking went on among the works operators and I occasionally found myself joining in: I recognised that the men respected me for doing so.

I became concerned about how I'd behave during one of the occasional site visits of directors to the works. Wouldn't the directors think badly of me if I was jovial with the operators, and wouldn't the operators think that I was playing up to the directors if I was very serious or businesslike in front of them?

I resolved the dilemma by recognising that I could maintain my values while modifying my behaviour so that it was appropriate in dealing with directors and operators simultaneously. I decided that during site visits I'd sometimes be very serious and sometimes use humour appropriately . . . and it worked. I realised that I was in fact being respectful of each group by modifying my behaviour so that each group was comfortable with how I behaved.

Looking through the Johari Window

As well as looking at and inside yourself, I also encourage you to seek feed-back from other people to increase your self-knowledge. To show the extent to which people see (or crucially don't see) themselves effectively, I use the Johari Window – developed by Joseph Lufts and Harry Ingrams and shown in Figure 4-1. This model shows in the first column what you do know about yourself and in the second what you don't know about yourself, and helps to explain just why seeking feedback from others is so important. I refer to each quadrant in Figure 4-1 as panes in a window.

	Known to self	Not known to self
Known to others	Open	Blind
Not known to others	Hidden	Unknown

Figure 4-1: The views through the Johari Window.

'Open' pane

Like everyone, I'm sure that you're comfortable sharing a certain amount of self-knowledge or information about yourself with other people. Figure 4-1's 'open' pane represents this type of knowledge – which is known to both your-self and others – for example:

- Describing the work you do and the jobs you've held.
- Talking about your personal life, including your family details, interests, hobbies and so on.
- Revealing your preferences, likes and dislikes.

'Hidden' pane

In contrast to the 'open' knowledge, some information you may deliberately choose not to share with (or may indeed deliberately hide from) others (the 'hidden' pane in Figure 4-1). Choosing not to share such information is equiv-alent to painting over this pane so as to obscure from people what you prefer to keep to yourself. This knowledge may include, for example, things you've done in the past about which you're embarrassed.

'Blind' pane

The first two panes – 'open' and 'hidden' – comprise knowledge about yourself that you know and then choose to share with others or hide. In contrast, the other two panes consist of knowledge that you don't know about yourself.

Other people may well hold different views about you than you hold of yourself. For example, you may see yourself as a strong assertive character while others perceive your behaviour as being aggressive. If people choose not to share their views about you with you – probably bits of your behaviour or attitude that they'd like you to change – then what's apparent to them remains 'blind' to you (the 'blind' pane in Figure 4-1). This pane is equivalent to one-way glass: people see you but you don't see yourself. Because you don't notice the effect your behaviour has on other people (but that effect is apparent to them), this crucial pane is the one that you can illuminate by getting feedback from others. (Refer to the later sidebar 'I can't change if nobody tells me!' for an example of me giving feedback to a senior manager about the effect his behaviour was having on his staff.)

Many people don't share their views about you with you, however, if they think that you're going to be embarrassed or threatened by what they say, or they themselves feel embarrassed or threatened by sharing their views with you. Despite the potential awkwardness, try to seek out the views of others so you can gain insights into the effect you're having on your staff and other work colleagues. This process is the basis of 360-degree feedback used in leadership development programmes in many organisations, when feedback is sought from people who work for and with the leader about the extent to which the leader is considered to have certain competencies that the organisation considers to be important.

'Unknown' pane

Certain aspects of yourself exist that no one has yet discovered or seen. The information, under the 'unknown' pane in Figure 4-1, contains those aspects that neither you or other people know at the moment, and this pane indicates that you're on a lifelong journey of discovery. You can discover more about yourself through having new experiences and assessing how well you cope with them.

You can accelerate developing into the leader you want to be by actively seeking feedback from the people who report to, and work with, you about the effect you have on them and how they perceive you. Play to your strengths and work on your weaknesses. By seeking and using the views of your colleagues to improve yourself, you set a great example and are encouraging others to do the same.

I can't change if nobody tells me!

Pete was a Technical Director in a company he'd started with a partner. The company had grown over several years and now employed almost 100 people, many as engineers. As Technical Director, Pete had the right to check on all the designs for the engineering projects being worked on and took on this responsibility with gusto, almost as if he were holding court standing at a big table in the centre of the open-plan design office. Engineers brought their designs to the table and gave updates on how their projects were progressing.

Being a great engineer, Pete quickly spotted flaws or identified improvements in the designs. He had a booming voice, and everyone in the design office knew about the flaws and improvements required in each design as well as the relevant project engineer. Consequently, engineers weren't enthusiastic about having project reviews!

When, as part of a leadership development programme, I explained to him the effects of his behaviour on the engineers, it was immediately clear that nobody had ever mentioned this problem to Pete: he was totally unaware of the impact his project reviews had on engineers. He commented: 'I wish someone had pointed this out to me years ago and I could've done something about my behaviour!'.

Enhance your self-knowledge by asking people who report to you and other work colleagues for their views about you: that is, how they perceive you. Then compare and contrast how their views 'fit' with your own views of yourself.

As everyone is different, two people are never going to see things exactly the same. You can test this fact by completing the following short exercise and, at the same time, practise your skills in seeking and using feedback from others:

1. **Select an event or experience that you shared with a friend or colleague.** It may be a television programme or film you both saw, a speech you both heard or even a meeting you both attended.

2. **Ask your friend or colleague to describe her interpretation of the event and then share your interpretation.** Seek the other person's perspective *before* you share your own view.

3. **Give your friend or colleague your full attention while she's talking and suspend judgement while listening.** Don't interrupt or make decisions about whether you agree or disagree with the other person's interpretation. I'm not suggesting that you let go of your views or beliefs about the event, only that you stay open to another interpretation. When you become open to other interpretations, you sometimes find that those interpretations are more meaningful than your own: you discover how to be open to changing some of your views, assumptions or beliefs because you're questioning them.

Now apply this approach to seeking feedback about yourself:

1. **Seek the views of a colleague about you and notice any differences between how that person perceives you and how you see yourself.**

2. **Notice your own reactions to what the person says, because noticing differences in viewpoints can sometimes surprise or even shock you.** Make a mental note of you reactions or write them down.

3. **Question yourself about why you reacted that way.** For example, if someone's view surprises you, you must have been assuming that something else was true. If something someone says shocks you, you must believe something contrary to what the person is saying. Being surprised or shocked by another person's view or belief can expose and help you clarify your own views, assumptions and beliefs.

Questioning yourself about why you hold particular assumptions and beliefs can also lead you to change them.

Developing Self-Confidence

Most leaders have doubts about their ability to succeed at one time or another, especially when faced with difficult situations. Some leaders even see themselves as imposters in certain situations (as I describe in Chapter 6). Developing your self-confidence is an essential part of you becoming a great leader because:

- ✔ You're willing to step outside of your comfort zone (Chapter 6 helps you to clarify those situations that are inside and outside your comfort zone).

- ✔ You're more likely to think through and be prepared for the risks involved in stepping outside of your comfort zone.

- ✔ You're enhancing your leadership skills through confronting and dealing with difficult situations and problems that you've never previously encountered.

You can work on building your self-confidence by:

- ✔ **Acknowledging that nobody is perfect, including you.** Try to be the best you can be without beating yourself up for not being perfect. Check out the sidebar 'I want to be brilliant at everything!' to see how easily you can fall into this trap.

✔ **Catching yourself being successful.** You probably tend to notice problems and failures more than successes, and you can boost your confidence by actively looking for and recognising your successes. Praise yourself for doing a task well, although you may want to do so quietly to avoid receiving strange looks from your colleagues!

✔ **Appreciating that 'good enough' is okay when, for example, you're working on completing certain tasks.** Yes, you want to do the best job you can because it reflects on you, but recognising when a task is good enough (in that it meets the requirements) helps you to recognise that sometimes your work, and therefore you, are good enough.

✔ **Sharing the problems and difficult situations you experience with someone you trust and respect.** You often gain insights into what to do just by talking through problems, and doing so can enhance your confidence to tackle effectively the problems you're experiencing.

Leaving Thomas to doubt himself

On the leadership development programmes that I facilitate – in which people describe their problems or dilemmas in doing their job – I hear leaders in the early stages of their careers make the following typical comment: 'I thought it was only me.' They're surprised to find that other people also experience doubts about themselves.

Having doubts about your ability to handle or cope with certain situations is normal: almost everyone has such doubts at one time or another!

Acknowledging that other leaders are also experiencing similar problems or difficult situations can boost your confidence, because you recognise that you're not the one causing all the problems: encountering such problems is normal.

Questioning your approach to leading people or being self-critical is healthy because you can enhance your self-knowledge and leadership ability through questioning your motives, attitudes and reasons for behaving as you do in situations that require leadership. At times, however, you can be too self-critical and question or criticise yourself too much.

Be careful about thinking that you've solely caused the problems you encounter: other people involved are also likely to be contributing to or causing the problems. For example, you may well have come across a situation in which someone who reports to you didn't complete a task to the standard or deadline you expected. Perhaps you criticised yourself and concluded that you didn't explain clearly enough what you expected the person to do, or that you failed to train that person to do the task correctly and so on. The truth may well be, however, that the person was simply lazy!

I want to be brilliant at everything!

Jean is an ambitious person who strives to be the best she can be. She mentioned during a conversation that she compared herself with the best attributes in every successful person she admired with the aim of being as good as each of them in each attribute. Jean used a simple one to ten scoring system and always scored herself low in comparison to the best in the people she admired. I pointed out that although her aspiration was admirable she was doomed to always putting herself down, because she was striving to be perfect: striving to be someone who doesn't actually exist!

Avoid being so self-critical that you start to:

- ✔ Doubt your leadership ability
- ✔ Develop a 'can't do' mentality
- ✔ Lower your self-esteem

Being your best critic

One way of building your self-confidence is to take responsibility for solving problems or handling difficult situations that you come across, including those to which you contribute or cause. You can continually enhance your skills in solving problems and handling difficulties by learning from your experiences.

Being your own best critic involves adopting a 'critical friend' approach in which you constructively critique – rather than destructively criticise – yourself. Focus on questioning your motives, attitude and behaviour in leading people, because you're intent on enhancing your self-knowledge and leadership ability. You're on a journey of discovery, trying to find out how to prevent problems and difficult situations occurring or reoccurring.

Being your own best critic requires you to do the following:

- ✔ Construct a positive 'I want to (learn to) be better' mentality to encourage yourself to examine and improve on what you do.

  To recognise the value of continuously working on your development, take a few minutes to think about and note how you've developed as a leader over the last year, and how the changes you've made in how you lead have benefitted you and the people who report to you. (Discover the different language used by people with positive and negative attitudes towards facing up to and handling difficult situations in the next section 'Learning from adversity'.)

✔ Be objective in constructively critiquing the action you took and why you took it in dealing with recent problems and difficult situations. Use facts and evidence about each situation wherever you can when conducting your analysis.

✔ Build progressively on your leadership strengths by working on the personal insights you gain from constructively critiquing yourself. Note the progress you're making and tell yourself 'well done [use your name here]' for solving the problems you encounter.

Always use your own name when giving yourself praise for doing a job well, because the praise is more powerful as personal recognition and reinforcement when your hear your name attached to the praise. For the same reason, always use the person's name when you're praising a colleague.

Find out more about learning from your experiences in the later section 'Discovering How to Lead from Your Experiences'.

Learning from adversity

In the early stages of my career, an occupational psychologist once described me as a 'maximiser', because I was always keen to explore the dilemmas I was experiencing in leading people and find out as much as possible about how to handle 'people problems' – or perhaps I should say 'problem people'. I'm certainly not suggesting that you create or cause problems just so that you can learn from them, but I do encourage you to see problems, difficult situations and dilemmas as opportunities to find out how to handle them effectively.

Adopt a positive rather than negative attitude towards difficult situations so that you can learn as much as you can from adversity.

The following short exercise helps to see whether you need to work on developing a more positive attitude:

1. **Take a few minutes to think about and note down the words or phrases that typically come into your mind when you're faced with a problem or difficult situation.**

2. **Compare your notes with the words in the first column of Table 4-1.** If most of the words or phrases in your list are the same as or similar, you probably don't like, or try to avoid, adversity. Try using the equivalent words or phrase in the second column when you're faced with adversity, because using these words and phrases give you a more positive attitude to dealing with adversity. You're then more likely to discover how to deal with such adversities effectively.

3. **Compare your notes with the words in the second column of Table 4-1.** If most of the words or phrases in your list are the same as or similar, you're probably willing to tackle adversity. Give yourself a pat on the back and keep up the good work!

Table 4-1	Negative and Positive Language
Negative Language	*Positive Language*
I can't (handle this).	I can (handle this).
I should/need to (do. . .)	I will (do. . .)
It's not my fault (that this problem exists).	I'm responsible (for solving this problem).
It's a problem.	It's an opportunity.
I don't know how (to solve this. . .)	I will find out how (to. . .)
We will do it but it will be difficult.	We will do it even though it will be difficult.

Discovering How to Lead from Your Experiences

Taking on board lessons from your experiences is a very powerful form of learning, because you remember your successful actions – the ones that achieve your aims – and discard or change your behaviour when you fail to achieve your aims. This process is the basis of learning through 'trial and error'. Unfortunately, 'trial and error' can be quite a slow and painful process because you:

- ✔ Tend mainly to notice and learn from significant events: those that go really well or very badly.

- ✔ Have to keep having new experiences from which you can learn and develop your leadership ability.

In this section, I show you how to accelerate and increase learning from your experiences.

Achieving more by learning quickly

You can speed up learning from your experiences by adopting a more structured approach called the *learning cycle*, a technique made famous by experiential learning and organisational behaviour expert David Kolb. The learning cycle contains four steps or activities:

1. **Acting:** Taking action and appreciating the immediate impact or effect the experience has on your knowledge, understanding and skills as a leader.

2. **Reflecting:** Reflecting back on the experience after the event to clarify and identify the main or significant actions you took, and possible causes or consequences of those actions.

3. **Theorising:** Acquiring insights and learning lessons about what works and doesn't work from the links you make between actions and outcomes.

4. **Planning:** Making plans to apply the lessons you've learnt.

The cycle then starts again by you taking the action you plan to take, reflecting on it and so on. Making this cycle part of your everyday practice enables you to accelerate developing your leadership skills through a more structured and thorough approach than simple trial and error, enabling you to use these skills to achieve more in leading your team.

The following example demonstrates how the learning cycle can be applied to finding out how to ride a bicycle. Assume that you're only a few years old and have just had the stabilisers removed from your bicycle. You've come to a steep descent and are peddling quite hard. Your speed increases more than you expect and your exhilaration at going fast suddenly turns to fear for your safety:

You take *action* that causes the bike to stop suddenly and tip forward throwing you over the handlebars.

By *reflecting* on the experience, you identify that you pulled the front brake on immediately before the bike tipped forward.

By *theorising*, you learn the lesson that pulling the front brake on when you're going fast causes the bike to tip over, and you learn to pull the rear brake to stop the bike safely without you being thrown over the handlebars.

You *plan* to use this newly acquired knowledge about riding a bike as soon as you get back on your bike.

Use leadership learning plans as part of your structured approach to planning how you're going to work on your leadership and management development needs. Table 4-2 provides a structure of a leadership learning plan and contains an example of how to use the plan.

In Chapter 3, I present exercises on your expectations of leaders and managers. If you haven't already, complete these exercises and use the leadership and management development needs you identified to complete the following exercise:

1. **If you think that the leadership development needs you identified in Chapter 2 are too vague, now's your chance to rewrite them as learning objectives.**

2. Complete a plan for each leadership development need or objective by answering the questions at the top of each column.

3. Use the learning plans you complete to develop your leadership skills as quickly as you can, and then to assess how well you're applying the knowledge and skills you acquire in the workplace to improve your own and others' performance and behaviour.

Table 4-2	Example of a Leadership Learning Plan		
Description of my Learning Objective	*How I'm Going to Achieve my Learning Objective*	*My Deadline for Achieving This Objective*	*How I'm going to Measure my Success in Achieving my Learning Objective?*
To be skilled in constructively challenging unacceptable behaviour and performance	Attend an influencing skills workshop that meets my learning objective	By 30 June 2011	I'll be confident and effective in resolving interpersonal problems.
	Practise using the knowledge and skills I acquire in working with my colleagues	By 30 September 2011	The performance and behaviour of each individual I work with will meet the standards I expect/require of them.

Harnessing the power of reflection

Your working day is probably the same as that of most leaders: hectic! Busy, busy, busy, with so much on your mind, as you strive to get through all your work, hit your deadlines and deal with the crises that keep cropping up. You don't have time to be still, and you may well ask why would you want to be still when you've so much to do? Because being still and calming your mind is necessary for you to be reflective.

Perhaps an analogy may help. Cars and other vehicles have reflectors on the back of them. The purpose of these reflectors is to catch light from the headlights of other vehicles and reflect the light back so that the vehicle can be seen. Reflecting involves you shining a light into your past experiences so that you can see into, and make sense of, them.

Reflecting enables you to notice and see things that may not have been immediately apparent to you when the experience occurred. You gain insights into each experience by making connections between, for example, the actions and reactions of yourself and others involved in the event. These connections enable you to identify the causes and effects of these actions and reactions.

Reflecting is an important enough activity for you to spend time doing it.

Most leaders find that reflecting on and learning as much as they can from their experiences is difficult because:

- ✔ They've so much to do and feel under pressure to complete their workload and hit deadlines.

- ✔ They've no pressing deadline for the activity of reflecting and so it can keep dropping towards the bottom of the 'to do' list.

- ✔ They don't appreciate the value of reflecting.

- ✔ They aren't skilled in reflecting.

Make time every day to reflect on and learn from your experiences of the day and get into the habit of asking yourself questions such as the following:

- ✔ What did I do well today?

- ✔ What could I have done better?

- ✔ What action(s) did I take that helped me and/or my team succeed?

- ✔ What action(s) should I have taken, and what were the outcomes or consequences of my inactivity?

- ✔ What would I do differently if I were in a similar situation again?

- ✔ What have I discovered from reflecting on today's experiences?

Developing skills in reflecting

Although some people are naturally more reflective than others, you can develop your skills in reflecting on and learning from your experiences.

Become a more skilful reflector by starting to do the following activities:

- ✔ **Being more self-aware.** Practise noticing what you do in, for example, meetings. Do you tend to speak up more or less than your colleagues? Reflection involves looking back into your experiences, and so you may want to conduct a review of your contribution to a meeting after the meeting finishes or even during the meeting itself. However, be careful to avoid becoming so engrossed in yourself that you miss important points being made by your colleagues on the topics being discussed.

✓ **Questioning yourself.** As you become more aware of your behaviour in meetings and other situations, question yourself about the reasons for behaving the way you do in these situations. Questioning yourself about the assumptions or beliefs that cause you to behave as you do provides valuable insights into whether your assumptions and beliefs are valid . . . or whether you need to change some of them!

✓ **Noticing what's significant.** People who are skilled in reflecting on situations or events are able to pick out the actions that were significant in contributing to or causing or affecting the outcomes of each situation. Taking meetings as an example, outcomes may include such things as decisions made, the commitment of individuals to take the actions that were agreed, the attitude of attendees towards the value of the meeting and much more.

Practise your skills in noticing what's significant by observing and noting down how people act and react to each other and what's said in meetings. Examine your notes after the meeting to identify connections or 'causes and effects' between the points you note, and use your analysis to enhance your understanding of how individuals are influencing and being influenced by the arguments, actions and behaviour of people at the meeting.

The next time you go along to a professional gathering or event, actively listen to what others from different industries to your own say. See whether you can include one or two of their ideas in your own situation.

✓ **Calming your mind.** Being reflective doesn't involve thinking about and planning what tasks you're going to do next: reflecting is a backward-looking and not a forward-looking activity. When you're busy, reflecting can be difficult because your mind is full of things you have to do, and so initially you need to practise clearing or calming your mind as follows:

Find a calm or quiet place in which you can be reflective. Choose a place where your mind won't be distracted: perhaps a quiet office, a quiet corner of a café, your journey home on the train or somewhere similar.

Relax your body by settling into a comfortable chair. Take a few deep breaths and feel any tension leave your body as you slowly exhale. Let go of irrelevant thoughts by refocusing on the situation or event on which you're reflecting. Writing brief notes about the situation and focusing your thoughts on your notes help you to stay focused. (*Mindfulness For Dummies* by Shamash Alidina (Wiley) has a wealth of advice for calming your mind.)

Using leadership learning logs

The main value in you keeping a leadership learning log is for you to optimise your learning by critically reflecting on your experiences, and through this activity improve your reflection skills. Table 4-3 provides the structure for critically reflecting on your experiences, and in the second and third rows I provide an example (of attending a meeting) to show how you can complete it.

Table 4-3	Example of a Leadership Learning Log	
Describe the Experience	*Reflect on and Review the Experience*	*Learning and Application*
Give a brief account of what happened, describe your behaviour, thoughts and feelings, and then the behaviour of others involved in the situation.	What was especially significant about what happened? How do you now feel about the experience? What conclusions can you draw from your experiences, including any possible causes and/or potential consequences with regard to what happened?	What have you found out from reflecting on your experiences? What insights or interpretations have you gained? For example, confirmation of something you already know, a new way of looking at an old issue or something new that you didn't know before. How, and when, do you plan to use this knowledge and/or skills?
I attended one of my occasional meetings with senior managers regarding a potential new book. I had several good ideas but didn't speak up because I wasn't confident that my ideas were good enough. Other people then made proposals similar to my own, which were accepted. I felt annoyed with myself for not speaking up.	I now recognise that I tend to hold back too much in meetings until I become familiar with the people. Senior managers probably see me as not being creative, which is untrue. I don't get recognition and may be overlooked for future promotions. I'm still a bit annoyed with myself, but am using this feeling to prompt myself to act differently in future meetings.	I'm going to practise speaking up more in all types of meetings I attend. I recognise that I may sometimes feel embarrassed when my ideas and opinions aren't accepted, but I'm telling myself that I can cope with any criticism. I'll become more confident as people accept my good ideas, and will overcome feeling embarrassed through more exposure to my views being questioned.

Finding and working with your own coach

Finding and working with your own coach enables you to accelerate becoming the leader you aspire to be. Use your coach as follows:

- ✔ As a sounding board to provide independent and objective feedback to you about your ideas and plans.
- ✔ To examine significant events you want to explore, and offer alternative views, perspectives and interpretations to help you to better understand them.
- ✔ As a source of moral support to enable you to resolve difficult dilemmas.
- ✔ To support and challenge you in examining your intentions, motives and appropriateness of your behaviour in a wide range of work situations.

As your coach, seek someone you admire for their professional expertise and achievements and/or someone you can trust and respect: the latter two attributes are essential because you want to be open with the person and sometimes explore sensitive, confidential, personal or commercial issues.

Look for someone who:

- ✔ Respects and maintains the confidentiality of your conversations.
- ✔ Is a good listener and hears you out without interrupting.
- ✔ Asks searching questions to prompt you to question your own thoughts and decisions.
- ✔ Provides honest and independent feedback to you.

Pluck up the courage to ask the person you most admire to be your coach regardless of her position in your organisation. Most senior managers appreciate being asked to perform this role because you're paying them a compliment by letting them know that you value them. If the person agrees to be your coach, you need to clarify the following items:

- ✔ Their role as your coach.
- ✔ The expectations you have of each other.
- ✔ How frequently you're going to meet.
- ✔ How you plan to review jointly whether the relationship is working for both of you.
- ✔ How you'll know when to end the coaching relationship, and how you're going to end it.

Good luck in your search!

Chapter 5

Singing Your Leadership Song: Being in Tune with Your Values

In This Chapter

▶ Knowing when you're out of tune with your values

▶ Appreciating the value of your values

▶ Getting into tune with others

*U*nlike me you may have a great singing voice, and yet sometimes when you sing you're going to be out of tune! When this situation happens, your singing talent is wasted because people don't want to listen to you. Being a great leader is sometimes similar to being a great singer: you can have all the skills required for leading effectively, but your colleagues can choose not to follow you when they think that you're not being authentic. In other words, you appear to be out of tune with yourself!

In Chapter 4, I demonstrate the negative consequences when the people who report to you perceive you as being inauthentic: they begin to question themselves and whether they should follow you, and may even decide not to do so. They may comply superficially with what you expect of them, but they don't give you their full commitment.

Chapter 4 also describes two of the key attributes of authentic leaders: they know themselves and they're genuine. In other words, they know what's important to them – they know their values – and their actions and behaviour are always aligned or congruent with those values.

In this chapter you discover how to recognise when you're out of tune with your core values and how to compose your own tune: that is, how to communicate your values to the people who work for you through your words and actions.

Recognising When You're Out of Tune

You may think that you have to know what being 'in tune' means before you can recognise when you're out of tune, but in fact that isn't always the case. Sometimes you just don't feel right about whether or how you need to address a situation. Or when you're aware that you could have handled a situation better, you continue to feel uneasy or uncomfortable about what you should have done or, indeed, did do. Typical situations can include some of the dilemmas covered in Chapter 6, such as how to lead friends effectively.

Occasionally, this unease or discomfort can exist for weeks or months or even longer, perhaps not continually but the sensation keeps coming back. You can feel that something is 'gnawing away at you' and you can't put your finger on the problem.

What's wrong with me?

I share this personal story to explain what I mean about feeling vaguely uneasy. When I was in my late 20s, I was interested in starting my own business. I can recall having conversations with people who ran their own companies about how to start my own business, but having two young children and a hefty mortgage I got on with building my career.

When I was in my early 30s, I became more aware of being upset in certain situations. Those situations tended to be times when I wasn't busy. When I was at work I was focused on the jobs I had to do and the deadlines I had to hit, but when I was at home and my mind wasn't so occupied with tasks and deadlines I became irritable. My wife noticed the change in my behaviour and mentioned it to me.

I knew something wasn't right but I was unable to put my finger on it. We talked about various aspects of our life, but concluded that the unease wasn't about any of the typical aspects of family life. Eventually, I sat down and analysed my life by asking myself and answering

simple but difficult-to-answer questions such as:

✔ When have I been happy and what were the reasons?

✔ When have I been sad and what were the reasons?

✔ What do I enjoy doing?

✔ What do I dislike doing?

From this analysis, which took me a few months to complete, I distilled five words that were important to me: achievement, variety, change, helping (people) and management. Through this long process of questioning myself, I realised that I was out of tune because I wasn't working for myself doing what I really wanted to do, and I was becoming more frustrated because I wasn't working towards making this happen. I decided then to take voluntary severance from the organisation I worked for and started to build a career working for myself based on the five words that were important to me.

Invest time in finding out what's causing your discomfort. If the sensation keeps returning, it may be a symptom of you being out of tune with yourself regarding something that's important to you: it may even be about something as fundamental as what you want to do or achieve in your life!

Acknowledging when 'it just doesn't feel right'

My personal story in the sidebar 'What's wrong with me?' shows that acknowledging when you just don't feel right is certainly worthwhile. The cause of your discomfort doesn't have to be as profound or go on as long as mine did: it can be as simple as you not behaving in accord with one of your core values for a time. (I describe the importance of core values in the later section 'Questioning what underpins your leadership').

I encourage you to notice and acknowledge any persistent feelings or sensations that something feels wrong to you for the following reasons:

✔ When something is causing you to feel uneasy, you're likely to carry that emotion and the associated behaviour into working with your colleagues or being with your family and friends. You may upset others even though that's not your intention. Working on clarifying and resolving whatever's upsetting you so that you're more 'in tune' with yourself and 'feel right' is necessary for you to behave appropriately when you're around colleagues, family and friends.

✔ When you experience a sense of something not being right, that feeling can keep grabbing your attention. Staying focused can become difficult and you may even be, or appear to others to be, preoccupied. Being in such a state not only wastes your time, but also makes you less productive than you can be.

Act on, rather than ignore, any feelings or sensations of discomfort that persist over a period of time; they're probably symptoms of something important to you, perhaps that one of your core values isn't being fulfilled.

Questioning what underpins your leadership

The values that are important to you have mainly evolved from the following:

✔ Your DNA: your personal make-up (not the stuff you may put on your face!).

✔ Your upbringing: the way your parents or guardians brought you up.

✔ Your life experiences: critical, perhaps life-changing, events and how you interpret them.

The exercise in Chapter 3 about working through your own experiences of leaders and managers helps you to gain insights into the values and associated behaviours that are important to you, and about how you prefer to treat, and be treated by, people.

Your values are descriptions of what is important to you or what you value, but not in a material sense. Some of your values are core values because they're the most important ones to you.

Your values, especially your core values, underpin your approach to leadership because they:

- **Have a significant bearing on what you do and how you behave.** For example, if you value being trusted and trust people to get on with their work you're likely to give them more autonomy. But if you believe that people can't be trusted, no doubt you check up on and monitor them closely.

- **Guide how you evaluate people and events.** For example, you're more likely to get on well with people who have the same or similar values as you. You may also react strongly towards people who behave in ways that conflict with or undermine your core values.

Like most people, you may well spend little time thinking about what's important to you.

Invest time in clarifying your values, because when you're clear about them you can use them:

- To establish principles or reference points when making decisions about how you lead and manage people.

- To set standards for many aspects of work for yourself and the people who report to you.

- To resolve dilemmas about how to handle difficult situations and people.

- To ensure that you act fairly and consistently in working with people who report to, and work with, you.

You discover how to clarify the values that are important to you in the later section 'Working out what's important to you'.

Leaving your old baggage behind

Through my coaching work in organisations, I've met leaders who were carrying significant baggage from their formative years. I noticed that such baggage is often unintended interpretations of phrases that the parents or guardians of these leaders said to them when they were younger.

Although the parents and guardians had good intentions in saying these phrases to their children during their formative years, the unintended interpretations aren't helpful in their subsequent development as leaders. Here are a few such phrases, with the intended and unintended interpretations and associated consequences for becoming an effective leader:

> ✔ **'Children should be seen and not heard.'** *Intention:* Behave well in public. *Unintended interpretation and consequence:* Don't speak up or express your views and opinions.
>
> One individual is unlikely to have all the answers to solving difficult problems as work and organisational life become more complex and demanding. Solutions to complex problems are more likely to come from an amalgam of the ideas and views of everyone involved. Leaders need to express their ideas and opinions, and draw on the ideas and expertise of everyone in their team to solve the complex problems they and their teams encounter.
>
> ✔ **'Keep a stiff upper lip.'** *Intention:* Keep control of yourself and don't fall apart in a crisis. *Unintended interpretation and consequence:* Hide your emotions.
>
> Leaders have to be emotional because they're expected to be enthusiastic and even passionate about the aims and objectives that they and their team have to achieve. Also, although sometimes you have to control your emotions – such as needing to control your anger or temper when someone makes an important mistake – you can still describe your emotion: for example, you can still say how disappointed or upset you are about a mistake being made.
>
> ✔ **'Try harder.'** *Intention:* Make more effort. *Unintended interpretation and consequence:* You and your work are never good enough.
>
> A typical story that intelligent individuals tell me relates to examination results. A person achieves top grades in every subject except one, for which he's awarded a 'B' grade. The individual then remembers his parents or guardians focusing on what went wrong with the solitary 'B' grade and saying that he must try harder. Unfortunately, such comments can sow doubts in individuals' minds that they can never be good enough, and therefore adversely affect their self-confidence in the future.

If any of the above or similar phrases are familiar to you and you think that hearing them a lot during your formative years resulted in unintended consequences for you being an effective leader, you need to work on leaving this baggage behind as follows:

✔ Recognise that the baggage probably results from unintended interpretations and consequences of the good intentions of those who raised you.

✔ Translate the unintended interpretation or consequence into a personal learning need or objective, and use a leadership learning plan to develop your attitude and ability to leave the baggage behind. Check out Chapter 4 for how to write and use leadership learning plans to achieve more by learning more quickly.

✔ Find a coach you can trust and respect, to talk with and help you work through any baggage you're dragging around with you. Refer to Chapter 4 for guidance on finding a coach.

Composing Your Own Leadership Tune

You discover in the earlier section 'Questioning what underpins your leadership' that your values are the foundation of your approach to leadership, because they've a significant bearing on what you do and how you behave, as well as how you evaluate people and events.

In this section you discover a few techniques to clarify your values and communicate them to your work colleagues. Investing time in clarifying your values is equivalent to you composing your leadership tune, because being clear about your values and behaving in ways that are in accord with and promote them enables you to be 'in tune' with yourself. When you're 'on song' in this way, your staff recognise that you're being authentic: they see that you know your core values and are behaving in ways that fit with them.

Being an authentic leader requires you to show a genuine interest in other people, as well as being true to yourself by behaving in accord with your values. You can't be authentic by focusing on what's important to you while ignoring the needs and values of other people.

Working out what's important to you

When meeting you for the first time, many people ask the following question: 'What do you do for a living?'. This question is fairly easy to answer, but what do you say when someone asks 'Who are you?' or 'What's important to you?'. You may well find these questions more difficult to answer unless you've invested time in getting to know yourself. Take time now to start knowing yourself better by completing the following exercise on clarifying your values:

1. **Take a few minutes to consider the questions at the end of this list.** Identify the ones that seem most relevant or helpful in clarifying what's important to you and copy them into a notebook, leaving plenty of space to answer each question.

2. **Try to come up with and note down any other questions that you think may help you to identify what's important to you.**

3. **Start to answer your questions when you've created a sufficient number.** As a guideline, form a list of between four and seven useful questions: any less than four may cause you to be less thorough than you should be, whereas more than seven can prompt you to start digressing into more general philosophising about your life!

   Take as much time as you need to answer your questions: the quality of your thinking in answering each question is much more important than answering it quickly. Leaving the questions partially answered for a time is fine: come back to them when you may want to add to or refine your answers after you've reflected on them.

4. **Pick out recurring or significant words, phrases and themes that run through your answers.**

5. **Use these words, phrases and/or themes to produce a list of your values.** In addition, note one or two behaviours that demonstrate that you're behaving in accord with each of those values.

6. **Record these words, phrases and themes in Table 5-1.** Insert a bullet point for each value so that you can refer to it when you're working on becoming an authentic leader and a great role model (I cover the latter subject in Chapter 11). In the table, I provide one example of a value and two appropriate behaviours.

Here are the questions to select from, to help discover your values:

✔ What's important to me about being a leader and how I lead people?

✔ What are my values, especially my core values?

✔ What's important to me about how I'm treated and how I treat others?

✔ What's important to me about how people work together?

✔ What work topics and issues generate most energy, positive or negative, within me?

✔ What positive impact or difference do I want to make to my organisation and/or my work team?

✔ What would need to happen at work for me to have a real sense of fulfilment?

✔ What topics tend to grab my attention and/or what do I talk about a lot at work?

✔ In terms of what is right and wrong, what are my absolute standards?

✔ What mark do I want to leave on the world, the organisation, and the people around me?

✔ What would my organisation's values be if I could choose them?

Table 5-1	Values and Behaviours that Demonstrate I'm Behaving in Accord with My Values
My Values	*Appropriate Behaviours*
Respect everyone.	I encourage people to express, and I consider, their ideas and opinions.
	I treat everyone fairly.

Walk your talk! Live your values by behaving in ways that fit with them because doing so is the best way to promote and reinforce them: people who report to you take more notice of what you do than what you say.

Questioning your assumptions

You may assume that you always act in accord with your values, but unfortunately this may not always be the case. For example, you may value treating people with respect and not notice when talking to them about completing a task that you're being curt, because you're anxious and under pressure to hit a deadline.

Instead of simply assuming that you always behave in accord with your values, try the following:

- ✔ Question and challenge yourself about whether you always behave as you intend to behave.

- ✔ Try to notice how you behave in different situations – especially when you're under pressure – and compare your behaviour with the behaviours you listed next to your values in Table 5-1 in the preceding section, 'Working out what's important to you'.

- ✔ Share your values, and how you intend to behave, with the people who report to you: seek feedback from them about whether you always behave as you intend, and how your behaviour affects them.

You may also find yourself assuming that other people place the same importance, or equally value, on what's important to you, or presuming that the way you prefer to work is the same for them. You may be right, but you may also be wrong!

If significant differences exist in the values or the preferred ways of working among the people in your team, including you, you're likely to experience problems in leading them and how well they work together. You can find out how to involve members of your team in clarifying and agreeing the values and behaviours to guide how they work together in Chapter 15.

Singing Your Leadership Song

One of my colleagues tells leaders that they're 'teachers without a voice', meaning that leaders are role models: the people who report to you take notice of and copy what you do. Modelling the behaviours that you want other people to adopt is a powerful way of communicating the values and behaviours that are important to you.

Communicating your values

Whenever possible, use face-to-face communication to convey your values, and the associated behaviours, to the people who report to and work with you.

I'm sure that you're relieved to find out that you don't literally have to do a song and dance act to share your values with your staff! Your words and actions, however, do need to be aligned or congruent with your values for you to be authentic and help reinforce your intended message to your work colleagues.

Using face-to-face communication gets across your important values and the relevant behaviours far better than email or other written forms of communication because:

- ✔ You're trying to achieve more than just informing your work colleagues about your values: you have to influence them so they appreciate that your values are important to you and how your team works. Face-to-face communication is a more effective means of influencing people than other forms of communication because you can see the effect you're having on your colleagues and act accordingly, such as by expanding on or clarifying certain points.

- ✔ You're using both sight and hearing, and research indicates that people take in more information through their sight than through just hearing the words.

- ✔ You can engage your colleagues more effectively in exploring the values and behaviours that you're sharing with them and what they mean in practise for how you all work together.

Face-to-face communications in which you sit around the same table as your colleagues is best, but having a video conference may be necessary if some of your staff are in different locations or even on different continents. Get close to the camera when using video conferencing so that people can clearly see you, especially your face.

Harmonising with others

As the buck stops with you in the sense that you're accountable for ensuring that your team achieve objectives and complete tasks to the right standard by the required deadline, you may think that you've the right to impose your values and behaviours on your staff.

As Chapter 3 describes, generally people don't respond well to being told what to do, especially when they feel they're being treated disrespectfully or made to feel inferior. A simple way to cause people you work with to feel inferior or disrespected is to emphasise your values and ignore the values that are important to them.

Be careful to avoid promoting your values over the values of people you work with especially when the national culture of some of your work colleagues is significantly different to your own national culture.

To help you harmonise your values with a work colleague, perhaps a team member, peer or even your boss, have a meaningful dialogue with him as follows:

1. **Approach your colleague and suggest that you explore what's important to you both in how you work together, with the aim of better understanding each other and improving workflow and productivity.**

2. **Agree to produce separately a list of the values that are important to each of you and note what you expect of each other in working together.** You may need to explain the importance of values by drawing on the content of the earlier section 'Questioning what underpins your leadership'.

3. **Complete your lists before you next meet.**

4. **Take turns during your next meeting to share each of the values and the expectations that you have of each other.** Look for similarities to reinforce how close you are to each other already, and explore differences and the ways they can be reconciled in order to agree how you're going to work more effectively together in the future. Agree when and how you plan jointly to review how well you put the agreements into practice.

5. **Conduct reviews using facts and evidence of how you've worked together – particularly emphasising successes – to build progressively on good practice and strengthen your relationship.** Where evidence emerges that you could work better together, jointly suggest and agree how you're going to make improvements.

For a way to harmonise your values with everyone in your team, complete the relevant exercise in Chapter 15 on creating a set of team values with your staff.

Chapter 6

Stepping Up to Leadership: Handling Dilemmas

*S*ometimes you choose to step up to becoming a leader and sometimes you're offered the role: and sometimes, of course, you've no choice – you have to take it! Whatever your particular route to finding yourself in your first (and each new) leadership position, you're likely to come across a few dilemmas that test your mettle and even your strength of character!

In this chapter I urge you to step back in order to help yourself step up to leadership, as I consider the dilemmas you may experience and work through how you can handle them successfully. I offer suggestions on how you can support and challenge yourself to succeed in what's probably the most demanding and difficult role that you've held at work up to now.

Dealing with Dilemmas

A dilemma is a real or perceived situation that causes you to be unsure, concerned or worried about what to do, and of the consequences of taking or not taking action to address the situation. Remember that a dilemma for you may be an opportunity for other people to demonstrate their capabilities, and so in this section you work through clarifying your own dilemmas.

A good start is to write down your dilemmas to get them clear.

1. **Get a notebook and divide the page into four columns as shown in Table 6-1.**

2. **Write 'Current Dilemmas' for dilemmas that you're currently experiencing about stepping up to leadership, followed by a column for the reasons for the dilemma.** Also, make a list for 'Potential Dilemmas' for situations that don't exist now, but you'd have concerns about if you did experience them.

3. **For each dilemma, write a few words that capture the reasons why the dilemma is a concern or worry for you.**

Table 6-1	Your Current and Potential Dilemmas		
Current Dilemmas	*Reasons for the Dilemma*	*Potential Dilemmas*	*Reasons for the Dilemma*
Being thought of as an imposter.	I feel embarrassed and inferior when I compare myself with my colleagues.		

When you to step back and reflect on your dilemmas, be careful not to create dilemmas that don't or may never exist. For example, if you're being promoted to your first leadership position, you may worry about getting the sack for failing to perform to the required standard. But if you think about how many people you know of in your organisation who've lost their job because they failed to step up to their first leadership role, your answer is almost certainly 'nobody'. Be aware of dilemmas that don't really exist.

The following sections cover a few dilemmas that may be on your list, and how to deal with them.

Surviving being thrown in the deep end

Have you ever been worried about being out of your depth in a swimming pool? If so, you may well remember thrashing around in the water, grasping for air and stretching out to reach the safety of the side. Being promoted to your first leadership position can feel like being thrown in at the deep end, although without the immediate risk to life!

As a new leader, you can feel up to your neck in problems, drowning in dilemmas and exhausted from trying to get everything done, while the lifeguard – your own manager – doesn't even notice that you're struggling. Okay, this analogy may be a bit dramatic, but more similarities exist between the two scenarios than you may at first think.

You're bound to have a few basic questions about your new role as leader, and I pose three questions to highlight similarities between being a new leader and being thrown in the deep end:

- ✔ Did anyone fully explain the depth and breadth of the leadership pool – the boundaries of your new leadership role and the limits of your authority – which you're expected to glide through effortlessly like an Olympic swimmer?

- ✔ Have you been guided in how to co-ordinate your breathing and swim strokes – your priorities and tactics for achieving them – so that you move gracefully through the depths of your duties and responsibilities?

- ✔ Do you know how to get and keep the attention of the lifeguard – your manager – to ensure that you get the right level of support necessary to be able to survive the choppy waters of competing priorities and multiple demands caused when everyone around you is thrashing about under intense pressure?

Being thrown in at the deep end is akin to being expected to perform your job well without enough direction, guidance, development and support to make sense of and perform your role. Consequently, all these questions are appropriate ones to ask yourself, and then your manager, to enable you to be clear about what's expected of you to become a high performer in your leadership role.

Think about the questions that you want answered so you can be clear about what's expected of you to be a success in your current leadership role. List these questions, leaving sufficient space under each question to write your answer. I pose the following questions to help you get started:

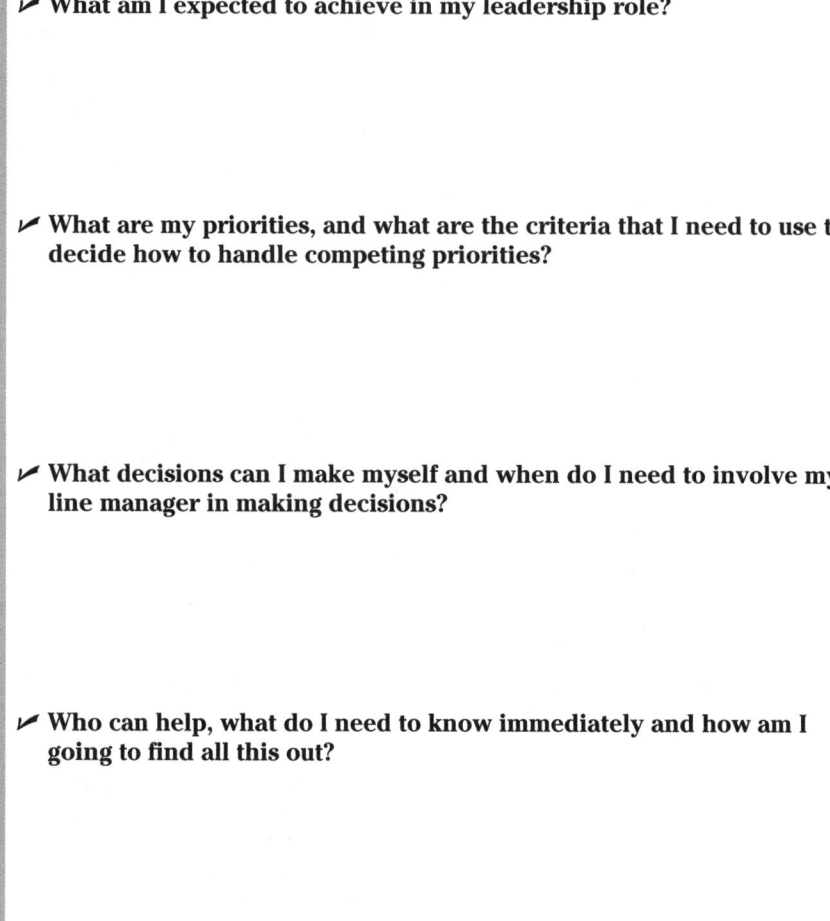

✔ What am I expected to achieve in my leadership role?

✔ What are my priorities, and what are the criteria that I need to use to decide how to handle competing priorities?

✔ What decisions can I make myself and when do I need to involve my line manager in making decisions?

✔ Who can help, what do I need to know immediately and how am I going to find all this out?

When you've completed your list of questions, try to answer them yourself first before involving your manager. Thinking fundamentally about your role and what's expected of you is a great way to help you develop your ability to make sense of unclear or complex situations. Answering the questions before you share them with your manager also demonstrates that you've taken the initiative to think things through and are simply seeking confirmation.

Being chosen for the right wrong reasons: Few new leaders arrive fully trained

Many people are chosen for promotion to their first leadership position because they show the necessary potential to perform at the next level in the organisation's management structure. Perhaps you demonstrated good skills in the technical or professional aspects of your work and displayed a great work ethic. You may have been recognised for the latter through an excellent attendance record and a track record for 'going the extra mile', perhaps by being willing to work late to complete a task, taking the initiative to solve problems and so on. You're almost certainly seen as a good team player who gets on well with people.

Although all these skills and attributes are commendable, they're not necessarily the crucial skills and attributes that determine whether you're going to be successful in your first leadership role. Consequently, you can find yourself promoted to your first leadership role for the right wrong reasons: by which I mean that you show certain skills and attributes, but not necessarily all the right ones to succeed. Recognise that because you've been promoted for the right wrong reasons (you were brilliant at your last job, not the new one), you've a whole lot more to learn. Immediately therefore, you're going to find yourself facing dilemmas for which you feel unprepared.

(You can find information on the crucial skills for leading people in Chapters 2 and 3, and much more on the skills required to be an engaging leader in Chapters 8 and 9.)

When you're about to step into your first leadership position, or recently have done so, recognising that being promoted without having all of the necessary skills to succeed is a common aspect of organisational life is useful for you. Experiencing dilemmas in your first leadership role can be a consequence of poor practice within your organisation as much as, if not more than, you having doubts about whether you're capable of being a good leader. Understanding that promoting people before they've been developed to succeed in their first leadership role is common practice can boost your confidence, because you see that the situation you're facing is common: the underlying causes of you experiencing dilemmas rest with the organisation more than with you.

Organisations also have dilemmas! One is whether to develop people before they step up to their first leadership role or develop them after they've been appointed. In my experience, people who participate in leadership development programmes before they take up their new position have more difficulty fully understanding and appreciating the difficulties and dilemmas that other people on the programme want to work through, simply because they haven't experienced these dilemmas. On the other hand, waiting until people acquire enough experience to enable them to gain the most benefit from participating in a leadership development programme means that they're more likely to encounter dilemmas for which they're unprepared.

Newly appointed leaders need to be coached by their line manager to handle dilemmas and succeed in their role, and participate in a leadership development programme to accelerate developing their leadership skills after they've gained a few months experience leading people.

Every time that you're promoted into a more senior leadership position, you're likely to encounter situations that you haven't experienced before: or put another way, handling dilemmas is part of leadership! The sooner you accept this fact, the sooner you can start to work on enhancing your leadership skills through tackling the dilemmas you experience. (You can find out in Chapter 4 how to look for your own coach if your line manager isn't giving you the support you feel you need.)

Becoming comfortable with being uncomfortable

Most people prefer to be comfortable rather than uncomfortable. For example, when you arrive home after work you may well sink into your most comfortable chair or sofa instead of settling for a seat in which you can't totally relax.

 Similarly, in the work environment, most people prefer to remain in their comfort zone. *Comfort zone* is a term used widely in personal and leadership development to describe the state in which a person feels safe or at ease: a mental and emotional state I also describe as 'comfortable'. When you're operating in your comfort zone, you're at ease with yourself. You're in a situation or doing an activity that allows you to work within the limits of your perceived skills and abilities: or put another way, you feel comfortable because you're confident that you can do the activity well or deal with the situation.

Staying in your comfort zone is therefore risk-free because you don't expose yourself to potential failure. But developing your leadership skills can never be risk-free, otherwise you never discover how to handle potentially difficult problems.

Instead, you need to face up to and deal with difficult situations, and therefore you can expect to feel uncomfortable in your new leadership role. Unfortunately, too many new leaders don't accept this reality and refuse to face up to difficult problems or people. Instead, they delay dealing with them or even ignore them, which often means that the problem gets bigger as the work situation deteriorates.

Figure 6-1 gives a couple of examples of the types of situations that may be outside your comfort zone. Add your own dilemmas to the diagram (if you're yet to identify your own dilemmas, complete Table 6-1 in the earlier section 'Dealing with Dilemmas') and create a picture of your own, personal comfort zone. Write those dilemmas that are just outside your comfort zone closer to the centre circle, and those that you feel involve more risk farther away from the centre. Also, include a few examples of situations that are inside your comfort zone to ensure that you also recognise your strengths.

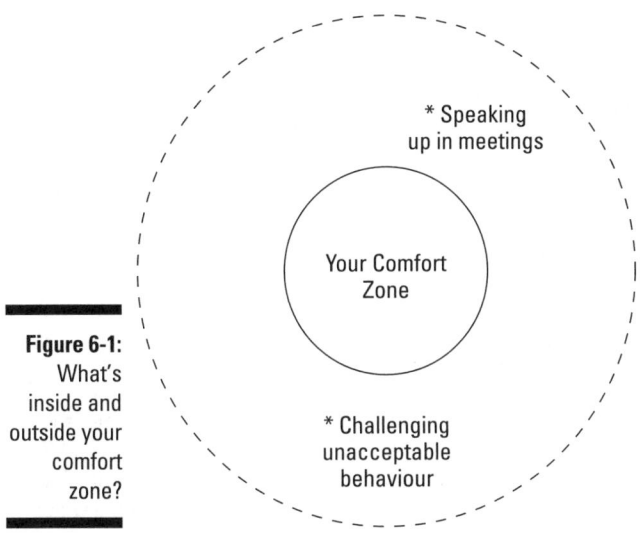

Figure 6-1:
What's
inside and
outside your
comfort
zone?

* Speaking
up in meetings

Your Comfort
Zone

* Challenging
unacceptable
behaviour

Facing up to problems and exposing yourself to new potentially difficult situations involves stepping outside of your comfort zone and being uncomfortable. In this way you can discover how to become 'comfortable being uncomfortable' and build the confidence that you can cope with new situations and be successful in dealing with them.

Finding out how to be comfortable being uncomfortable also enables you to stretch yourself and develop your leadership abilities. Working through how to deal with difficult situations and problems enables you to develop your problem-solving and decision-making skills, convey the standards of work and behaviour you expect from others, practise your skills in working effectively with difficult people and so on. Developing your leadership abilities also enhances your self-confidence in handling new situations, which in turn enables you to expand your comfort zone because you then feel more at ease when you're exposed to new difficult situations in the future.

To encourage you to face up to and address a difficult situation or put yourself into a new situation that involves a degree of risk, consider and answer the following questions:

- ✔ **What's the worst possible outcome if I address this situation?**
- ✔ **What's the best possible outcome of this situation?**
- ✔ **What's the outcome that's in the middle of these two outcomes?**
- ✔ **What's the probability of each of these outcomes happening?**

Behind every problem lurks an opportunity

One of my early leadership roles involved managing several water treatment works spread over a large geographical area. The area hadn't been managed properly for several months due to my predecessor being absent on long-term sickness and, consequently, superintendents from surrounding areas taking turns to 'cover' the area as well as manage their own areas.

During the first few months in my new position a senior operator tried to make life really difficult for me because I curtailed his time driving to several treatment works so that he spent more time doing productive work. This senior operator was also a union official who, in the absence of a permanent manager, had been regularly going to other works simply to visit 'his men' and he was influential with the rest of the employees.

I recall spending many hours being uncomfortable, tossing and turning most nights, wondering how to handle all the problems and difficulties that this man was creating. I often asked myself the questions, 'Why have I got the most difficult employee working for me?' and 'Why can't I manage another area that's a lot easier to manage?'.

My state of discomfort continued until I realised that the problems and difficulties I was experiencing were great opportunities for me to discover how to handle dilemmas. Realising this fact enabled me to become more comfortable in situations in which I wasn't sure about what to do: I had in fact become more comfortable being uncomfortable because I appreciated that my senior operator was, unintentionally, helping me to acquire invaluable experience about leadership and managing difficult people.

I discovered that status and recognition were important to the senior operator, and I found a way in which he could fulfil his union responsibilities and perform the duties I required him to do.

Answering these questions may well confirm that you're overestimating the seriousness of the problem or the likelihood or it occurring. New leaders often don't face up to situations because they're concerned about the outcome, without objectively assessing what the outcome may be: they're concerned about the worst outcome even though the probability of it happening is miniscule!

One of the most common outcomes that people tell me they're concerned about is feeling embarrassed due to not dealing with a difficult situation very well. When I enquire how long they feel embarrassed, most people say a few hours or a day or two at most. In fact, the chances of you dealing so badly with a situation that you're left with an emotional scar is extremely rare. Clarifying the best and middle outcomes can encourage you to address the difficult situation because you place equal emphasis on the positives as well as the negatives. Recognising and appreciating the benefits of dealing with the situation can also prompt you to act.

Getting caught in the middle

Unless you're a managing director, you're going to be in the middle of two other levels in the organisational structure of your company. People in their first leadership position are typically in the middle between their staff and their boss, the equivalent of a corporal in the army who's between the front line troops and their sergeant. Being in the middle requires you to communicate the views of senior managers to your staff and the views of your staff to your manager.

Being in the middle, though, involves far more than just communicating and liaising between these two groups: you need to represent both groups as well, which is where you can get trapped!

At times, the views of more senior managers, or your immediate manager aren't going to align with the views of your staff, and vice versa. Both sides are likely to expect you to side with them: your manager expects you to reinforce the company view while your staff expect you to support and speak up, or even stand up, for them! This dilemma can result in some leaders avoiding taking sides and end up 'sitting on the fence'.

You may have come across this situation before you become a leader: if so, take a few moments to remember how you felt about the 'fence-sitter'.

Some of the main dangers of sitting on the fence are:

- ✔ Being seen as indecisive.
- ✔ Losing credibility with your manager.
- ✔ Losing credibility with your staff.
- ✔ Permitting changes in systems, procedures or other ways of doing things that don't work.
- ✔ Risking your staff becoming more anxious, frustrated or angry about changes that the company are introducing.

You have to get off and stay off the fence if you want to avoid these and other dangers of being caught in the middle. Listen carefully to both sides of an issue – to the views of your manager and your staff – and then make an objective assessment of the situation and decide on your own view. Inform your staff about the reasons behind decisions and why you agree with them, and be willing to acknowledge their concerns.

If you disagree with decisions that your own or more senior managers take, and you're expected to implement them, ask for clarification about the reasons for the decisions. Also be prepared to let your manager know your view and the views of your staff, as well as your and their reasons for questioning or challenging the decision. You may not be successful in changing the decision, but at least you can try to ensure that all parties have a good understanding of the reasons for and against the decision.

You're certain to experience situations in which you understand the business reasons for a decision, and yet have concerns because the decision is going to have an adverse effect on your staff. You may need to ask yourself whether to tell your staff that you disagree with the decision. I suggest that you act in ways that maintain your integrity with your staff and encourage them to do what's reasonable to help the business achieve sustainable success. You can find more insights and guidance on leading people, especially during periods of change, in Parts III and IV.

Accepting that leadership can be lonely

Leaders of all types of organisation are expected to be brilliant at leading their organisation and staff. In a way, people expect their leader to be super-human and have x-ray vision to foresee every threat, the ability to fly to get all around the organisation and incredible strength to carry and support everyone.

Leadership can be lonely, because leaders often have difficulty sharing their concerns and doubts about decisions and even their own abilities with the people who report to them: they don't want to undermine this image of perfection. Many managing directors engage me as a mentor or coach because they're lonely and need a 'sounding board' or critical friend who's willing to challenge and support, but not judge, them.

Similarly, people in their first leadership role can also be lonely, because they find that sharing their concerns and dilemmas with their manager and staff is difficult. Your current manager probably appointed you, and you may be reluctant to share your concerns and doubts in case doing so reflects badly on you. You may also be reluctant to share your doubts with your staff because you're concerned that they may lose confidence in you and decide that you don't know what you're doing.

Many organisations now use external or internal coaches to be critical friends to support the development of managers and leaders. If your organisation is yet to adopt this approach, take the initiative and find your own coach. Choose a leader with more experience than you – someone who you admire, respect and trust – and ask that person to be your coach. In doing so, you're paying that person a compliment: you're acknowledging that you value her knowledge, skills and wisdom. Talk through what you expect of each other, and agree what you can talk about and how often you're going to meet. (You can find more in Chapter 4 about finding your own coach.)

Avoiding the imposter syndrome

People who are promoted and then question whether they're worthy of having a seat at the table with their new colleagues can experience the 'imposter syndrome'. If you feel like an imposter, you fear doing or saying something that causes you to be embarrassed in front of your colleagues; that is, you fear being revealed as an imposter because you're not up to performing your new role. You tend to be cautious, speaking only when necessary when you're confident and knowledgeable about the topic or issue being discussed (check out the earlier section 'Becoming comfortable with being uncomfortable', on the dangers of being stuck in your comfort zone.) People who've felt like an imposter tell me that the sensation exists until they realise that they feel comfortable with, or as good as, their colleagues. They observe and listen to their colleagues, and in doing so come to realise that their colleagues are human rather than superhuman: the thinking and contributions of their colleagues aren't always brilliant and they also make mistakes.

To avoid falling prey to the imposter syndrome, make sure that you talk yourself up and build your self-esteem. Remind yourself that you've been promoted to your new position because others appreciate your talents, and praise yourself for making useful contributions, such as to group discussions. Take time to observe your new colleagues and notice what they do well and what they can perhaps do better. Recognising that they're not perfect – and that some of your abilities and talents are the equal of or even better than those of your colleagues – helps you to appreciate yourself and feel that you're worthy of your seat at the table.

Leading Friends

Stepping up to your first leadership role can cause all sorts of dilemmas if you're promoted from among a group who were your peers and are your friends. Dilemmas normally result from you and/or your friends perceiving that a fundamental shift has taken place in the relationship: at work, you're no longer 'one of them'.

Perhaps, previously, members of the group took liberties with timekeeping, spending more time than they should chatting in the office or surfing the Internet. Now that you're responsible for setting the standards for the group, you may be concerned about changing everyday practices that you used to condone as a group member.

If you fear being accused of having double standards and lacking integrity, this section gives tips to help.

Achieving success while keeping your friends

One question that may occupy your mind is: can I succeed in my new leadership role and keep my friends?

Yes you can, because although the work context has changed – that is, you're now the manager – the relationship as friends hasn't. You do, however, need to consider the implications of the change in work context on the relationship. One implication is that you're expected to consider fully the needs or requirements of your company, and therefore any consequences of, for example, the behaviour or performance of your staff on the success of your company. This new reality may mean that you now have a different view towards timekeeping, time spent chatting or the extent to which people surf the Internet.

Another implication is that you probably used to share most, if not all, information with each other when you were peers. In your leadership role, however, your manager may include you in considering options such as potential changes in organisational structure or procedures, or share commercially sensitive information with you that you can't share with your staff, at least not straight away.

Talk through the implications of the change in work context with your staff, especially those that are your friends, so that everyone fully understands these implications and you can continue to work well together. This discussion can be a tough thing to do, but you and your staff can all experience success while you keep your friends.

Your true friends support you in everything that you do. And if you're getting things wrong for any reason, it's much better to have people that you know and trust coming to you with their views. You can listen in full confidence and if things need adjusting, you have advice from sources that you know have your best interests at heart, as well as those of the organisation.

Knowing where and when to draw the line

Most organisations have policies and procedures that are designed to provide general guidance for managers on how to lead and manage their staff. These policies probably cover a range of issues such as health and safety, attendance or absence, training and development, and performance, as well as procedures for dealing with situations in which individuals are significantly under-performing in their job: the discipline procedure. Providing detailed guidance on every possible aspect of staff performance or behaviour, however, simply isn't feasible: the reference document would be far thicker than *War and Peace* and nobody would use it. In any case, foreseeing every possible scenario is impossible.

As a leader, you need to consider each situation on its own merits and no documentation can be a substitute for you or other leaders making the best decisions and taking everything into consideration. Put another way, you're expected to make difficult decisions about the performance or behaviour of your staff with the assistance of your organisation's policies and procedures and, where available, the advice of the Human Resources department or personnel specialists.

You need to be clear about the standards you expect from yourself and the people who work for you so you can make decisions about what's acceptable or unacceptable behaviour and performance, and to enable you to know where and when to draw the line! Being clear about your standards helps you to deal with dilemmas and, eventually, prevent a lot of dilemmas through sharing and reinforcing your standards with your staff and other work colleagues.

In Table 6-1 in the earlier section 'Dealing with Dilemmas', I suggest that you make a list of the dilemmas you're currently experiencing or you may potentially experience. Refer to this list and copy any dilemmas that relate to behavioural or performance issues regarding leading friends into the first column in Table 6-2.

Can we still be friends?

During a management development workshop that a client asked me jointly to facilitate with another person, a manager asked the following question: 'Can you still be friends with people you're managing?' The other facilitator responded immediately: 'No you can't, you have to keep your distance!' I disagreed with this viewpoint and shared my concerns with the group, as follows.

Describing a person as a friend means that you've established a mutually beneficial relationship. You've common interests or values and a commitment to help or support each other even if this support is implicit rather than explicit. To accept that this person can no longer be a friend means that you have to break the relationship that exists, and everything that this relationship represents. My concern is that if you suddenly stop valuing a person, how can you expect that they're going to value you? For me, you can't! You damage the trust and respect that you've established, and when you lose the trust and respect of the people who work for you, you also lose the foundations of working well together.

Using this table, describe the standard you expect from yourself and your friends (in the second column), making sure to consider fully the needs or requirements of your company, and therefore any consequences of, for example, the behaviour or performance of your staff on the success of the company. Then describe in the third column how you think that your friends would prefer to work. The first rows of the table give examples of possible differences in the preferred ways of working, as regards timekeeping and Internet use, so that you can see how the exercise works.

Table 6-2	Clarifying Your Standards	
Description of the Behaviour or Performance Issue	*Description of the Behaviour or Performance Standard I Expect from Myself and My Friends*	*Description of the Behaviour or Performance Standard My Friends Would Prefer*
Timekeeping	Always arrive at work by the agreed time	Arrive at work when I choose to
Use of the Internet	During lunchtime and other reasonable breaks	Whenever I want to

You can also complete the above exercise for all aspects of work and help explore the potential differences in preferred ways of working between you and any of your work colleagues. Having a conversation with people about their and your preferred ways of working enables you to share your standards with them and clarify any differences in expectations. Clarifying the gap is the first step to bridging it and resolving dilemmas.

You can also experience dilemmas even after you've clarified and shared your standards with your friends and other work colleagues. At certain times, common sense dictates that you allow a member of staff to work outside the standards you expect from yourself and others. An example is when someone wants to come into work late or leave work early because they've a valid personal reason for doing so. Don't be concerned that making an allowance on one occasion means that have to agree to every similar other request in the future: you don't. You only have to use your common sense and standards as a point of reference in making your decision each time in order to decide what's reasonable and fair.

Part III
Leading Others

'The trouble is that they <u>all</u> want
to be leaders.'

In this part . . .

If raising people's commitment and optimising their performance is your major interest, then this is the main part for you. In these chapters you find out about the importance of purposeful work, and I explain how you can really engage people so that they want to follow you and do their job to the best of their ability. You discover how you can become an engaging leader and modify your leadership style to suit different situations. You find out how to handle people who aren't achieving your standards, and coach good performers towards gaining exceptional results.

Chapter 7

Developing a Sense of Purpose

. . . .

. . . .

*W*hat's the point?' Have you ever asked this question, or maybe heard a work colleague ask it, about a change being introduced to the way your department, team or you work? Perhaps you've experienced occasions when you and/or your work colleagues think that proposals to change the organisational structure, systems or processes (or perhaps instructions from senior management to follow a particular course of action) are completely pointless!

People like to know the point, or purpose, of their work: you can't expect people to do a job or task to the best of their ability if they don't understand the purpose or reasons for doing so. In this chapter you find out how to create a clear sense of purpose that you can use yourself – and communicate to the people who report to you – to focus everyone's efforts on achieving the objectives and results required of you and your team. You also discover how to increase your sphere of influence to encourage people you don't have authority over – including your boss! – so that they act in a way that helps you and your team to be successful.

Having Clarity of Purpose

Your job description, if you have one, describes your duties and responsibilities, but does it clearly describe the purpose of your job and how you contribute to the success of your organisation? For example, does it describe your priorities or how you measure success in doing your job? Probably not!

Or things may have changed so much since your job description was written that it's now out of date, for example, in changes in systems, procedures and even the tasks that you're asked to do. In addition, most job descriptions include the vague phrase '. . . and anything else that is required to . . .' near the end of the description. A good chance exists that you haven't even looked at your job description for ages! With all these uncertainties in mind, developing clarity of purpose can be difficult, which is where this section can help.

I often use the following scenario to challenge leaders on development programmes about how clearly they understand their role in their organisation. I ask them to assume that I'm the new Chief Executive Officer or Managing Director, and that I'm walking around the Head Office stopping individuals and asking them to tell me in 30 seconds:

> *What's the purpose of your job and how do you add value to this organisation?*

To add a bit of spice I also say that I'm looking to make savings and that I'm going to form my initial opinion about the value of each individual's job on the strength of his answer. When answering the question, people tend to tell me what they do rather than describing the positive impact they have in, or the value they add to, their organisation. How well would you answer this question in 30 seconds?

Be so clear about the purpose of your job and your team that you can concisely describe your and their role to them in 30 seconds or less so that they understand how they contribute to the success of your organisation. (Flip to the later section 'Clarifying how you add value' for how to achieve this aim.)

Avoiding being a busy fool

Have you ever experienced any of the following sensations:

- ✔ Feeling like you're on a rocking horse, being furiously active but getting nowhere?
- ✔ Feeling like you haven't stopped all day and yet have achieved nothing?
- ✔ Feeling like you get sucked into the details of your team's work so often that you can't get on with what you're paid to be doing?
- ✔ Feeling like you're running around like a headless chicken?

To really add value to your organisation, you need to avoid becoming one of those busy fools who're less productive than they could be.

You may think that you're being effective and efficient because you're very active, but as the song goes 'it ain't necessarily so'! You may, for example, be spending time on tasks or activities that are less valuable or important than other work that you need to do, or so busy because you're disorganised, with one of the following results:

- ✔ You're effective, but not efficient.
- ✔ You're efficient, but not effective.
- ✔ You're not effective or efficient.

Many of the inexperienced and experienced managers that I've worked with on leadership development programmes misunderstand the terms *effective* and *efficient*:

- ✔ Being *effective* means focusing on, and spending time doing and completing, the most valuable or important tasks or activities that you have to do and doing them well: it means doing the right things!
- ✔ Being *efficient* means using the minimum time and resources to do a particular task or activity: it means doing things the right way!

To help, I use the four-box grid in Figure 7-1 to explain these terms in simple language. The top-right box is the way towards high effectiveness and efficiency.

Figure 7-1:
Simple
explanation
of the terms
effective
and
efficient.

	Efficient	
High **Effective** Low	Doing the right tasks the wrong way	Doing the right tasks the right way
	Doing the wrong tasks the wrong way	Doing the wrong tasks the right way
	Low	Efficient High

You can avoid being a busy fool by focusing on being effective and efficient: that is, doing the right things the right way!

Being bold: leading with conviction

The people who report to you expect you to be a decisive leader: they don't want you to 'sit on the fence' (check out the dangers of being a 'fence-sitter' in Chapter 6). You may, however, sometimes be indecisive because you're unsure about what to do: being bold and leading with conviction in this situation is risky and potentially foolhardy!

Being clear about the purpose of your job, the objectives and results you have to achieve and your priorities enables you to be bolder than you may normally be because you:

- ✔ Confidently communicate the direction that you and your team have to take, and the necessary objectives, targets and results.

- ✔ Convey the direction, objectives and results in ways that the people who report to you understand so that their work becomes meaningful to them.

- ✔ Are more confident that the decisions you make are leading you towards achieving the purpose of your job and your priorities.

- ✔ Follow through on your decisions and act with commitment to positively influence people and achieve your objectives.

- ✔ Can explain to anyone and everyone where value is being added and lost in everything that you do.

Clarifying how you add value

Along with everyone else who has a job, you're in the conversion industry: you take *inputs* and convert them into more valuable *outputs*. That's how you add value to the organisation you work for.

Being in the conversion industry doesn't apply only to manufacturing – where companies convert materials into products – it also applies to every service. For example, every time you eat in a restaurant the employees are using information, knowledge, skills, ingredients, equipment and much more to create a great experience and meal for you. Figure 7-2 provides more examples of inputs and outputs.

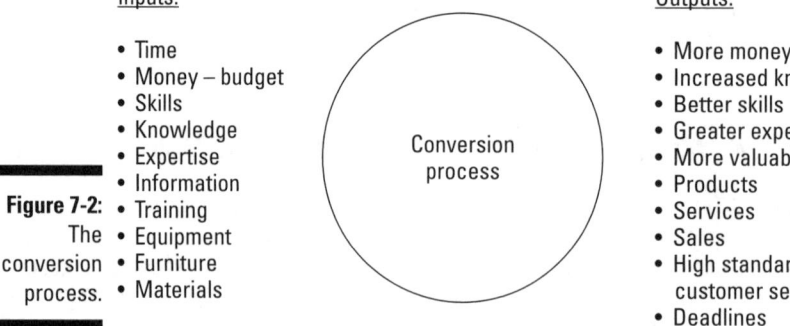

Inputs:

- Time
- Money – budget
- Skills
- Knowledge
- Expertise
- Information
- Training
- Equipment
- Furniture
- Materials

Conversion process

Outputs:

- More money – profit
- Increased knowledge
- Better skills
- Greater expertise
- More valuable information
- Products
- Services
- Sales
- High standards of quality, customer service and so on
- Deadlines

Figure 7-2: The conversion process.

Seeing yourself as being in the conversion process may help you to look at your job from a new perspective. Complete the next exercise to start to clarify how you add value to your organisation by describing the purpose of your job.

Take a look at the lists of inputs and outputs in Figure 7-2:

1. **Tick or circle the words in the first list that describe inputs that you use or consume in carrying out your job.** Add any inputs that you use or consume that aren't on the list, but keep the inputs generic, similar to the points already on the list, instead of dropping in a lot of detail.

2. **Repeat step 1 for the list of outputs.**

3. **Write a sentence that describes the purpose of your job based on some of, if not all, the outputs and inputs you ticked or circled.** I provide two examples below of how the broad purpose of a publisher's job for academic books may be written.

    • **Example 1:** To source, sign and publish the targeted number of books to the required standards and deadlines within budget.

    • **Example 2:** To enhance the knowledge and skills of students, and achieve my profit target by sourcing, signing and publishing academic books.

Which example appeals most to you in terms of the purpose of a publisher's job being most worthwhile or adding most value to the publisher's company, and even to society?

The right answer of course depends on the 'why'! I suggest Example 2 is more appropriate because how value is added – enhancing knowledge and skills, and making a profit – is more explicit in this example than in example 1. So when you write your sentence, make sure that you can support and justify (and if necessary defend) the position that you've taken.

When you're writing a sentence describing the purpose of your job, try to capture the essence or fundamental reason for doing your job: how you add value rather than only 'to earn money'! The purpose of your job needs to capture what's important and worthwhile – and be meaningful rather than meaningless to you and other people when you explain it to them.

The purpose of my job is:

_____

Now work on further clarifying how you add value to your organisation through the work you do by building on the exercise you have just completed.

Before you can be highly productive, you need to have a clear understanding about how what you do helps your organisation to be successful. You need to know what being a 'high performer' in your job means in practice. Completing the following exercise enables you to be clear about what you're expected to achieve and how you can measure your success, which, in turn, helps you to make the right decisions to attain the right results.

Refer to the outputs and inputs you identified and the purpose of your job that you produced when completing the previous exercise and complete the following steps. I give an example of how partially to complete these steps in Table 7-1. (By all means complete these steps in a notebook first while you clarify your thoughts about each step, but also note the outcomes of each step below so that you can use them to focus your efforts and time on achieving the required results. Find out how to do this in the next section, 'Focusing on your key results'.)

1. **List the most important parts of your job.** I suggest that up to five or six most important parts of your job exist: if you're noting more than six, you're probably getting into too much detail:

   A:

   B:

   C:

   D:

   E:

   F:

2. **Write the objectives and/or results that you're expected to achieve in each of the most important parts of your job and how you measure how successful you are in each part.**

	Objectives and/or Results I have to Achieve:	*How I Measure Success:*
A.		
B.		
C.		
D.		
E.		
F.		

Some measures of success may be key success measures, perhaps more commonly known as key performance indicators (KPIs), because those measures or indicators are the most important indicators of performance.

Table 7-1   A Partially Completed Description of a Publisher's Job, and Measuring Success

	Most Important Parts of a Publisher's Job:	
A	Publish books to schedule	
B	Enhance the knowledge of students in the subject area	
	Objectives and/or Results a Publisher has to Achieve:	*How a Publisher Measures Success:*
A	Publish 30 books on schedule in this financial year	Number of books published by the set deadlines
B	Achieve the required uptake and use of books on selected courses	Quality and appearance of subject content
		Feedback from course leaders and students
		Recommendations by course leaders
		Subsequent sales achieved

Share the outcomes of this exercise with your line manager to discuss and agree that you're focusing on the required results, and are working to the right priorities to achieve those results. You may be surprised to find that your manager's views on the purpose, results and/or priorities are slightly (or even significantly) different to your views. Agreeing these items with your manager helps you to work well together by avoiding misunderstandings about what you should be or are doing.

You can only measure whether anything you do is a success or failure against what you set out to achieve.

As the leader of your team, your overall job purpose and objectives are the same as your team's purpose and objectives. Enthusiastically convey the purpose of your team and the objectives and results that you're all aiming for to everyone in your team and to other departments that your team works with and rely upon to succeed. (You can find out how to involve members of your team in clarifying your team's purpose and objectives – if you prefer this alternative approach – in Chapter 15.)

Focusing on your key results

You probably think that you have a lot, perhaps too much, work to complete within the hours stated in your employment contract. Being clear about the objectives and results required to make a valuable contribution to the success of your organisation helps you to be highly productive, but it doesn't guarantee your success. For that, you need a little help from a guy called Vilfredo Pareto.

Pareto was an economist who looked into how land was distributed among people who lived in Italy. Surprise, surprise! Pareto discovered that 20 per cent of the people owned 80 per cent of the land and the basis of the Pareto principle or 80/20 rule was born.

Applying the 80/20 rule to your job means identifying the 20 per cent of the tasks and activities to spend your time on that enable you to be 80 per cent successful in your job. You have to focus on the most valuable tasks and activities: out of all the things you can spend your time doing, you need to decide which tasks and activities are a priority for you to achieve what you need to.

The following descriptions help in understanding how I'm using these terms:

- A *task* is a specific piece of work that you need to do such as one of the steps to complete a project or achieve an objective or result.
- An *activity* is something you do regularly such as holding meetings with your team to discuss how your team is making progress in achieving your team's objectives.

An *urgent* task or activity is one that's very close to the deadline by which it has to be done or completed, whereas a less urgent task is one further away from its deadline.

An urgent task is typically one that has to be done in the next one or two hours or even minutes. For example, completing a document that has to be posted to a client today may be considered to be urgent if the last collection time for the post is within the next one or two hours.

The urgency of a task or activity may change: all you have to do for a task or activity to become more urgent is to not do it and notice how it becomes more urgent as time passes!

An *important* task or activity is one that, by completing, you add a lot of value to your organisation; or put another way, one that contributes significantly to you achieving your objectives and results.

The importance of a task or activity doesn't tend to change unless:

✔ Senior managers decide to change a company policy or objective, such as to attack a new market, which affects the work you do.

✔ A change in legislation or another significant external event impacts upon your work responsibilities, such as health and safety legislation.

Figure 7-3 and the following list explain the different combinations of urgency and importance that you may allocate to a task or activity:

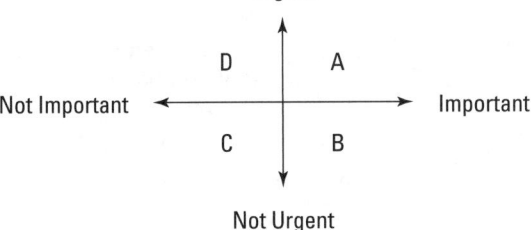

Figure 7-3: Importance and urgency of tasks and activities.

The figure is based on the time management matrix featured in Stephen Covey's Seven Habits of Highly Effective People *(Simon and Schuster).*

✔ **Category 'A' task.** An 'A' task is both urgent and important because completing it significantly contributes to you achieving one of your key objectives and you're close to the deadline for completing it. You may feel under pressure or stress when doing an 'A' task because too little time may be available to do the task as well as you'd like to, and consequences apply if you don't complete it by the required deadline or to the required standard.

✔ **Category 'B' task.** A 'B' task is important but not urgent: completing it significantly contributes to you achieving one of your key objectives, but you're not close to the deadline for completing it. You probably feel more relaxed and in control when doing a 'B' task because you've the time you need to do the job well.

✔ **Category 'C' task.** A 'C' task is less important than other tasks you have to do and isn't urgent: completing it doesn't significantly contribute to you achieving one of your key objectives and you're not close to the deadline for completing it. You may ask yourself why you're doing a task that you categorise as a 'C' task, which is probably a good question – challenge yourself as to whether it's worthwhile doing it!

✔ **Category 'D' task.** A 'D' task is urgent but less important than other tasks you have to do: completing it doesn't significantly contribute to you achieving one of your key objectives, but you're close to the dead-line for completing it. An example of a category 'D' task is one that a work colleague has asked you to do at short notice, but completing it adds little value to your organisation.

Question how important a task or activity is as well as how urgent it is when trying to decide on your work priorities.

Use these categories to make decisions about your work priorities and how you plan and organise use of your time. You can apply the following approach to a workday, week or even a month or longer:

1. **Make a list of all the tasks you have to do in the period you have chosen.**

2. **Go down your list and decide how important and urgent each task is by giving it an 'A', 'B', 'C' or 'D' rating.** If you have given several tasks the same rating, allocate these tasks a secondary rating such as A1, A2, A3 and so on based on the lower the number the higher the priority.

3. **Use the ratings you've given to each task to decide the order in which you're going to do them.**

Bear in mind the following guidelines:

✔ Do more important tasks before less important tasks.

✔ Do 'A' tasks – those that are important and urgent – before 'B' tasks, but make sure that you start 'B' tasks early enough to avoid them becoming 'A' tasks.

✔ Do 'D' tasks if by doing them you stop worrying about them or get a sense of achievement, but do them as quickly as you can.

✔ Leave 'C' tasks alone and only do them if you don't have any 'A', 'B' or 'D' tasks to do.

Spending the right time on the right job

Although deciding on the order in which you're going to do your tasks helps you to 'do the right job' to be effective, it doesn't necessarily make you efficient. (You can find out about the importance of being both effective and efficient in the earlier section 'Avoiding being a busy fool'.) To be efficient, you have to spend the right time on each task: the minimum time required to do the job well.

Use the following techniques to spend the minimum time on each task or activity you have to do to do it well:

✔ Question yourself whether the job really needs to be done to the standard to which you normally do it. Can you do the job in less time and it still to be good enough or 'fit for purpose'?

✔ Ask yourself, and others, 'What would happen if I didn't do this job?'. Your manager or colleagues may ask you to do extra tasks such as provide additional monthly information or reports to them, but never tell you that they don't need you to do them anymore.

✔ When you're estimating how long a big job or project may take to complete, break the project down into steps and estimate how long each step is going to take. Then add up the time for each step to produce a more accurate estimate for completing the whole project.

Becoming a Visionary Leader

Many visionary leaders have captured the attention and admiration of the public, and influenced the direction, thinking and behaviour of a large group, society and even a nation. Martin Luther King, Jr. is one of my favourites: I get a tingling sensation every time I hear a recording of his 'I Have a Dream' speech that he gave in 1963.

You don't have to be able to capture the attention of society, but you do have to capture the attention of, and positively influence, the people who report to you if you want them to do a great job for you . . . and being a visionary leader may help you to achieve this aim. I explain how to come up with your vision in the later section 'Creating your own vision', but I introduce being a visionary leader by briefly covering a common process used in many organisations for influencing employees to contribute to the organisation's success: sharing the strategic direction of the organisation.

You probably expect that the direction that your organisation is going in, and why and how it's going to get there to be shared with you because, like most people, you want to contribute to something worthwhile. The direction that your organisation is going in is probably described by the strategic goals, objectives and plans to achieve them, and these may be cascaded down from your Chief Executive Officer or Managing Director, depending on the type of organisation you work for, to you and your colleagues via directors and managers who are more senior than you.

As well as understanding your organisation's goals, you also need to know how the objectives that your immediate line manager requires you to achieve fit with those wider goals. By clearly understanding this connection, you can appreciate how you're adding value and contributing to the success of your organisation. (The earlier section 'Clarifying how you add value' shows you how you can work out how to add value to your organisation.)

Just as you expect your immediate line manager to help you clarify how your objectives connect with your organisation's goals, your staff probably also expect the same from you.

 Being a visionary leader, and sharing your vision of how your team is going to carry out its work in the future, complements sharing the objectives or results you expect them to reach, because it enables them to see a more attractive way of working in the future.

Valuing having a vision

Have you ever flipped through a magazine or perhaps surfed the Internet and come across a picture of a location that grabs your attention so strongly that you start to dream of being there? Well, your vision needs to have this effect on your team . . . and more! Your vision, and how you share it, needs to be so attractive to members of your team that they become committed to making your vision become reality.

Your vision of your team depends upon your position and role in your organisation. Your vision may be for your whole organisation if you're the Managing Director, your function or department if you're a director or head of department, or your section or team if you're at another level in your organisation's management structure.

Your vision needs to fulfil the following roles:

- Present a picture or image of how you want your team to be at some point in the future.
- Describe what you want to create because this vision is focused on a future that is better than that what currently exists.

✔ Describe how your team will be working together in achieving its purpose or how it adds value to your organisation and/or its customers.

✔ Reflect and reinforce high standards of excellence regarding the work of your team in serving its customers, and how people in your team work together and with customers.

✔ Give a sense of what's possible: share it with enthusiasm and passion to inspire and encourage people to believe that they *can* create it.

✔ Be unique, important and worthwhile: people are more enthusiastic and committed about creating something that they want to be part of and which is important to them.

The value of your vision of how you see your team doing its work in the future lies in the quality of the vision you create and how well you share it with the people who report to you.

Creating your own vision

You may create a vision of how you want your team to be by yourself and then share it with them, or you may involve part of or all your team, depending on how many people comprise it, in creating the vision. The approach I describe for producing a vision is based on you doing it yourself, but you may follow the same steps in involving your team.

To create your vision for your team, first you need to clarify your team's purpose, and the required goals necessary to make a worthwhile contribution to the organisation as a whole. (You can discover how to clarify the purpose of your job and how you add value in the earlier section 'Clarifying how you add value'.) The overall purpose of your job is probably the same as that of your team because you're the leader of your team and are responsible for its work.

Keeping the purpose of your team in the back of your mind, start to create a picture or vision of how you see your team working in achieving its purpose by reflecting upon and answering the following questions.

You may prefer to draw a picture or write a few words that represent your vision for your team in answering the following questions:

1. **Get a notebook and copy the following questions, leaving enough space to answer them.** Then add your own questions to this list to help you to think about anything that's significant to you in creating your vision:

    • What will people in my team be doing?

    • How will members of the team be working together?

- How will the team be working with and serving its customers and/ or colleagues in other departments?

- How will people be treated?

- What impression will the team be making on the different groups of people it works for and with?

- What will these different groups be saying about my team?

- How will members of the team be feeling about their work and about each other?

2. **When you've answered all the questions, reflect upon your answers to draw out the key words or themes that are significant to you.**

3. **Combine the significant words or themes to produce a short statement or paragraph that captures your vision of your team.**

4. **When you're satisfied with the statement or drawing that captures your vision, share it enthusiastically with your team so that they want to be part of it and make it come true.**

5. **Talk to your team regularly about the vision to reinforce what you're striving to create, and discuss the progress your team is making in creating it with them to acknowledge the team's achievements.**

The more you involve people in creating a vision, the more they feel part of it, own it and be committed to achieving it. A good starting point for involving your team in shaping and creating its future is to work with your staff in clarifying the team's purpose by working through the exercises in the earlier section 'Clarifying how you add value'. Just a simple step is then needed to involve them in working through the above exercise to create their vision for the team with you.

Fluffy white robes and slippers

I heard a Chief Executive of a hospice invite guests attending a fundraising ball to talk to her about contributing to the work of the hospice. I took up the invitation and subsequently met the Chief Executive to talk about the future plans for the hospice.

The Chief Executive described her vision for the hospice and I share with you now the picture that she described to me.

'My aim is to build a new hospice that fully utilises our position overlooking the valley and countryside for the benefit of our residents and staff. We will have six residential rooms, each with one wall of glass so that patients will be able to enjoy the panoramic view from their bed. Each room will also have its own secluded terrace so that residents and their families will be able to sit outside on fine days and enjoy the location and each others' company in private.

We will have a large treatment centre and a spa where people can enjoy a wide range of complimentary treatments provided by our wonderful staff. Residents and patients visiting for day care will mix with paying guests who are hiring the facilities (to generate income to sustain the hospice) in the spa and other areas. People will be shuffling around in white robes and slippers, enjoying and benefitting from the excellent skills of our staff and the facilities, and you won't be able to tell who are paying guests and who are residents or patients here for day care.'

This vision of caring for people, especially of building a community of people mingling together regardless of their health or wealth, inspired me to become a volunteer with the hospice and commit to sharing and using my expertise in how to build successful organisations.

Expanding Your Sphere of Influence

I'm sure that, like most managers, you want to have more influence and control over your working life. For example, greater influence may mean:

- All the necessary resources to do everything you have to do being available without you needing to work extra hours.

- Everyone that you rely upon to provide the necessary information and so on to complete your work giving it to you on time, every time.

- Senior managers taking more notice of your views and opinions when making important decisions that affect you and your team.

In this section I encourage you to question and challenge yourself about the amount of influence you have, and work on expanding your sphere of influence over your work and, perhaps, in your organisation.

Discovering that you have more influence than you think

Your success in influencing people and situations is as much down to your mindset as to you having a particular skill! I use the term *mindset* in this context to mean a way of looking at or viewing something: in this case, the potential to influence a person or situation.

I describe two approaches that you can adopt – depending on which one of two different mindsets you may have – towards changes happening in your organisation that affect you. These two opposing approaches (one negative, one positive) demonstrate the importance of your mindset when you're trying to influence people:

✔ **I'm a victim of change.** If you see yourself as a victim of change, you don't think that you can do anything to influence whether or how changes are introduced. You typically wait for the change to happen and then cope as best you can with the consequences of the change.

✔ **I'm an agent of change.** If you see yourself as an agent of change, you're likely to look for opportunities to improve the performance of your organisation and to influence people to change processes, ways of working and so on, outside and within your area of responsibility.

Managing Directors and Chief Executives prefer people who work for them to be agents rather than victims of change.

Cultivate a positive mindset and attitude towards influencing people and being an agent of change by:

✔ Developing your ability to step outside of your comfort zone. Find out how to do so in Chapter 6.

✔ Recognising the words or phrases that typically come into your mind when you're faced with a problem, and then working on thinking about and using positive words and phrases whenever you encounter a difficult situation or notice an opportunity to bring a change about at work. You discover words and phrases that you can use to develop a positive attitude when facing and learning from adversity in Chapter 4.

Questioning whether something really is outside your control

Like all employees, you have some but not total control over the work you do. Expanding your sphere of influence requires you to identify the factors that impact on your ability to work towards achieving the required results, and then invest your time and effort in having a greater influence over those factors. The following exercise helps you to do so:

1. **Draw three large concentric circles on a page in a notebook, as shown in Figure 7-4.**

2. **Take time to reflect on and list the factors that help you to be highly productive in doing your job.** Your list may include, for example, competent staff, reliable equipment and so on. Question yourself about whether you're making full use of these factors. For example, can you delegate more tasks to competent staff to increase your and their productivity.

3. **Now reflect on and identify the factors that hinder you from being highly productive in doing your job.** As you identify each factor, use the following guidelines to decide on the extent to which each factor is inside or outside of your control, and write each factor inside the relevant circle in your notebook:

   - **Within my control.** These factors are those about which you can decide what to do, when and how, without having to refer to or ask for permission from your manager or any other person.

   - **Within my sphere of influence.** These factors are those that aren't directly within your control, but you can influence somebody to act on them if you spend time gathering and analysing information, and make a robust argument for justifying that your proposals should be acted upon.

     You can influence most factors providing that you present a compelling and well-reasoned justification for action. For example, you may want to influence your attendance at (or the timing or duration of) meetings, or the level of priority that other departments give to your team's work.

   - **Outside of my control.** These factors are those that you can't influence regardless of how much time or effort you invest in trying to influence someone about them. Don't waste your time on the few factors that you can't influence or change, for example changes in legislation that affect the work of your team.

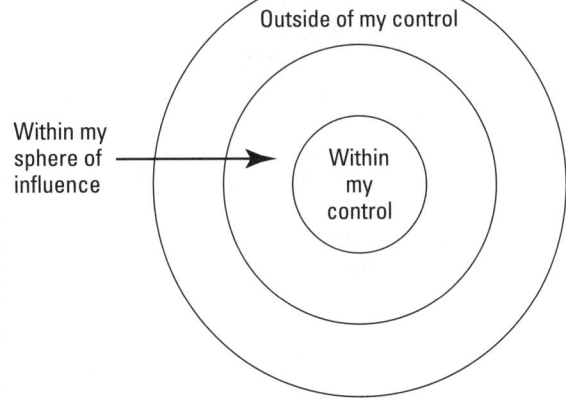

Figure 7-4:
Factors
within and
outside your
influence
and control.

Targeting the people you want to influence

To be successful in expanding your sphere of influence, you need to be able to persuade people to change their minds, for example, about factors that are hindering your, or your team's, performance.

Identify the key decision-makers that you have to influence and try one of the following approaches to influence them to make the decision and/or take the action that you desire:

✔ Focus on building your relationship with individuals rather than focusing solely on what you want people to do for you.

✔ Work hard at really engaging people to create a mutual understanding about the actions that are necessary, important and worthwhile. Explain the benefits and consequences of taking/not taking action to the organisation as well as to you.

✔ Seek to gain people's commitment rather than just compliance to the action you want them to take. Try to find out what's important to people and how you can help them to achieve what they need – their motivations – as well as them helping you to achieve what you want. Strive for a win-win outcome.

✔ Build your networks to expand your sphere of influence by identifying who has the capability, knowledge and/or contacts to make things happen. (Some of these people aren't going to be in senior management positions.) Spend time with them, finding out what's important to them and showing a genuine interest in them.

✔ Question and challenge people about how urgent and important their requests and requirements of you and your team are to the success of the organisation. Be a critical friend by always striving to be positive in how you question and challenge people.

Be careful about using your power – whether this power is based on, for example, your authority, technical knowledge or expertise about how your organisation functions – to force people to do what you want them to do. You may win this battle but lose the next one: strive to avoid win-lose outcomes!

Chapter 8

Employing the Power of Engaging Leadership

*E*mployee engagement has received a lot of press over the last few years as a way of improving the performance of businesses and other organisations. In this chapter I define *employee engagement* and explain why engaging employees is so important to business and organisational performance. As leader of your team, you have the biggest impact on the extent to which your team members are engaged in contributing to the success of the overall organisation.

You find out about the four foundations for effectively engaging people – foundations that also underpin you being an engaging leader – and discover the secrets that enable engaging leaders to be brilliant at engaging everyone who works with them.

Engaging People: The Key to Unlocking Commitment

Businesses and other organisations are always on the lookout for ways of improving their performance, and employee engagement is increasingly seen as one such method. Many descriptions of employee engagement exist, but almost all recognise that the overall aim of employee engagement is as follows:

To encourage employees to contribute all that they are capable of contributing to the success of their organisation: to put all the skills, knowledge, expertise, ability to think and effort that is at their disposal into their work and into working with their colleagues, or put another way to go the extra mile.

The people who report to you have control over whether they apply *all* their knowledge, skills and so on in doing their work. Almost all employees want to do their job well and are at least compliant: they put enough effort into their job to achieve a reasonable level of performance, one that's more than good enough to avoid them being disciplined for not doing what's required of them. Many employees do a lot more than this and perform their job to a higher standard, but still don't do their job to their full capabilities.

You may sometimes have to use the authority that comes with your job to get less-motivated individuals to comply with your requirements and do their job to the standard of performance you expect from them, but each and every individual chooses whether to put in the extra effort required for high performance: every individual chooses whether to give you their total commitment. If you want all your staff to perform to their full capabilities, you have to be skilled in engaging them in ways that unlock their commitment. You find out more about engaging people in the later section 'Building the Foundations for Engaging People'.

1. **Take a few minutes and reflect upon occasions when you've been highly committed to doing a task or activity in your current or a previous job.** Then consider occasions when you've been only compliant in doing a task, and answer the following questions:

   • What were the reasons that caused you to be so committed, and how did you feel about the work you were doing at the time?

   • What were the reasons for you being merely compliant, and how did you feel about the work you were doing at the time?

2. **Now reflect on your reasons.** See whether one common theme exists for you being committed and another theme for you being merely compliant when you do a task. Can you spot a significant difference between these two themes?

Probably the most significant difference is that you wanted to do the task to the best of your ability when you were committed, but you were only doing the task because another person, perhaps your manager, wanted you to do it when you were only compliant.

The key to unlocking the commitment of people to perform a task to a high standard is engaging them in ways that mean that they take ownership of the task and hold themselves accountable for successfully completing it: they do the task to a high standard of performance because they commit to doing it to that standard.

Avoiding the black hole of meaningless work

People's work is a crucial part of their identity, as well as often being an important source of meaning. To test this notion, answer the following simple question:

> *When you initially meet a person, what's the first question you tend to ask to find out more about that person?*

The question that most people ask is, 'What do you do?'.

Obtaining the answer not only gives you information about the person, but also enables you to relate to the person because – if you're like most people – you tend to associate certain characteristics with certain job titles such as barrister, engineer or accountant. Each of these roles has a certain meaning for you: perhaps, for example, you associate high earner, clever, articulate and so on with a barrister.

As well as job titles having meaning, the work that you do in carrying out your job is also a source of meaning for you: your work can be meaningful or meaningless . . . or somewhere in between:

- ✔ **Meaningful work.** When you view your work (whether a task or activity) as being meaningful, you see it as being important and worthwhile, and you're committed to doing it well. You're likely to be totally engrossed in doing the work because you apply all yourself – your knowledge, skills, expertise, thinking and so on – to making sure that you do it well.

- ✔ **Meaningless work.** When your work seems to be meaningless, you probably can't see a good reason for doing it well, or even at all. You're more likely to cut corners, delay or even not bother doing it until someone reminds you to do it.

Make sure that you avoid your staff perceiving their work as meaningless. I describe some of the problems of this situation occurring in the sidebar 'The Dreaded Ds'.

Making work meaningful

Your starting point for making work meaningful for your staff is to help them understand what's expected of them:

- ✔ Share your team's purpose and direction with the members. (Check out Chapter 7 for all about communicating the objectives and results that your team needs to achieve.)

- ✔ Explain what and how every member contributes to the success of the team. (Chapter 2 describes how to engage people in enhancing mutual understanding and commitment, to work better together towards achieving the necessary objectives.)

The Dreaded Ds

My first job was as a Chemical Technician in a large company that employed almost 5,000 people at the location. My job responsibilities included testing the chemical quality of materials, components and the finished products that were being produced and/or assembled in manufacturing household goods. I came into contact with hundreds of people who worked at the location because my work rota involved working day, evening and night shifts.

I progressively realised, partly because I chatted to people I worked alongside as I was checking the quality of the products, that many employees were so disinterested that they didn't really care about the company, were disheartened doing the same work day after day

and disillusioned by how they were treated by dysfunctional management. I was aware that management were experiencing problems with the quality of products, timekeeping, attendance, morale and motivation of employees, and so on.

I started to think that better ways of managing people must exist than the way I was experiencing people being managed. The notion of the 'dreaded ds' – employees being disinterested, disheartened, disillusioned – as I subsequently named it, had been sown as the seeds of my vocation to find ways of engaging people to want to perform to the best of their ability and be fulfilled in doing their work even though I didn't totally realise this at the time.

Engaging members of your team to build mutual understanding is a great way to make work meaningful:

✔ Mutual understanding means that you and members of your team have a common and shared understanding about an issue, objective, priority, task, problem and so on: no room is left for misunderstandings!

✔ Mutual understanding involves you and members of your team agreeing on the importance and worthwhile nature of a particular objective, task or activity. When people have a common understanding that a task is important, they also have a common commitment to completing the task.

✔ Mutual understanding is created by everyone being involved in contributing ideas, views and thoughts, and asking searching questions to seek clarity. You and members of your team are more likely to:

• Come to better decisions by involving the relevant people in making a decision simply because people see things from different perspectives, and contribute different ideas, highlight different potential problems and so on.

• Work better together by people sharing their views on how well the team is working, and build a sense of camaraderie and team identity. (You discover in the preceding section that work is an important source of identity and meaning in people's lives. You can also find out a lot more about how to build teamwork in Part V: 'Leading Different Types of Teams').

✔ Mutual understanding means involving people by having a genuine interest in them and asking for their thoughts and ideas, and listening to what they say; this approach reinforces the connection between you and them, and strengthens the relevant relationships.

Talking to a member of your team to enhance mutual understanding about the importance of a task or activity isn't the same as management by consensus. As team leader, you're ultimately accountable for the decisions made and actions taken by your team, and at times you're going to need to make decisions that some team members disagree with. Involving people, however, enables them to:

✔ Better understand the reasons for your decision.

✔ Appreciate you seeking and considering their views.

✔ Give you a higher level of commitment than they would if you hadn't engaged them.

Realising that engaged people go the extra mile

You discover in Chapter 2 that research into employee engagement has shown that employees expect their line manager to:

✔ Keep them well informed about what's happening in the organisation.

✔ Treat them well.

✔ Seek and listen to their ideas and opinions.

✔ Show an interest in their well-being.

Engaging your team to establish common and shared understandings about important objectives, tasks and activities, demonstrates that you respect and value your team members: you seek their views and take notice of what they say.

Engaging people involves much more than seeking their views: you need to engage them in conversations and establish what's worthwhile, which requires you to seek and consider what's important to each individual as well as to the organisation. If you're interested only in getting people to commit to achieving the organisation's objectives, they may well perceive that you're putting the needs of the organisation and/or yourself before their own, and that reduces the level of commitment people give to you and the company. Being an engaging leader requires you to have and show a genuine interest in the work-related needs, hopes, aspirations and concerns of each individual who reports to you as well as you being interested in your organisation's required objectives and results. In my experience, people reciprocate the genuine interest that I show in them, and you're likely to find that your team members are then more committed and go the extra mile towards achieving what you need them to.

You have biggest impact on the extent to which the people who report to you are engaged in contributing to the success of the organisation, due to how you treat them and the extent to which you show a genuine interest in them.

Your focus in engaging work colleagues needs to be on working together to create optimum outcomes for everyone involved so that everyone is unified in striving to achieve common goals. Engaging people requires you to find out what's important to people and find ways of enabling them to fulfil their needs through working towards achieving the required objectives and results.

Building the Foundations for Engaging People

In this section, I expand on my description of engaging leadership in Chapter 2:

> *Engaging leaders engage their staff to enhance mutual understanding and commitment to work better together towards achieving their objectives.*

Engaging your staff so that they're always highly committed to working with you to achieve the necessary and expected goals is difficult for the following reasons:

- **People are different.** You can't treat everyone the same way to get the best from them, but you can act with integrity and in accord with your values. (Refer to Chapter 5 to discover how to clarify the values that are important to you and use them in working with people.)

- **People can change.** Their needs and motivations may change depending upon changes in their personal circumstances, such as an employee becoming a parent for the first time and wanting to spend more time at home.

- **People may react differently to changes in their work situation.** Individuals and groups may react differently to, for example, changes in organisational structures, systems and processes.

- **People can misunderstand.** Misunderstandings can easily occur about aims, objectives, decisions and actions, especially when people don't articulate their thoughts clearly and concisely, don't listen carefully or make assumptions.

To gain and sustain the commitment of your staff, you have to be highly skilled in engaging people so as to notice or discover the factors that are impacting upon them, or that have to be addressed. In the next four sections, you find out about the four foundations for effectively engaging people (these foundations also underpin you being an engaging leader):

- ✔ **Relating.** Really connect with individuals and groups by showing a genuine interest in them.

- ✔ **Proacting.** Share and seek information, and critique each others' thoughts by 'speaking your mind' and asking searching questions.

- ✔ **Sensing.** Switch on your senses to gather data and information about others' thoughts, emotions, needs and commitment to act.

- ✔ **Inter-interpreting.** Interpret and reinterpret data and information, including views and opinions, to create mutual understandings and commitment to act on work issues and problems.

These four foundations are intimately connected with each other and are sub-processes of the overall process of engaging people.

For you to be an engaging leader – someone who's effective at engaging staff and work colleagues – you have to become skilled in using these four sub-processes simultaneously.

Relating to people

Many people see their relationships as being stable and longlasting, but in fact the relationships between you and many of your work colleagues can change. You may have strong relationships with, perhaps, just a few individuals: you may not see or even speak to these people for many years, but you can pick up the relationship immediately and have a conversation as if you'd spoken only a few days before.

You have less strong relationships with most people: these relationships are less stable, or even fragile, simply because of how you both relate to one another. As a result of your interpretations of your experiences of each other, these types of relationships can change more quickly than you realise. (Refer to Chapter 2 to find out more about how leaders and followers affect and are affected by each other through the process of leadership that is occurring between them.)

Relating to people is a more appropriate way of thinking about how you and your staff connect with each other (instead of thinking of stable *relationships*), because the term more effectively conveys the potential for, and rate of, change in the relationship. Here's my description of *relating* (to a person):

Connecting with a person through having, and demonstrating, a positive interest in them and their needs (as a human being).

The benefits of developing your skills in relating to your work colleagues include the following:

✔ You're more likely to be conscious of the effect you have on people and that they have on you when you recognise that how people relate to each other is a dynamic, fluid process.

✔ You develop a better understanding of people when you have a genuine interest in them and find out more about them. You're more likely to develop more meaningful and important relationships through this approach.

✔ People show more interest in, and have a greater commitment to, helping you to achieve what you want when you demonstrate that you have a positive, genuine interest in them.

✔ People are more likely to acknowledge and accept your explanations of the need for changes in organisational structure, systems or policies that have an adverse effect on them if they appreciate that you have a genuine interest in them as individuals.

Strive to develop your skills in relating to people to really connect with them, and through this approach build mutual respect for one another and stronger, more meaningful, lasting relationships.

When you're relating effectively to your work colleagues, you've adopted the approach of 'working with' rather than 'doing to' them. 'Working with' a person is based on you having and showing total respect for people and striving to really understand them.

Work through the following exercise to examine those occasions when someone's adopted the approach of 'doing to' you rather than 'working with' you:

1. **Get a notebook and divide the page into four columns as in Table 8-1.**

2. **Write brief notes that describe situations in which you felt that a work colleague was 'doing to' you in the first column.**

3. **In the second column note brief details that describe what your work colleague did or said that caused you to feel that the person was 'doing to' rather than 'working with' you.**

4. **Describe the effect of your work colleague's behaviour on you in the third column.**

5. **Describe how you then related to the person as a result of the effect that she had on you.**

I give examples in the first row to help you get started.

Table 8-1	'Doing to' Versus 'Working with' People		
Brief Details of the Situation	*Brief Details of What my Colleague Did or Said*	*The Effect on Me*	*How I Then Related to the Person*
The situation was a team meeting when I was giving a progress report on my project.	My boss interrupted me and spoke for me, but she didn't express what I wanted to say correctly.	I had mixed emotions of embarrassment, being undermined and anger with my manager – although I hid my emotions.	I feel that my boss undermines me every time she does this even though I suspect she thinks she's actually supporting me.

You've probably noticed that certain work colleagues often adopt an approach of 'doing to' you and others because they're trying to be helpful. Unfortunately, such good intentions are in fact unhelpful because they can have unintended consequences such as:

✔ Undermining a person's self-confidence.

✔ Taking responsibility off a person by, for example, speaking for her.

✔ Imposing the doer's views on people, which can be particularly damaging when done in meetings.

✔ Giving an impression that the doer is self-centred by promoting her own views and even herself, especially when this act is done in large meetings.

✔ Causing people to disconnect from the doer and undermine relationships with her.

Beware of unintentionally adopting an approach of 'doing to' rather than 'working with' your work colleagues, because your behaviour can have unintended consequences for them and for you. (You can find more on how to 'work with' people in Chapter 9.)

Being Captain Courageous: Speaking your mind

You may be wondering why I use the term 'Captain Courageous' for this section? My reason is simply because you need to have courage to speak your mind: to express your thoughts openly and honestly. In my experience many managers, including senior managers, don't openly and honestly express their thoughts in meetings, as you see in the later sidebar 'I was just going to say that!'.

'Speaking your mind' is more than being open and honest in expressing your thoughts because it also involves encouraging others to speak their mind: to express their thoughts. As thoughts may include questions as well as views and opinions, 'speaking your mind' may also involve critiquing the thoughts of your work colleagues, as well as encouraging them to critique your thoughts.

I've coined a new word for this combination of activities – *proacting* – because the word captures being proactive in prompting and having meaningful conversations to share and clarify thinking in order to make something happen. The purpose of you and your colleagues proacting – seeking, sharing and critiquing each others' thoughts – is to:

✔ Generate and clarify information.

✔ Use this information to enhance mutual understanding about, for example, a work issue or problem that then:

• Enables better decisions to be made.

• Generates commitment to take action to implement those decisions.

I encourage you to be courageous because expressing your thoughts and encouraging your colleagues to critique your thoughts is risky: you and/or they may feel embarrassed or threatened because:

- ✔ Your views about a work issue or problem may be significantly different to those of your colleagues.

- ✔ Your colleagues may cause you to question your thoughts and views.

- ✔ Both of these scenarios may happen in a meeting when other people, perhaps more senior managers, are observing or are involved in the conversation.

You may need to develop your self-confidence to handle the perceived risks of speaking openly and honestly (this self-confidence is explored in Chapter 4), and of being vulnerable to having your work colleagues question, critique and challenge your thoughts (see the later section 'Building strength through vulnerability'). You can discover in Chapter 9 how to develop the ability to be courageous in having meaningful conversations with work colleagues.

Be a great role model for the people who work with you by demonstrating your willingness to express your thoughts, critique others' thoughts and encourage your work colleagues to do the same in working with you.

I was just going to say that!

At many senior management meetings I've heard the statement 'I was just going to say that'. Here's just one example.

The purpose of the meeting was a quarterly performance review when the Chief Executive was visiting one of the Divisions in the company to conduct a review with the Divisional General Manager and his team. The Chief Executive was renowned for asking searching questions to enable him to understand how well the various departments in the Division were performing and, I suspect, to be confident that managers' thinking and decision-making was robust.

A presentation had just been given on proposed expenditure on a major project when the Chief Executive asked one of his searching questions:

'Can someone please explain to me as if I was a child why we need to spend several tens of thousands of pounds on this initiative and what the benefits will be?'

A long pause followed while managers looked anywhere in the room except at the Chief Executive; then one of the less experienced managers gave a concise and succinct explanation justifying the proposed expenditure. Immediately, a chorus arose from many of his colleagues of 'I was just going to say that!'.

This is just one example of managers not openly and honestly expressing their thoughts and views in meetings . . . until someone else has had the courage to make the comment they would like to make.

You can find out how to step outside of your comfort zone and be more willing to address situations that you find risky in Chapter 6.

Switching on your senses

Have you ever been so consumed by your thoughts that you fail to notice something? For example, your partner may be talking to you and you don't notice what she's saying until she criticises you for not listening! Or you're watching a drama on television and realise that you've missed an important incident, because your thoughts drifted to a real incident that you experienced earlier that day.

You don't consciously switch off your senses so that you don't notice things happening around you, but you're just not as well tuned into those senses as you could be. Also, I suspect that our senses have become dulled over generations as we notionally have more control over our surroundings in a modern society by adopting technology such as air-conditioning in buildings and cruise control in cars!

In my experience, one of the main causes of people being disengaged at work is that they perceive that their manager doesn't give them enough attention, listen to them or show enough interest in their well-being.

One of the biggest compliments that you can give people is to give them your total attention, because by doing so you're demonstrating that you respect and value them.

To give a work colleague your total attention, you have to be good at *sensing* what's going on around you:

✔ **Bring yourself 'into the moment'.** Focus your attention on the here and now, on the person(s) you're working with at that moment.

✔ **Switch on your senses.** Bring your senses into a heightened state of awareness so that you're highly alert and attentive to what's going on around you. In particular, turning up or tuning in your visual and auditory senses is crucial for you to notice small and subtle changes in the person or people you're working with, as well as in yourself. (You can discover the importance of recognising your thoughts, feelings and behaviour and how they impact on other people in Chapter 4). Switching on your senses enables you to better notice nuances in another person's and your own:

   • Emotions, especially from noticing the expressions on a person's face.

   • Behaviour or body language.

   • Energy, particularly regarding whether a person is enthusiastic or not about the issue or topic being discussed.

   • Use of, and emphasis on, words to clarify and understand fully the meanings that the person's attempting to convey to you.

The purpose of switching on your senses is to gather data and information that you can then interpret to enhance your own understanding of people including:

- ✔ Their priorities.
- ✔ Their perspective on, and views about, an issue.
- ✔ Their level of enthusiasm or commitment to taking an agreed action.

You find out how to switch on your senses or, put another way, improve your *sensing* ability, in Chapter 9.

Creating shared meanings

I was recently working in Brazil and I used an interpreter to explain and help me to understand the meanings of the views and opinions expressed during meetings with groups of employees in a company that I was working for. Your staff and work colleagues expect you to be your own interpreter: they expect you to explain clearly the meaning of information you're sharing with them, such as the reason for decisions or actions that you want them to take.

As discussed in Chapter 2, employees expect their line manager to seek and listen to their views: they want to contribute to making decisions. Members of your team also have a responsibility to you and their colleagues to be their own interpreters and clearly explain the meaning of their views and opinions.

As you can discover in the earlier section 'Making work meaningful', engaging members of your team in order to enhance mutual understanding is a great way of making work meaningful. Enhancing mutual understanding requires you and members of your team to create shared meanings: common and shared understanding about, for example, the causes of problems, the reasons for decisions, agreed actions and so on.

Creating shared meanings requires you and your work colleagues to do more than just be your own interpreters, however, so that you can clearly convey and explain your views. Creating shared meanings involves an activity or process that I describe as *inter-interpreting*, which involves the following:

- ✔ **Interpreting together.** This part of the process means helping each other to come to better understandings instead of imposing one's thoughts, perspectives or interpretation on another person.
- ✔ **Striving to acquire understanding from each other's perspectives as well as your own perspectives.** This activity is more than just being empathetic and more than appreciating how another person is feeling about an issue: it involves opening up your mind to different and new perspectives.

✔ **Working together to help each other to understand each other's thoughts.** To better understand each other's interpretations and meanings of the information that you're sharing with each other, you and your colleagues have to be each others' interpreter as well as your own interpreter!

✔ **Seeing things in a new or different light.** This activity helps to gain insights that enable you and your team to create new meanings that lead to better understandings of complex problems and better decision making.

You can find tips on how to be better at *inter-interpreting* in Chapter 9.

Knowing the Secrets of Engaging Leaders

You probably know someone who's brilliant at engaging people, but you're not sure quite why that person is so good. Well, the earlier section 'Building the Foundations for Engaging People' can help because it provides a clear understanding of how to engage your work colleagues and staff effectively.

This section adds to those foundations and provides you with two secrets of engaging leaders.

Being open to everything

'Being open to everything' means being open to the opinions, views, ideas, proposals, arguments and so on of the people you work with. Being open to others' views doesn't mean that you have to accept them, because you're bound to have your own views. Instead, 'being open' means having an open, rather than a closed, mind: being willing to at least consider others' views and opinions.

You can develop an open mind as follows:

✔ Recognise that you're not your thoughts: they're simply expressions of what's going on in your mind. You may be attached to some of them, but you don't have to be!

✔ Value contrasting perspectives that your work colleagues may have towards a work issue.

✔ See work colleagues who are questioning or challenging your views or decisions as critical friends: almost all will be acting with good intentions because they want to improve an aspect of work.

✔ Give people space and time to express themselves.

Building strength through vulnerability

You may think that encouraging your work colleagues to express their views openly and honestly is risky, because they may put you on the spot and you may not be sure about how to respond. More specifically, you may feel more vulnerable encouraging a colleague to question, critique or even challenge your point of view because they may:

- ✔ Highlight that you haven't thoroughly thought through a decision.
- ✔ Undermine your view.
- ✔ Prove you wrong!

I suggest that you to have the courage to invite colleagues to be open and honest in conversations with you – and each other – because:

- ✔ Your role as a leader is to get to the right decision regarding a work issue or problem: you don't have to come up with the answer yourself!
- ✔ Only through encouraging your colleagues to:
  - Share their ideas, suggestions and viewpoints, can you tap into their knowledge and expertise in, for example, solving complex problems.
  - Question, critique and challenge your thinking, and that of their colleagues, can your team members develop their ability to improve how they think; and improving the quality of thinking leads to improved mutual understanding of work issues, better decisions, greater commitment and improved results.
- ✔ By setting an example that you're willing to have your views challenged and even proved wrong you can encourage your colleagues to take risks in expressing their views and have their own views challenged.
- ✔ You develop self-confidence and are more able to have 'difficult conversations' by being put on the spot and coping with potentially or actually being embarrassed.

Thinking precedes action and having the right thoughts precedes taking the right action. Work with your colleagues to improve the quality of thinking, create shared meanings and common understandings about work issues and problems to enable you (and them) to act to solve problems and achieve the desired results for all concerned.

You can discover in Chapter 9 how to be more vulnerable by coping with situations that you find embarrassing and threatening.

Chapter 9

Becoming an Engaging Leader

*T*he great news is that you already have some skills in engaging people, and you can build on these skills to become an engaging leader. In Chapter 8, I show you the four foundations for engaging your team members: *relating* to people; *proacting* to seek, share and critique each others' thoughts; *sensing* – switching on your senses to gather data and information; and *inter-interpreting* – interpreting and reinterpreting together.

In this chapter you find out how to enhance and effectively deploy your skills in these four foundations, and how to engage people effectively. I also show you how your improved performance as an engaging leader is linked to building your personal confidence, maintaining focus and clarity within your team, and increasing your team members' commitment.

Recognising Your Existing Skills

Chapter 8 describes how the four foundations for engaging your staff are intimately connected with each other. They are sub-processes of the overall process or activity of engaging people, and to be brilliant at engaging people you have to become skilled in using these four sub-processes simultaneously.

Before I explore using each of the four foundation sub-processes in more detail, take a few minutes to reflect on situations when you were in a conversation with an individual or group of people in which one or more of the following events occurred:

✔ You were all totally engrossed in the conversation.

✔ Individual and group understanding of the subject were significantly enhanced.

✔ One or more 'aha!' moments happened: for example, when new insights were gained into the subject being discussed.

✔ The people involved experienced a strong sense of togetherness or camaraderie.

✔ A common commitment to act resulted from the conversation.

Now try the following exercise.

1. **Get a notebook and divide the page into three columns as shown in Table 9-1.**

2. **Write a brief description of the situation in which the first conversation occurred.**

3. **In the second column, list the actions that you took – briefly describe what you did or said – to make a valuable and meaningful contribution to this conversation.**

4. **Describe the effect that your contribution had on you and/or the other people involved, or the outcome of the meeting.**

5. **Repeat steps 2 to 4 for other situations that you identified.**

I give an example in the first row to help you get started.

Table 9-1	Examples of Situations When I Used Skills in Engaging People	
Brief Description of the Situation	*Brief Description of What I Did or Said that was a Significant Contribution to the Conversation*	*The Effect that it Had on Me and/or Other People Involved, and the Outcome*
Weekly team meeting in which I thought that we were, as normal, meandering off the topics and wasting time.	I pointed out that we were going off-track and I questioned whether this way of holding meetings was the most effective use of our time.	Some people were initially defensive about why they had introduced new topics, but my questions prompted the team to re-evaluate how well we were holding meetings, and we agreed changes to improve the productivity of the meetings.

Brief Description of the Situation	Brief Description of What I Did or Said that was a Significant Contribution to the Conversation	The Effect that it Had on Me and/or Other People Involved, and the Outcome

Take a look at the notes you make in the second column: these comments are examples of the skills that you already possess in engaging people, and ones on which you can build to become an engaging leader.

Enhancing Relating to People

As I reveal in Chapter 8, most working relationships are less stable, and sometimes more fragile, than you and other people may realise; the way that you relate to, or connect with, each other changes due to your interpretations of your experiences of working together. You find out how to enhance your skills in relating to and connecting with your work colleagues in the next four sections.

'Working with' and not 'doing to' people

In my experience, people want to make a positive difference or contribution to the organisation that employs them. I explain in Chapter 8 that, in trying to contribute, some people may be too helpful in working with their colleagues in the sense that they take responsibility off, or undermine, them. Examples of actions – and the reasons for taking them – when you may notice colleagues (or even caught yourself) taking responsibility off people include:

✔ Interrupting a colleague and finishing his sentences by expressing what you think your colleague was going to say.

✔ Taking a task off a colleague, especially a less experienced one, because you know how to do the task better. You may indeed complete the task quicker, but your intervention stops the less experienced person from discovering how to do it correctly and may undermine his self-confidence.

These are examples of unintentionally 'doing to' rather than 'working with' people, but you may perceive that some people deliberately impose their views or actions!

Work on improving your approach to working with your colleagues by:

✔ Having and showing total respect for every individual: respect the rights that you and each person have such as:

• The right to express your views and opinions.

• The right to express how you feel.

• The right to be listened to and heard.

• The right to change your mind.

✔ Striving to get to know and really understand them. (Refer to the next section 'Having a genuine interest in others' to find out more about how to do this successfully.)

✔ Being empathetic: put yourself 'in their shoes' and try to appreciate things from the other person's perspective.

Having a genuine interest in others

You may sometimes find that showing a genuine interest in others is difficult. For example, in a work context you may have demanding targets or results that you have to achieve, and think that you have to focus all your attention and effort on achieving those results. Focusing in on your targets has a similar effect to looking down a telescope: you can clearly see your targets but you can't see much else!

From my experience of working in numerous organisations, 'silo management' – which is when departments become inward looking and don't consider the needs of, or how they impact on, other departments – tends to happen when managers of departments focus on achieving their own department's targets. In doing so, managers tend to become blinkered to the needs of, or how their work affects, their peers in other departments. I describe this effect in the later sidebar 'Hitting your KPIs'.

Hitting your KPIs

The most senior manager of a large business asked me to work within the company to enhance the quality of leadership in order to deliver improvements in business performance. I interviewed all the senior managers, many middle managers and a representative sample of employees to acquire an understanding of the factors affecting leadership and how well the company was functioning as an organisation.

I discovered that a lot of emphasis had been placed on clarifying and using key performance indicators (KPIs) over recent months. The effect was that managers were very clear about the results they were expected to achieve, and were primarily focused on hitting their own KPIs. As a result, although improvements in performance had been seen, the improvements weren't as great as was expected.

I also discovered that the emphasis on using KPIs to focus managers' attention and efforts on achieving the results expected of them was having unintended consequences. The following comments made by managers capture some of these consequences:

✔ 'Managers aren't working together as well as they used to and departments are becoming 'silos.'

✔ 'Some KPIs conflict with each other.'

✔ 'There isn't any collective responsibility among senior managers for the success of the business.'

The emphasis on KPIs was having both positive and negative effects on (and between) managers.

An unintended side effect of focusing on your own targets is like putting blinkers on a horse to prevent it being distracted in a race: you stop noticing and showing an interest in what's going on around you!

Practise developing a genuine interest in your work colleagues by:

✔ **Challenging yourself: 'How well do I really know each person?'** Ask yourself how well you know each person who works with you, especially the people who report directly to you. Can you accurately describe their personal circumstances, interests and hobbies, hopes and aspirations, any concerns about their work and so on? What makes them tick? If you don't know, invest time in finding out by talking to them.

✔ **Asking members of your team about whether they think that you show enough interest in them.** If your organisation has an appraisal process, invite each person who reports to you to give you honest feedback about how well you lead, support and work with them. If your organisation doesn't have an appraisal system, take the initiative to have informal conversations with each person to obtain their views about you.

✔ **Checking your plans.** Take a look at your schedule, plan or 'to do' lists for the last month and estimate how much time or how many activities were focused on people: getting to know or understand them better, train, develop, guide and support them, and so on. What insights do your findings tell you about how much of a genuine interest you show in people?

Reflect on the benefits and consequences of how often you're showing a genuine interest in people, especially if your initial assessment indicates that you're thinking about people issues less than 20 per cent of the time – depending on the size of your team.

Building strong connections

When you build strong connections with your work colleagues, you also construct strong bonds and more stable relationships with them and throughout your team.

1. **Refer to Figure 9-1 and get a notebook to draw a figure to represent how closely connected you are with the people who report to you.**

2. **Draw a small circle in the centre of the page and write your name inside it.**

3. **Draw a small circle representing each person who reports to you around your circle and put their name in it, the position of each circle being closer to or farther away from your circle based on how strongly you're connected with the person.**

4. **For each close connection that you have with a person ask yourself:**

    • What are the reasons for this connection?

    • What have I done to create this connection?

    • How do I treat this person?

    • How much time do I spend with the person?

5. **Repeat step 4 for the connections that you have with other people who are less close.**

List the actions that you take that help you to build close connections with people, and plan actions that you're going to take to show a genuine interest in and build strong connections with all the people who report to you. Repeat this exercise for other key people who you work with.

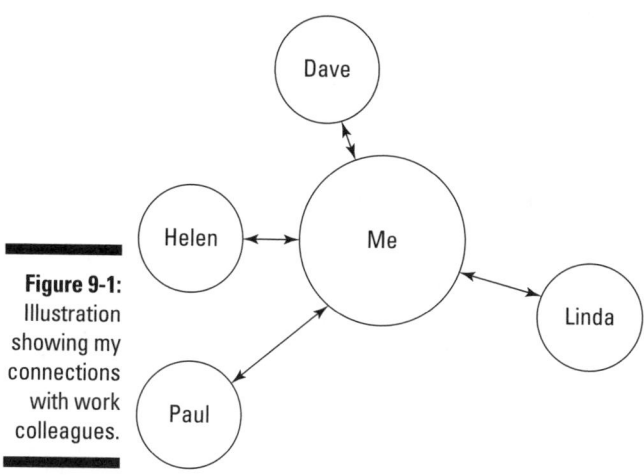

Figure 9-1:
Illustration
showing my
connections
with work
colleagues.

You strengthen the connection between yourself and colleagues when they sense that you have a genuine interest in, and concern for, them. Plus, when you show this kind of interest, they're highly likely to reciprocate the interest in you, and the objectives and results that you're trying to achieve.

Being non-judgemental

You may not realise, but being judgemental – that is, forming an opinion about whether a person is good or bad – is all too easy, as is then allowing that opinion to affect adversely or unfairly how you treat the person.

I often use the following exercise on leadership development programmes to explore how easy becoming judgemental with people can be:

1. **Take a few moments to think about the person you most enjoy working with: a person who perhaps does great work, is helpful, reliable, takes initiative and so on.** Does the person's face appear in your mind?

2. **Now think about the person you least like to work with: someone who perhaps causes you a lot of problems, is difficult to work with, causes you to worry about work, who you like to avoid if you can and so on.** Can you see this person's face?

3. **Now reflect on how you work with each person, and question yourself about whether you're always fair regarding how you treat these two people.**

In my experience, virtually everyone who I ask to do this exercise agrees that they quickly see that they treat people differently. My concern is that you, if you also see different people, may unconsciously be carrying baggage about each person with you: views or opinions that prompt you automatically to treat people in a certain way.

For example, if you have an opinion that a person is difficult to work with, you may go into a conversation with the person about a problem with his work expecting to have a difficult conversation: you've already formed a judgement that the person is going to be difficult! If you do so, you're likely to contribute to causing a difficult situation because you don't have an open mind and may be less objective in asking questions about the problem and listening to what the person has to say.

Practise being non-judgemental by:

✔ Recognising and appreciating that each person is unique and, therefore, different. The best teams in my experience are those in which members have different perspectives, styles and ways of thinking because such diversity enables people to make a wide range of contributions to solving complex problems. (You can find out more about how to manage diversity in teams in Chapters 15 and 17).

✔ Increasing your self-awareness by noticing the thoughts and opinions you have, or assumptions that you're making about individuals, and the implications of your opinions and assumptions for how you treat people. (Discover how to increase your self-awareness in the later section 'Being in the moment'.)

✔ Being empathetic towards each person; try to put yourself 'in the shoes' of a person to see things from, and to understand, their perspective. 'Doing so may involve you trying to understand their background, culture and so on. Improving your understanding of a work colleague's background may enable you to view his behaviour differently without lowering your standards regarding work or behaviour.

Developing the Courage to Speak Your Mind

I'm occasionally asked to work with groups that are very dysfunctional, and I've noticed that one of the main reasons for this condition is that people don't feel able to 'speak their minds' in order to resolve problems between members of the group. For such a situation, I put a lot of effort into finding an appropriate venue that would help to create the right environment for people to open up and share their thoughts with each other.

Although the physical environment is important, the crucial factor that determines whether people open up to each other by speaking their minds is the environment created by members of the group. You discover in the earlier section 'Enhancing Relating to People' that having and showing a genuine interest in a person helps you to understand that person: this approach is a good starting point in encouraging members of any group, especially a dysfunctional group, to work better together.

In this section I show you how to develop the courage to speak your mind as a complement to showing a genuine interest in people and enhancing your skills in engaging people in one-to-one and group situations.

Standing out from the crowd

You have probably noticed when walking in the countryside how sheep tend to follow each other: it appears that one decides to go in a certain direction and all the rest follow in a long line. I sometimes experience a similar condition in working with management groups: one person, often the most senior manager or strongest character in the group, proposes a decision and everyone goes along with it. This behaviour often leads to the condition known as *groupthink*.

Be aware of groupthink, where the thinking behind decisions goes unchallenged in a group, leading to poor-quality decision-making.

Overcoming groupthink requires someone to have the courage to stand out from the crowd and speak his mind, to propose an alternative solution or challenge the proposed view.

Take the lead in speaking your mind in situations in which you experience groupthink, because by doing so you can:

✔ Assist the group to make more robust decisions by:

- Providing alternative and contrasting perspectives, options and solutions.

- Questioning the validity of proposals already put forward.

- Encouraging your colleagues to critique constructively, instead of automatically accepting your suggestions and proposals.

✔ Show leadership by being a role model and attempting to influence the rest of the group to follow your lead by sharing their views and critiquing the quality of thinking and decision-making.

✔ Challenge group norms of behaviour such as not questioning each other's views and encourage members of the group to strive continuously to improve how they work as a team.

Chapter 7 describes how the people who report to you expect you to be bold and lead with conviction. You're more likely to be bold and speak your mind when you're more sure of yourself, when you're confident that the thoughts you want to express are relevant and valid.

Being clear about the purpose of your job, the objectives and results that senior management expects you and your team to achieve, together with having a clear understanding of the goals and objectives of your department and/or organisation, enables you to be bolder and speak your mind. This clarity helps generate confidence that the points that you want to make and the questions you want to ask are relevant.

You probably perceive that 'standing out from the crowd' by expressing your thoughts – especially if they're different to the group's view or involve critiquing the views of a senior manager or strong character – would put you in a difficult situation. Refer to Chapter 6 to discover a technique to help you to be more comfortable with being uncomfortable and willing to address difficult situations.

Remaining aware of being dishonest

I don't think that you deliberately intend to be dishonest, but you may well have difficulty always being honest and saying what you really think! Complete the next exercise to check whether you do sometimes hold back.

Take a few minutes to reflect on situations in which you held back from expressing your honest views or opinions with an individual or group. The situation may be one that you experienced at work or in your personal life.

1. **Divide the page of a notebook into three columns as shown in Table 9-2.**

2. **Write a brief description of the situation in which you held back from expressing your true or honest thoughts.**

3. **Describe in the second column the thoughts that you had at the time.**

4. **Describe in the third column your reasons for not sharing your thoughts.**

5. **Repeat steps 2 to 4 for other similar situations that you identified.**

I provide a simple example in the first row to help you to get started.

Table 9-2	Examples of Situations When I Didn't Share My True or Honest Views		
Brief Description of the Situation	*Brief Description of What I Really Thought but Didn't Say*	*My Reason for Not Sharing My Thoughts or Opinions with the Individual/Group*
One of the people who reports to me was again late for work by several minutes.	I thought the person shouldn't be late so often and should be better organised.	I didn't want to create a scene in which the person reacted badly and I wouldn't know how to cope with it.

People hold back from sharing what they really think for two main reasons: they want to avoid being embarrassed or threatened, or they don't want another person to feel embarrassed or threatened.

I suspect that many people don't want to embarrass a person because they care for them. Read the true story in the later sidebar 'You're behind time!' as an example of a group not being able to criticise the behaviour of a colleague they cared for.

You may feel threatened in a situation in which you say what you really think about a work colleague's performance, behaviour or attitude to work, and the person reacts angrily, verbally or emotionally towards you. Colleagues may feel threatened by you sharing your thoughts if they then have to do something that they don't want to do, your comments reflect badly on them or they feel that their job security is under threat.

'You're behind time!'

A group of General Practitioners (GPs) wanted to improve the way that daily surgeries were run to cope with a high demand for their services from the local community. The GPs agreed that every GP needed to see patients at the rate of 12 patients per hour to cope with demand at peak periods.

One GP who liked to have in-depth consultations with his patients took longer with each patient and as a result he didn't finish his consultations on time. The effect was that his colleagues had to see all the patients who attended the emergency clinic that was held at the end of the normal day surgery.

His colleagues thought that this situation was unfair and that he ought to finish his surgery sooner and see his share of the emergency patients, but they felt unable to tell him because he was a caring GP – even though the problem was causing ill-feeling among some GPs in the practice.

I facilitated a meeting between the GPs to discuss openly the differences in rates of GPs consultations with patients and agree a protocol for consultations that all GPs accepted. The GPs used this protocol to guide how they ran their surgeries, and as a reference point to raise any issues about non-compliance with the protocol in GP meetings.

Although certain occasions exist when saying what you really think isn't appropriate or worthwhile – such as when a work colleague makes a rare minor mistake on a task – you don't want to allow standards of work and behaviour to slip by holding back. You can find tips to help in the later section 'Coping with embarrassment and threat'.

Asking searching questions

Perhaps, like me, you've been discouraged from asking people searching questions, especially personal ones, because your parents or guardians think that doing so is impolite. You may have difficulty changing behaviour that you picked up when you were a child. The fact is, however, that as a team leader you're sometimes going to have to ask difficult questions.

In general, you're going to have one of three main aims when asking searching questions of work colleagues:

✔ To engage people with their own thoughts, by questioning the meaning of words, phrases and language that your colleagues are using in order to:

- Enable them to think things through.

- Clarify their thinking on the topic or subject being discussed.

- Prompt them to question or test the assumptions that underpin their point of view.

📐 To gather more information to enable:

- You to better understand people's points of view.

- You and your team to improve your understanding of the topic, subject or problem being discussed.

📐 To encourage and promote the activity of asking searching questions as a valuable activity in decision-making.

Practise your ability to ask searching questions by:

📐 **Being curious.** Rekindle the hunger to understand and seek the truth that young children have, as demonstrated by them asking questions such as 'Why?'.

📐 **Keeping the conversation going.** A good question can be a statement such as 'Tell me about. . .' or 'Talk me through. . .'.

📐 **Using open questions.** People feel obliged to give you more information about the topic or subject you're discussing when you ask a question starting with *what, why, where, when, how, who* or *which*.

📐 **Becoming comfortable with silence.** Most people I've worked with don't like silence when they've asked a question, and ask another question or answer their own question within 20–30 seconds of asking the first question. Practise being silent for up to 90 seconds after you've asked a really good question.

📐 **Building up, not putting down.** Always have the positive intention of building up people instead of ridiculing, undermining, making them look foolish and so on in asking searching questions. People respect you when you act with integrity.

📐 **Remaining clear about your values or principles.** You're more likely to question and challenge others' views and even unacceptable behaviour in a group when you're clear about what's important to you. (Refer to Chapter 5 to find out how to clarify your values.)

📐 **Rising to your biggest challenge.** You may be the type of person who prefers to tackle the most difficult challenge straight away, or alternatively practise on less difficult situations or people first to progressively build your confidence. If you prefer the latter approach, start by asking searching questions of someone who's more receptive to being questioned or having his views challenged in order to develop your skills in framing questions.

📐 **Enhancing your ability to cope with potentially being embarrassed.** You may sometimes ask an inappropriate question such as one for which you should already know the answer. Checkout the later section 'Coping with embarrassment and threat' to find out how to handle being embarrassed.

Inviting challenge

One of the best ways of encouraging work colleagues to become used to others asking difficult questions and challenging their views is to set an example by inviting others to question and challenge your own views.

Be a good role model for inviting challenge by:

✔ Keeping an open mind to find the best solution to a problem. You may demonstrate this approach by admitting that you may not have the best suggestion or solution to the problem being considered, but that you want to get to the best solution.

✔ Maintaining a calm composure and vulnerability to having your views or decisions questioned or challenged. You discourage colleagues from sharing their views with you when you criticise them for taking the initiative to do so.

✔ Praising colleagues who effectively question and challenge your views and decisions.

Coping with embarrassment and threat

Chapter 8 describes how expressing your thoughts and encouraging your colleagues to critique your thoughts is risky, because you may feel embarrassed or threatened. You can also develop the courage to speak your mind by being able to cope with situations that you perceive to be embarrassing or threatening.

Here are a few ways to work on being able to cope with embarrassment and threat:

✔ **Recognise that embarrassment almost always fades with time.** Think about occasions when you felt embarrassed and you often realise that the emotion fades after an hour or two, or perhaps a day or two. Rarely are occasions so embarrassing that you're left with an emotional scar!

✔ **Nurture an 'I will survive' mentality.** You're more likely to put yourself into potentially embarrassing situations when you believe that you can cope with them. Use positive language such as 'I can. . .', 'I'm good' or 'I will survive' to talk up your self-esteem, or listen to a song that motivates or inspires you to help you to feel more positive.

✔ **Assess the risk.** If you're the sort of person who tends to worry when you do something wrong, such as asking an inappropriate question or making an inappropriate statement in a meeting, assess the real risk of doing so. For example, how many people do you know who were actually disciplined or dismissed for asking questions? Chapter 6 provides simple questions to assess the real risk to you.

> ✔ **Recognise that every 'cloud has a silver lining'.** You learn by being exposed to difficult situations: you may not want deliberately to create situations in which you feel embarrassed, but you can certainly profit from them! (See Chapter 4 for ways to take lessons from adversity.)

Sensing for Success

Chapter 8 describes the importance of switching on your senses – especially your visual and auditory ones – so that you can notice subtle changes or nuances in another person's or your own:

> ✔ Emotions.

> ✔ Behaviour or body language.

> ✔ Energy or enthusiasm about the issue or topic being discussed.

> ✔ Emphasis on words that reflect that certain words have significant meaning.

You can then use the information gathered in this way to better understand your work colleagues, especially their commitment towards taking a certain course of action or doing a task that needs to be done to achieve an objective. In this section you discover techniques for using your senses more effectively.

Being in the moment

Take a few moments to relax. When you feel relaxed, turn your attention to your mind and notice how still your mind is and any thoughts that are on or come into your mind . . . .

You probably notice that your mind is still for only a few seconds before a thought jumps into it! Your active mind keeps grabbing your attention: you may sometimes find that this happens to such an extent that colleagues may occasionally notice that they don't have your attention, prompting them to enquire whether something's on your mind or even whether you're day dreaming! You yourself may sometimes notice that your attention is some-where else – that is, not in the moment – when, for example, you're in a meeting and you miss comments made by your colleagues.

 'Being in the moment' is the act of bringing your attention into the here and now, and enables you to focus your total attention on the person(s) you're working with at that moment.

Practise the following techniques to enhance your ability to bring yourself into the moment:

- ✔ **Calm your mind.** Let the thoughts that clutter your mind and disturb your attention slip away, and as new thoughts jump into your mind let each of them go. You may want to find a calm place to help you practise, but you can also practise this technique in public places such as on public transport.

- ✔ **Be aware of a single object.** Select a single object that you can see and increase your awareness of it but don't think about it. For example, I can see the shape of an apple on the computer I'm using: I'm increasing my awareness of the detail of the shape without associating lots of thoughts about apples with it. Practise holding your attention on a single object without thoughts entering your mind.

- ✔ **Relax your body.** Breathe slowly and relax your body. Let the excess energy that's causing your muscles – and you – to be tense slip away as you gently exhale each deep breath. You have probably heard the saying 'healthy body, healthy mind'; now you know another one 'calm body, calm mind'!

Seeing what others miss

'It's the little things that matter!' Such a comment is often made when describing exceptional quality of service provided by a restaurant, hotel and so on. I suggest the same is also true when you're effectively engaging a person: your work colleagues may rarely tell you how they feel and so noticing the subtle changes that other people miss, especially in a colleague's facial expressions, is crucial for you to become an engaging leader.

Try the following techniques to enhance your skills in seeing what others miss:

- ✔ **Keep your head up.** You can't notice subtle changes in a person's facial expressions if your radar isn't pointing in the right direction! Frequently looking at someone's eyes (without doing it so intensely that you make the person feel uncomfortable) enables you to connect with and relate to people.

  In my experience, people may avoid direct eye contact with you when they don't want to commit strongly to doing something.

  Watch for subtle changes in a person's facial expressions, especially around the eyes, for clues about what a person is really thinking. Use subtle changes that you notice in a person's behaviour, such as a raised eyebrow, as prompts to enquire about the person's views on, for example, a statement you've just made that may have prompted the reaction. Enquire what the reaction meant instead of making assumptions.

- ✔ **Work your peripheral view.** Practise noticing what's on the edge of your field of vision, especially when you're working with groups. You may detect subtle changes in people's body language and behaviour that you may otherwise miss.

- ✔ **Scan in and out.** Practise focusing your vision in and out so that you can zoom in on, for example, a person and notice what's on your peripheral vision almost simultaneously.

Listening for meaning: Getting behind language

You're most likely aware that you unconsciously ignore background noise at work, such as the soft drone of air conditioning fans. Your mind appears to tune out such noises so that you can get on with the work in hand. Although this skill is essential for good concentration, you need to develop your listening skills when talking directly with people.

Practise listening for details and meaning by tuning your hearing and attention in to the words and phrases that a work colleague's using during direct one-to-one conversations:

- ✔ 'Listen with your mind' by concentrating on trying to understand what the person means rather than primarily focusing on your own thoughts.

- ✔ Hold your attention at two levels; be 'in the moment' and attentive to the person while maintaining at the back of your mind an overview of what a successful outcome to the conversation is going to be.

- ✔ Notice subtle changes in the tone of the person's voice that indicates he's placing more emphasis on certain words and phrases: emphasis that suggests that these words and phrases have a significant meaning to the person.

- ✔ Look out for a colleague repeatedly using certain words and/or phrases in a conversation. Repeated use of the same phrase may indicate that your colleague thinks that you've not fully discussed or considered the issue. For example, if your colleague keeps on repeating the phrase 'there wasn't enough time' when discussing why a particular job wasn't completed on time with them, I suggest this probably means that he thinks that you've not considered this 'lack of time' issue to his satisfaction.

- ✔ Suspend judgement. If you interrupt someone, you've probably already decided that you know what your colleague's going to say or disagree with him.

✔ Listen for *how* people say things; and especially whether people are using jargon such as 'thinking outside the box', 'blue sky thinking', and 'realising potential'. Make sure that you get people to explain what they mean in the particular situation and context.

✔ Listen for what people *don't* say; be alert to potentially different meanings of phrases and sentences that your colleague uses. For example, if a team member says the following sentence when explaining that he's experiencing problems obtaining information from another department: 'I tell them, but they don't take notice!' Does he mean:

  • 'People in the other department deliberately ignore me.'

  • 'I'm not very good at influencing people.'

  • Or does he have another interpretation of the sentence?

Being Brilliant at Building Commitment

The key to unlocking the commitment of work colleagues so that they perform tasks to a high standard is engaging them. (Check out Chapter 8 for much more detail.) When engaged, people take ownership of tasks and hold themselves accountable for successfully completing their work.

Work colleagues taking ownership of tasks is the difference between them being committed to doing tasks to the best of their ability and them doing their work just 'okay' simply because they're being compliant with your requests/instructions. When colleagues are only being compliant, they probably don't do their work as well as they could, unless you have a great relationship with them and they want to really please you.

In this section, you discover how to build and maintain the commitment of work colleagues to do all their tasks to the best of their ability.

Starting from pole position

My use of a motor racing metaphor isn't meant to imply that you're in a race with your work colleagues to get what you want! As the leader of your team, however, you may feel as if you have to be (or even that others expect you to be) in pole position: as if you're in front of your team as regards setting the direction that you want your team to go in and expecting them to follow you. You may even think that you know best about what's required from your team and individual team members for them to contribute to achieving your team's objectives. While you do need to be clear about these objectives, this section shows some of the difficulties that adopting an approach of always being in pole position can create.

(You can discover how to clarify the objectives and results that your team needs to achieve – and share these aims and your vision for your team with them to set the team's direction – in Chapter 7.)

I've observed hundreds of managers holding conversations with a work colleague to agree actions to complete a task, or agree a change of behaviour, when a colleague is underperforming, in real work situations or as part of leadership development programmes. In my experience almost every manager adopts an approach that I describe as 'having the endpoint in mind', in which the managers:

- ✔ Focus on the action they want their colleague to take or the change that they want them to make in their behaviour.

- ✔ Attempt to influence the person to act or change behaviour by using what they, the manager, believes to be a logical argument or appropriate evidence of the need for their colleague to act or make the change.

This approach can backfire and fail to achieve your aims. When you adopt this approach, you're focusing on the endpoint or outcome that you want to achieve through having the conversation. Your attention is primarily on your own thoughts as you follow your plan of how you intend the conversation to proceed: you may miss or ignore important information that your colleague is sharing with you!

When you take this approach, a typical response to any comment that your colleague makes that indicates that he disagrees with your views is for you to reinforce your viewpoint by restating the need to act or change and/or by using (more) evidence that you consider appropriate. You focus on your own interpretation of, for example, your colleague's underperformance and on your own meaning or understanding of the reasons for this underperformance.

If you fail to provide sufficient reasons or evidence for taking action or making a change that your colleagues agree with, or if they interpret the evidence differently, you and they are going to have different interpretations and understanding regarding the need for them to act or change. If these different understandings persist, your colleagues probably end up with a lower commitment to act or change their behaviour than you want them to have.

Approaching conversations with colleagues by starting from pole position is more likely to result in people only being compliant with what you want them to do, instead of them being genuinely committed to act or change their behaviour. The next section presents a more effective approach.

Beginning from their grid position

Instead of 'starting from pole position' (see the preceding section), a more appropriate and successful place to start conversations with colleagues to gain their commitment to act or change their behaviour is to start from their *grid position*. This approach means beginning from where your colleagues are regarding their view about the need to act or change their behaviour rather than you focusing only on the outcome that you want to achieve.

You're more able to gain the commitment of colleagues to act or change their behaviour when you fully understand the reasons why they do or don't do something or behave as they do.

Here's how to start from your team member's grid position:

✔ Focus on and find out your colleague's views or position regarding the current situation, standard of performance, need to change and so on. Strive to find out whether, and how important and worthwhile, your colleague perceives the need to act or change his behaviour.

✔ Be alert and attentive to notice words and phrases that appear to have significant meaning to your colleague (check out the earlier section 'Listening for meaning: Getting behind language').

✔ Explore the meanings that your colleague attaches to these words so that you improve your understanding of his views or perspectives by using phrases such as:

  • 'You mentioned [restate words] . . . what exactly do you mean?'

  • 'You seem to put a lot of emphasis on [restate words].'

  • 'It appears to me that [restate or paraphrase words] are significant to you.'

Focusing on winning together

Your aim in engaging work colleagues to 'go the extra mile' is to work together with a common commitment to achieve optimum outcomes for everyone involved (as I describe in Chapter 8). By doing so, everyone is unified in striving to achieve common objectives that directly or ultimately benefit your organisation, you and your staff.

Focusing on you working with one member of your team, striving to achieve a common objective, requires you and your colleague to arrive at a common and shared understanding about the importance of the objective and, depending on the difficulty of achieving it, the importance of tasks and activities that have to be done to achieve the objective. You *and* your colleague are *both* likely to be committed to achieving an objective, or doing a task or activity, when you agree that it is important and worthwhile because the objective or task is meaningful. (You found out about the dangers of work being meaningless to people in Chapter 8.)

Work with one of your colleagues to gain his commitment by agreeing that an objective, task or activity – or, perhaps, a change in his behaviour if he's underperforming – is important and worthwhile:

- ✔ Start from his grid position (see the preceding section for details).

- ✔ Explain the benefits of, for example, achieving an objective or doing a task, and the consequences of not doing it.

- ✔ Acquire a better understanding of each other's views and reasons for them.

- ✔ Gain new insights into the issue or problem, and identify more appropriate courses of action, through interpreting and reinterpreting together the views, ideas and information that you're sharing with each other.

- ✔ Notice any changes in your colleague's language during the conversation that indicates that he's accepted the need to act or change his behaviour, and that he's taking ownership and becoming committed to act or change.

  Examples include a move away from negative phrases such as 'I can't . . .' and 'I won't . . .', towards more positive responses such as 'Would it be possible for me to . . .', 'How can I/we . . .' and 'Can I . . . ?'.

- ✔ Agree some actions to take to work together more successfully (read the next section for details).

Strive to engage your colleagues to enable them to achieve their aims and objectives by working with you to achieve the team's objectives.

Agreeing actions to drive success

Having a meaningful conversation with a colleague to gain his commitment to act or change behaviour is pointless if you don't also agree the action and a deadline for taking that action. Sometimes, depending on the situation, both your colleague and you need to take actions to demonstrate your commitment to achieving an objective and/or to working better together.

Try to be absolutely clear about actions to be taken by:

- ✔ Describing each action clearly and concisely.

- ✔ Naming who's going to take each action.

- ✔ Agreeing specific dates as deadlines for taking action; don't leave room for any misunderstandings.

- ✔ Agreeing a method and date for reviewing progress or measuring success.

Avoiding meaningless language

Avoid using vague or cryptic language in any conversations in which you're agreeing actions to be taken as a result of gaining a colleague's commitment to act. Such language can cause misunderstandings and, potentially, disagreements and/or ill feeling if your colleague doesn't act as you expected him to.

Be wary of the implications of allowing colleagues to use the language set out in Table 9-3 when they're describing actions they're going to take.

Table 9-3	Examples of Meaningless Language
Meaningless Language	*Implication*
Hopefully I . . .	I hope but I can't be certain!
I'll try . . .	Is trying good enough for you?
I'll do it by next month.	With at least 28 days in a month, which day is meant?
I intend to . . .	How committed does this comment sound to you?

Keeping on track

One of the best ways to sustain the commitment of colleagues to take the actions that have been agreed is to recognise the progress they're making and their achievements.

Keep work colleagues on track by:

✔ Holding reviews at the time and date that you agreed. Put the review dates into your diary to prompt you to take the lead in organising and holding reviews.

✔ Asking your colleague in review meetings to take the lead in describing the progress he's made, his achievements, difficulties experienced and how he's going to overcome them and so on.

✔ Using your colleague's name when praising him to build his self-esteem, so that he hears success and praise associated with his name.

✔ Constructively challenging your colleague if you think that he's not maintaining his commitment, and providing any additional support that he needs from you to succeed.

Chapter 10

Modifying Your Leadership Style

· ·

In This Chapter

▶ Understanding why leading people is difficult

▶ Selecting an appropriate style for different situations

▶ Acting with integrity while modifying your style

· ·

As a manager you're going to encounter all sorts of different and varying situations and problems, and you need to be able to modify your preferred leadership style and approach as appropriate. In this chapter, you discover the main reasons why you may have difficulty leading people, and how different leadership styles affect the behaviour, attitudes and performance of your staff. In addition, I provide techniques for modifying your leadership style as you come up against different situations – so that your approach works for you and the people involved.

Having accepted the need to adapt your leadership approach as necessary, one question that then arises is: how can you remain authentic and act with integrity while also modifying your leadership style to suit the different requirements of different situations? This dilemma confused me in the early stages of my management career, when I experienced problems involving people, and in this chapter I help you find out how to handle it.

Appreciating the Need for a Range of Styles

Many factors impact on the attitudes, behaviours and performance of the people who report to you and they may also have implications for your choice of leadership style. These factors include:

✔ **People themselves.** Every person is unique, each having a different personality, preferred ways of working, needs, hopes, concerns, range of competences and so on.

✔ **Nature of the work.** The work that your team does may be, for example, extremely varied or repetitive in nature, or involve members of your team working in close proximity to you or out of your sight for most of the time.

✔ **Culture of your organisation.** Culture is often described as 'the way things get done around here', but essentially culture is the prevailing values, beliefs, attitudes and behaviours of people within your organisation.

✔ **Your boss.** Your boss's leadership style and how it impacts on you and your team.

✔ **You.** How you feel (that is, your current emotional state), your attitude towards each person and how you've treated people in the past.

Although you may have a preferred or natural leadership style in working with your colleagues, you need to be conscious of that style and display flexibility in your approach:

✔ Be aware of the impact that your preferred style has on the attitudes, behaviours and performance of your work colleagues.

✔ Work on developing an engaging leadership style that enables you to modify your approach to working with colleagues, in order to gain their commitment to working with you to achieve objectives.

✔ When you do find that you need to change your style, make sure that you do so without compromising your integrity or the overall quality of your working relationships.

Wondering why you seem to get the problem people

You may have accepted a job and then subsequently found out that you've more than your fair share of people reporting to you who aren't behaving or performing to the standard you expect. Such a situation probably reflects that those people haven't been led or managed well in the past: the leadership style of your predecessor was inappropriate! You may well come across situations in which people think that they're performing their job well because they've never been told otherwise.

You may inherit people problems that were caused by your predecessor mis-managing people, through perhaps having standards that weren't good enough for the work your team does or giving inappropriate feedback (that is, leading people to believe that they're doing their jobs well when they're not!).

If you've been leading the people for several months and some of them aren't performing or behaving to the standards you expect of them, ask yourself the following question:

> *What am I doing or not doing that's contributing to the current problems regarding underperformance or unacceptable behaviour?*

(Chapter 11 discusses the dangers of delaying taking action on behavioural and performance problems that you experience with your staff.)

Choosing horses for courses

Have you ever experienced a situation in which you treat two people the same way and find that they react differently to you? The same leadership style or approach may be effective in working with one person and less effective in working with another, which is just one reason why leading people can be difficult!

Consider modifying your leadership style when working with different people based on each individual's interests, needs, motives, preferred ways of working, skills and so on: all these attributes may affect the person's willingness and ability to do a required task. Leadership gurus Hersey and Blanchard describe this approach to leadership as *situational leadership* (in *Management of Organizational Behaviour, Utilizing Human Resources* (Prentice Hall)). They explain that leaders need to modify their directive and supportive styles of leadership to reflect the commitment and competence of each person who reports to them to do a particular task.

As well as the reasons I provide earlier in this section, other factors can also affect your choice of leadership style:

- ✔ How you're feeling at a given time and your attitude to work and each person who works for you. (Refer to Chapter 9 to find out about the problems that being judgemental of people can cause for you, and how to become non-judgemental.)

- ✔ Your own boss's style. You may have a similar or different style of leadership compared to that of your boss, and any significant differences may cause tension or even conflict between you about how you need to be leading your staff. You may sometimes decide to modify your leadership approaches to reinforce each other, such as when you both want to propose enthusiastically a change in an organisational structure or process to senior managers.

How individuals can change

Andy was an ambitious, young, financial accountant who worked hard to further his career and achieved several promotions. He married a lovely woman he'd met during the early stages of his career and eventually became a father for the first time. Andy's priorities regarding his career changed and he wanted to spend more time with his family. Although he continues to perform his job well, he's less keen to take on major projects that require him to spend periods away from home. Andy explained the situation to his manager, especially the short-term change in his career aspirations. Together they agreed that Andy would do less work on projects that involved working away for a period of time providing that Andy would help out, if required, on major projects.

Joan is an experienced and committed sales manager who encourages her staff to provide a service to customers that meets her high standards. One of Joan's staff changed quite quickly, and without any apparent reason, from being a fairly enthusiastic person to one who became critical of Joan and how she was managing. Such criticism was at odds with the views of the rest of Joan's staff, but the criticism was so strong that it significantly affected Joan's confidence in encouraging and challenging any of her staff to maintain her high standards, until her confidence was rebuilt through coaching sessions I had with her. I encouraged Joan to review all of the evidence regarding how she was working with each individual, and how each person was performing. Joan recognised that she was behaving fairly and consistently, and in accord with her own and the company's values. Joan regained her drive to hit her own targets and enthuse her staff to continue to achieve their targets, and, in the meantime, the employee who was critical of her decided to leave the company.

When you experience tension or conflict with your boss due to significant differences in your styles, try to influence your boss to, for example, accept your approach to leading your team or even to modify her leadership style, and in doing so work better together. Check out Chapter 9 for how to enhance your skills in engaging people, including developing the courage to speak your mind, and Chapter 7 for more on increasing your sphere of influence.

Working with chameleon people

Not only do you have to lead people who are different to each other, but you also may find that individuals change over time but, fortunately, not as quickly as a chameleon can change its colour. People's personal or work circumstances can change, which directly or indirectly affects their attitude to work, their needs, motives, performance and so on.

Understanding Different Styles of Leadership

In this section, I look at two basic approaches to leadership – one challenging and focused on targets and the other supportive of individual people – and the need to be flexible as a manager.

Modifying your leadership style helps you to engage your staff. Successfully engaging the people who report to you enables:

- ✔ You to gain their commitment to work together towards achieving the objectives that contribute to your organisation being successful.
- ✔ Them to fulfil their needs through working towards achieving those objectives.

To be brilliant at engaging people, you need to be skilled in the following:

- ✔ Relating to and connecting with people by having a genuine interest in them and their needs.
- ✔ Speaking your mind and asking searching questions.
- ✔ Noticing nuances in your own and other people's emotions, behaviour, enthusiasm and emphasis on words and language.
- ✔ Interpreting information together to create mutual understanding about, and commitment to, acting to achieve objectives, solve problems and so on.

Refer to Chapters 8 and 9 for more about these skills.

 When you're skilled in engaging people, you can modify your leadership style without undermining your integrity because you're simultaneously focusing on achieving your team's objectives, being sensitive and responsive to the needs of each member of the team, and consistently acting authentically in accord with your values.

Exploring leadership styles

In my work on developing high performance cultures in organisations, I interview managers and groups of employees in order to identify the factors affecting organisational performance. Although all managers have their own individual style, the prevailing leadership style is one major factor that affects the attitudes, behaviours and performance of employees in many organisations.

The prevailing leadership styles can range from leaders being highly challenging to being highly supportive of employees. The behaviours of leaders who have a challenging approach to working with their colleagues include:

- ✔ Agreeing (or setting) objectives or targets that stretch people.
- ✔ Holding each person, clearly and consistently, accountable for achieving her objectives and results.
- ✔ Challenging unacceptable behaviour, language or performance promptly when it occurs.

The behaviours of leaders who have a supportive approach to working with their colleagues include:

- ✔ Spending time getting to know people individually and building a close working relationship with each of them.
- ✔ Praising people for doing a good job.
- ✔ Recognising and helping people to solve any problems they're experiencing in performing their job.

The above descriptions of leadership styles also reflect a different emphasis that leaders may place on achieving the objectives and results that they and their teams have to achieve compared to how much emphasis they place on people and their needs. (If you want to find out more about how leaders' behaviours can be affected by how much concern they have for achieving results as compared to their concern for people, refer to *Leadership Dilemmas – Grid Solutions* by Robert R. Blake and Anne Adams McCanse (Gulf).)

During a typical workday, you may find that you experience situations in which you need to modify your style or approach in order to place:

- ✔ Equal emphasis on achieving objectives and peoples' needs.
- ✔ More emphasis on achieving objectives.
- ✔ More emphasis on people as individuals and their needs during the situation.

Figure 10-1 provides examples of how you can modify your leadership approach to place different emphasis on achieving objectives and on the people who report to you in different situations.

Style: Your focus in this situation is on achieving an important objective typically by an urgent deadline; you may be more directive by giving instructions, rather than consulting people about what to do, whilst still treating them with respect.	**Style:** You are focused on achieving objectives through involving people who report to, and work with, you to enable them to fulfil their needs through working towards achieving your team's objectives.
Style: Avoid being uninterested in achieving objectives and the needs of the people who work with you as your uninterest will achieve little and demotivate most people.	**Style:** Your focus in this situation is on the needs of individuals or your whole team with less attention, but not importance, given to progressing the achievement of work objectives. You may be building a person's self-confidence, developing their skills, discussing their concerns about a change in policy or procedure, and so on.

High ← EMPHASIS ON ACHIEVING OBJECTIVES → Low

Low ← EMPHASIS ON PEOPLE → High

Figure 10-1: Examples of how you can modify your style in different situations.

Adapted from Leadership Dilemmas – Grid Solutions *by Robert R. Blake and Anne Adams McCanse (Gulf).*

Realising how styles impact on people and performance

Choosing the right leadership style for each situation can be difficult. For example, you need to get the balance correct between putting too much or too little emphasis on achieving objectives and/or the needs of individuals in a given situation, and challenging or supporting an individual too much or too little!

Whatever leadership style you select has an impact on the performance of your staff and work colleagues.

Here's an exercise that helps you to discover whether you get the right balance in this area.

1. **Get a notebook and divide the page into three columns as in Table 10-1.**

2. **Write a brief description of a situation in which you placed too much or too little emphasis on achieving an objective.**

3. **In the second column, briefly describe the action that you took or should have taken, or how you behaved.**

4. **Describe the effect of your action or inactivity or behaviour.**

5. **Repeat steps 2 to 4 for other situations that you identified.**

6. **Repeat steps 2 to 5 for situations in which you placed too much or too little emphasis on an individual who reports to you, and on that person's needs.**

7. **Reflect on the contents of the last two columns.** Note how you want to improve your ability to work better with your colleagues to achieve objectives or to encourage and support them to achieve your standards, and meet their needs. (In Chapter 11, you can find out how to lead people towards achieving the standards of behaviour and performance that you expect.)

I provide an example in the first row to help you get started.

Table 10-1	Placing Too Much or Too Little Emphasis on Achieving Objectives and Individual Needs	
Brief Description of the Situation	*Action I Took or Didn't Take*	*The Effect of My Behaviour on the Team and/or Myself*
I needed Jim to stay late to help complete an important job for a client. I asked Jim to stay back but he said he had other commitments.	I didn't explain the importance of the job and wasn't assertive enough in asking Jim to stay late.	I cut corners to hit the deadline and the job wasn't completed to the correct standard. I felt that I let the customer and myself down.

Unintended consequences!

Here are a couple of examples of leaders putting too much or too little emphasis on achieving results, and on the needs of the people who report to them.

Bill is the sort of guy who gets things done. He sets demanding targets for himself and his staff, and he's totally focused on achieving results. He has a tendency to overlook the feelings of people through being so focused on hitting his targets, and he can rub some people – especially those who have high expectations about how they should be treated – the wrong way. These people comply with Bill's demands, but don't give him their commitment. People who are target-driven and who aren't too concerned about how they're treated respond well to Bill's drive to achieve objectives and aren't adversely affected by his demanding and brusque manner.

Jane is a caring person who likes to get on well with all her colleagues. She gives people a lot of autonomy, and is grateful when anyone does a job for her and tends to thank people profusely even when jobs aren't demanding or difficult to complete. Although everyone thinks well of Jane's good intentions, some of her staff would like her to set more challenging targets and only praise staff when they do a job exceptionally well.

Many of Jane's staff also think that she doesn't challenge certain people enough, and that they take advantage of her caring approach. They think that standards are falling because Jane allows certain people to get away with doing work that's not good enough, and they resent having to work harder because she doesn't challenge those people.

Modifying Your Leadership Style So That It Works for You and Others

In this section, you find out how to choose appropriate leadership styles that work for you and your colleagues.

Being true to yourself

Your work colleagues expect you to act with integrity! People generally have difficulty coping with a leader who acts inconsistently, for example, by displaying large, apparently irrational, swings in behaviour. For instance, if members of your team normally see you as being approachable, but you're occasionally brusque with them when you feel under pressure, they don't know how to respond to your changes in behaviour.

You confuse people if you act inconsistently by changing your behaviour without explanation, and if you change your mind about work priorities, standards of work and so on.

Make a conscious decision to modify your leadership style or approach based on the needs of each situation, but also ensure that you remain consistent by being authentic and by staying focused on the purpose of your job (Chapter 4 discusses the importance of authenticity as a leader). Clarity is vital in this aim, and Chapter 5 helps you get your values clear and Chapter 7 helps you clarify the purpose of your job.

Maintain your integrity by ensuring that how you act and behave with your work colleagues is always consistent with your values, while modifying your leadership style to reflect your work priorities and to meet the needs, motives, commitment, skills and so on of each individual.

Assessing first, choosing second

Your personal preferred or natural leadership style may cause you typically to adopt a certain approach to working with your colleagues, perhaps tending to be more supportive or more challenging. When deciding whether to modify your natural style or approach to dealing with different situations, consider the needs or requirements of each situation first before you decide how to modify your style.

The first step to assessing your approach to dealing with each situation is to assess yourself: for example, how your current work demands, emotional state and so on are affecting your approach to the situation and/or the people involved.

Other needs or requirements that, perhaps, you can consider include:

- Work priorities such as the importance of tasks and the urgency to complete them.
- Needs of the people involved such as their personal needs, their desire to understand, their preferred approach to being led or managed and so on.

Focusing on outcomes

Focus on clarifying the outcomes that you want to achieve in assessing your approach to any given situation. The questions listed below may be relevant for you to ask yourself to clarify the outcomes that guide you in modifying your leadership style and adopting an appropriate approach to a given situation. You don't need to ask all or even most of the questions unless the situation is a significant event such as a major reorganisation of the work of your team:

✔ **'What work objective or result do I want to achieve?'** Am I absolutely clear in my own mind about what I want to achieve, and can I articulate this objective clearly?

✔ **'To what extent do I need to enthuse people?'** Should I be really enthusiastic and upbeat or adopt a quieter approach in explaining the importance of this work?

✔ **'What are the individual and/or collective needs of members of my team that I need them to fulfil with regard to the subject that I want to discuss with them?'** How clear am I about the interests, needs, preferences and so on of each person, and how am I going to address these?

✔ **'Do I need to sustain current levels of enthusiasm and commitment?'** How will the news that I need to share affect each person?

✔ **'To what extent do I need to raise the bar regarding standards of performance or behaviour?'** Do I need to be more challenging or supportive in working with each person to get the best out of them in this situation?

✔ **'What are the consequences of me adopting the wrong approach to this situation?'** Could I make the situation worse if I choose the wrong approach?

Excelling through trial and error

You need to work continually on enhancing your skills in modifying your leadership style to suit the needs of different situations by treating all situations as opportunities to expand your knowledge and experience. Use the following techniques to learn through trial and error:

✔ Step outside of your comfort zone and become more comfortable at being uncomfortable when challenging or supporting – depending on your natural style – your colleagues. (Refer to Chapter 6 to find more on being comfortable being uncomfortable.)

✔ Become more self-aware and sensitive in order to notice how you impact on your work colleagues through switching on your senses. (Check out Chapter 9 for all about the importance of using your senses.)

✔ Reflect on your experiences by using learning logs. (Chapter 4 has more on keeping a useful learning record.)

✔ Seek feedback from your colleagues about how your style affects them using the Johari Window (which I describe in Chapter 4).

Strive to develop a leadership style in which you're normally putting an equally high emphasis on the following:

✔ Achieving the objectives that you and your team have to achieve *and* enabling members of your team to satisfy their needs through working towards those objectives.

✔ Challenging *and* supporting everyone in your team to achieve and maintain high standards of work and behaviour in working together.

✔ Being bold in leading with conviction *and* being sensitive to appreciating how you're impacting on the attitudes and performance of each member of your team.

And make sure that you modify your style accordingly.

Chapter 11

Leading People to Peak Performance

Sometimes you're going to find that leading people is a joy: you admire how everyone pulls together to scale new heights of performance and teamwork. At other times, however, leading people can seem like an uphill battle as they falter and fail to deliver the performance you expect.

Throughout this chapter I employ the metaphor of climbing to help you discover how to encourage your staff to strive towards achieving peak performance by setting standards for them and acting promptly when individuals fail to achieve those standards. You find out how to tackle the thorny issues of unacceptable behaviour and performance, as well as how to use coaching to lead people to even better performance.

Being a Great Role Model

I'm sure that you look up to and admire certain leaders, those individuals who you aspire to be like and, maybe, have learnt from. Take a few minutes now to identify those leaders: perhaps you have direct experience of working with them or maybe you know of them only through books, magazines, television or other media.

Get a notebook and take a few minutes to capture your thoughts about each leader that you identify using the following statements as prompts:

- The name of the leader and the position held.
- The characteristics, attributes, principles, knowledge, skills or actions that you admire in this leader.
- The effect that this leader has had on you.

This simple exercise allows you to identify the impact that role models have had on you, and prompts you to see that you have a similar influence on your staff. You find out about the importance of setting and maintaining standards in the next two sections.

Flying your flag on the summit

You're responsible for setting and maintaining the standards of work, behaviour and performance of your whole team and every member of it: you're the standard-bearer for your team! You want your team to rally round your standards, uphold and protect them just as an army unites around and protects its distinctive flag in battle . . . even to the last man standing!

As the standard-bearer for your team, you also:

- Promote and uphold your own, your team's and your organisation's values.
- Represent, promote and uphold the purpose, objectives and requirements of your team within your organisation to enable people to achieve the objectives and results expected of them.
- Create a team identity that enables your team to feel part of something special. (You find out about the importance of team identity in Chapter 15.)

Be a bold standard-bearer and carry your flag high: 'fly it from the summit' so that what you and your team stand for, in terms of purpose, objectives, values and standards, can be seen by everyone in your team and all the people your team works with.

Being a leader can be extremely hard! You need to set the standards for others to follow: you have to be the person that you want others to become in terms of your team's values and standards regarding the quality of work, how members of your team work together and with colleagues in other departments and so on.

Do what I say not what I do!

Brian is a busy person, always dashing around from one meeting to another, jumping from one task to the next. His team is also busy and time is a precious commodity to all team members. Brian's team recognise that he is always struggling to keep to deadlines and that he doesn't like to be kept waiting. In fact, Brian makes a point of heavily criticising any member of his team who arrives late to any of his many team meetings. Unfortunately, Brian is often late for his own meetings!

Brian's late attendance at meetings has resulted in his staff paying lip service to his criticism of them: people continue to be late for meetings.

Setting the standard doesn't mean that you have to be able to do every task that every member of your team does. As people do their jobs every day, they become experts. The range of your responsibilities and the size of your team are likely to grow as you climb up your organisation's management structure and as your leadership and professional talents are recognised and appreciated, and you can't possibly be an expert in everything.

Your staff members are always watching you: your team and other work colleagues take more notice of – and tend to copy – your behaviour more than they take notice of what you say. Inspire members of your team to achieve your team's objectives by conveying your enthusiasm and commitment to succeed. (You can find out about the importance of inspiring people in Chapter 1.)

Avoiding the crevasse of double standards

You can't expect the people who report to you to work to or maintain standards that you don't keep yourself. Therefore, you need to avoid having double standards! Developing double standards without realising it is all too easy, just as Brian describes in the sidebar 'Do what I say not what I do!'.

Be careful of unintentionally allowing double standards:

- ✔ Don't make allowances for a person falling below your standard regarding an aspect of work or behaviour just because that person is highly skilled in other aspects. Some people are naturally more skilled or proficient at doing certain tasks than their colleagues, and you need to organise work to make best use of the collective talents of your team;

but don't allow anyone to fall below the overall standards you expect everyone to achieve.

✔ Don't show favouritism towards certain team members. Be careful about turning a 'blind eye' towards people who fail to maintain the team's standards simply because you like them.

Noticing that the standards of work and behaviour in your team are falling can sometimes be difficult. Keep a constant lookout for early signs of standards falling because, just as a careless mountaineer can fall down a crevasse covered by snow, you need to discover problems sooner rather than later!

Acting Before Avalanches

When avalanches happen, they carry away everything in their path and bury it in deep snow. You may find that things come crashing down around you like an avalanche if you don't notice or ignore that standards are falling in your team as regards the work itself or how members of your team are behaving. Recovering from such problems can be difficult and time-consuming. I explore why and how you should avoid work avalanches in the next two sections.

Appreciating the dangers of delay

Putting off talking to someone about an unacceptable standard of work or behaviour can be all too easy, particularly if you:

✔ Are a busy person; you have good intentions regarding discussing the issue with the person but never get round to acting on them!

✔ Don't like having difficult conversations – and not many people do.

✔ Would be stepping outside of your comfort zone by raising the problem with the person.

Be aware of these common dangers of delaying taking action:

✔ **You accept a lower standard.** When people fail to meet your standard and you don't raise the problem promptly, they think that you're allowing it to happen. For example, if a person is occasionally late arriving at work and you don't raise the issue of timekeeping, that person may think that arriving late is okay. If you do not notice that the standard isn't being met, the affect on the other person is the same: he may assume you don't mind him arriving late.

✔ **You risk a bad apple infecting others.** If you allow one person's work or behaviour to fall below your expected standard, other team members may notice your inactivity and question why they should work to that standard when their colleague is being allowed to get away with not meeting it. For example, you may find that you've a growing timekeeping problem within your team if you don't take prompt action with a poor timekeeper.

✔ **Your credibility is damaged.** Members of your team who have high standards start to wonder why you don't take action: your credibility can be damaged by allowing a team member to fail to meet the team's standards.

✔ **Your job becomes more difficult.** Tackling the problem of unacceptable performance or behaviour becomes more difficult by not acting promptly because:

  • The problem grows due to the 'bad apple' effect mentioned above.

  • You may have to explain why you didn't act sooner; the person who's not meeting your standards may ask, 'Why didn't you raise this issue with me earlier?'.

Applying the golden rule of 'Now'

A golden rule to adopt regarding when to raise an unacceptable standard of work or behaviour is: *Do it Now!*

When you act as soon as you notice the problem, you can avoid the dangers mentioned in the preceding section and build your self-esteem by successfully tackling and dealing with problems with people – or people problems!

Another good general principle to adopt in leading people is to praise people in public and criticise them (constructively) in private. The following are the main benefits of adopting this principle:

✔ Praising people in public for achieving your standards means that:

  • They get the public recognition they deserve.

  • You reinforce high standards by talking publicly about a person achieving those standards.

  • Their work colleagues recognise that they also have to achieve those standards if they want to be recognised for doing a good job.

✔ Constructively criticising people who aren't meeting your standards in private means that:

- You're treating them with respect.

- You don't unnecessarily embarrass them in public.

Raising issues of unacceptable standards of work or behaviour straightaway may mean the following, depending on the severity of the problem and the work context:

✔ Raising the issue the minute you notice the problem, such as in a one-to-one meeting or conversation with the person.

✔ Raising the issue at a time convenient to you the same day. For example, you may decide to delay raising the issue for a few hours if you have to complete an important task by an urgent deadline.

✔ Delaying raising the issue until the earliest time at which you can have a private conversation with the person.

✔ Delaying raising the issue until the earliest time that you can gather the relevant facts or evidence to determine the severity of the problem.

Two exceptions exist to raising unacceptable standards of behaviour only in private. You need to raise the problem as soon as you notice it happening in a meeting also involving other people when the behaviour is:

✔ So severe that you can't appear to ignore it for even a minute. An example is the use of abusive personal language.

✔ Typical of the behaviour of several members of the group, and you want to discuss the behaviour in the group because the group is malfunctioning as a result. In such situations, you may describe and discuss the behaviour without naming the last person to behave that way. A simple example is when people interrupt and talk over one another, which demonstrates that people aren't fully listening to what the others have to say.

Leading Under-performers Towards Your Peak

You find out in the earlier section 'Flying your flag on the summit' that, as the standard-bearer for your team, you're responsible for setting and maintaining the standards of work, behaviour and performance of your whole team and everyone in it! Getting everyone in your team to own and work to your standards can be a challenge. The next four sections describe how to lead people whose performance and/or behaviour is unacceptable with regard to your standards.

Working on commitment and capability

Your approach to working with a person who fails to meet your standards for work or behaviour is affected by your assessment of the person's:

- ✔ Capability to achieve the standard.
- ✔ Commitment to do the task to the required standard or behave in accord with your values or standards.

The capability of people to do a particular task to the standard required depends on several factors including their knowledge, skills, experience, the ability to think through complex tasks or problems, and so on. The commitment of people to do a particular task depends on the importance that they attach to the task, whether they like or dislike doing it, how easy or difficult the task is for them to do, and so on.

In some situations, you may be tempted to be satisfied when an underperforming person simply complies with your requirements, but I encourage you always to strive to gain a person's commitment to meeting the required standards because:

- ✔ Committed people are more likely to achieve the standard.
- ✔ Committed people allow you to have confidence that they're going to achieve and maintain the standard.
- ✔ Committed people are easier to manage: you don't have to monitor that they're meeting the standard as much as you do if they're not committed.

Check out Chapter 8 for more on the importance of engaging people so that they take ownership of (and commit to) the task and hold themselves accountable for successfully completing it. Chapter 9 shows you how to hold conversations to become brilliant at building commitment.

Figure 11-1 summarises four different approaches to leading a person, whose performance or behaviour is unacceptable, towards peak performance based on your assessment of the person's capability and commitment to do a given task.

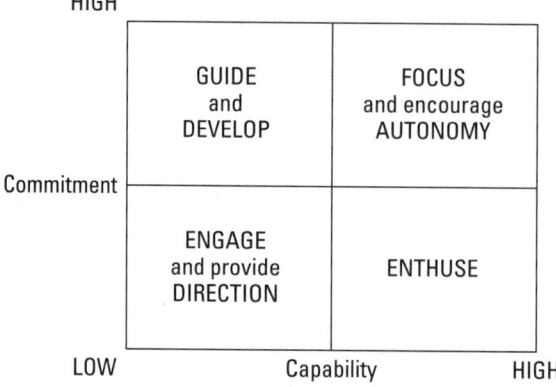

HIGH

GUIDE
and
DEVELOP

FOCUS
and encourage
AUTONOMY

Commitment

ENGAGE
and provide
DIRECTION

ENTHUSE

LOW   Capability   HIGH

Figure 11-1:
Approaches
to working
with people
based on
their com-
mitment and
capabilities.

(This model is based on the original work pioneered by Hersey and Blanchard on situational leadership. For more information on how situational leadership has been applied to executive coaching by Hersey and Chevalier refer to Coaching for Leadership, 2nd Edition (Pfeiffer).)

You can take four different approaches to leading a person. These are to:

✔ **Enthuse** (when someone is highly capable, but has low commitment to doing the task) the person by:

- Clarifying the reasons why the person isn't committed by exploring whether he has any expectations or needs regarding the job that aren't being met.

- Explaining the importance of the task and the reasons why you want the person to do it.

- Recognising the person's knowledge, skills and so on that are particularly relevant to completing the task.

- Helping the person to understand that doing the task to the required standard will enable him to make progress towards satisfying any unmet needs or expectations that he has about the job or role in the organisation.

- Agreeing actions and deadlines, and how progress is to be measured.

- Thanking the person for using his abilities.

✔ **Engage and provide direction** (when the commitment and capability of a person to do a task are both low) by:

- Exploring whether any expectations aren't being met.

- Clarifying how the person feels about how he's doing the job, showing an interest in his sense of self-esteem and the reasons for his view.

- Looking for ways for building the person's self esteem by agreeing small steps or actions that slightly stretch his ability but that he's likely to complete successfully – with your support if necessary – so that you can recognise and praise even slight progress.

- Agreeing actions or tasks that progressively stretch the person as his confidence increases.

- Providing on-going support to develop the person's ability and provide feedback emphasising his achievements (use the person's name when praising him).

✔ **Guide and develop** (when a person is highly committed, but has low capability to do the task) the person by:

- Explaining the main steps to complete the task.

- Encouraging the person to ask questions, and ask your own, to ensure that he clearly understands what you require.

- Agreeing milestones and deadlines when you want the person to report and discuss progress with you.

- Being available for reference.

- Praising achievements and using problems as opportunities for the person to grow and develop his capabilities.

✔ **Focus and encourage autonomy** (when the commitment and capability of a person to do a task are both high) by:

- Agreeing the objective or outcome and deadline to be achieved without discussing the method.

- Providing enough autonomy for the person to make his own decisions and take action to achieve the objective.

Be careful to avoid taking highly committed and capable people for granted: remember to thank people for showing a high level of commitment and doing their job well.

Approaching cliffhanger conversations

Most leaders dislike having conversations with people whose performance or behaviour is unacceptable. I call these conversations 'cliffhangers' because you:

✔ Are concerned that you may lose your grip on yourself and lose control of your emotions.

✔ Fear that you may slip up in what you intend to say, say the wrong thing and not achieve the intended outcome.

✔ Expect that the conversation may sometimes be on a knife edge: tense and uncomfortable.

✔ Perceive that the consequences of the conversation going wrong are huge – and it looks a long way down!

Here are guidelines to help you plan how to have really meaningful and successful conversations with someone who's not doing the job to your required standard.

✔ Preparing yourself:

- Be crystal clear about the standards you expect your work colleagues to achieve.

- Be objective but non-judgemental. (Chapter 9 shows that being judgemental can cause you to make the conversation difficult by, for example, expecting the person to be difficult.)

- Switch on your senses to enable you to give the person your total attention. (You discover the benefits and how to switch on your senses in Chapters 8 and 9.)

✔ Preparing your kit:

- Collect all relevant facts and evidence while keeping an open mind that further relevant evidence may be shared with you during your conversation.

- Clarify any gap between the standard expected and the current level of performance or behaviour as indicated by the evidence, while being responsive to fresh evidence being shared with you in the conversation.

- Consider how the person prefers to be treated. For example, some people like to get straight to the point in conversations whereas others prefer to talk around and lead up to a key issue.

- Be clear about the outcomes you want to achieve from the conversation including any actions that will demonstrate the person is capable and committed to do the task.

✔ Be wary of third party opinions:

- Sometimes you may have to seek the views of colleagues in obtaining facts and evidence about a person's performance or behaviour such as when the person is a member of a project group that doesn't include you. Check whether the work colleagues are giving you subjective opinions or solid facts: opinions can be challenged much easier than facts.

- Ask your colleagues' permission to reveal, if necessary during your intended conversation, that they're the source of the information. If they don't give you their permission, be wary of using the evidence: you may decide that you have to use it, but the credibility of the information may be challenged and undermined if you can't justify it.

Roping people into improvements

Spend time and work with people who are failing to meet your standards so that they identify and understand the gap between their current level of performance or behaviour and your required standard. Encourage them to come up with the actions necessary to bridge this gap so that they take ownership of, and are committed to, improving. (Flip to Chapter 9 for how to ask searching questions, listen carefully and interpret information when agreeing the importance of a particular objective or task.)

Be smart by agreeing improvements that are 'SMART':

- ✔ **Specific.** The outcome or actions agreed need to be so clear and concise that they can only be interpreted one way.

- ✔ **Measurable.** You both clearly understand how progress will be measured such as through observation, measuring outputs, progress reviews and so on.

- ✔ **Achievable.** Agree any support that you'll provide including 'on or off-the-job' training, access to you for advice and so on.

- ✔ **Relevant.** All improvements should contribute to the individual, and/or your team and even the organisation being more successful: if not, why are you seeking an improvement?

- ✔ **Time-based.** Agree dates and times for holding progress reviews rather than propose to hold reviews in one, two or more weeks, which is too vague and open to misunderstandings about deadlines.

People tend to achieve tasks when you agree deadlines as compared to when you leave actions open-ended!

Mapping progress towards peak performance

When working with people who fail to meet your standards, you need to demonstrate your commitment to encouraging them to achieve the required level of performance. Continue to challenge and support them following your initial conversation to discuss their performance.

Always put the date and time for conducting a progress review(s) straight into your diary system; that is, during or immediately after your conversation. This habit reminds you to hold the reviews, and forces you to think about moving or removing it from your diary and consider the implications of doing so.

Consider the following points when making decisions about the type and frequency of progress reviews to map how well a person is making progress towards the required standard:

- ✔ Recognising and reinforcing people's progress helps to sustain their commitment.

- ✔ Allowing space for people to learn from making mistakes may be risky, but 'trial and error' is an effective method of discovering how to do a job better. You may consider that taking a few well-considered risks is worthwhile to enable people who are committed to making improvements to learn through making their own decisions and taking action.

- ✔ Deciding whether any milestones or deadlines while completing the task are critical to achieve, and how to ensure that these are met.

Coaching the Good Towards Greatness

When trying to enhance the performance or behaviour of their staff, many leaders make the mistake of telling people what to do: the message often goes in one ear and out of the other one! People have to take *ownership* of the need for the change and become committed to putting the effort in to sustain a change in their performance or behaviour.

Your challenge in coaching the people who report to you is to have meaningful conversations with them so that they take ownership of and become committed to making the change . . . and, ideally, to managing themselves in achieving and sustaining the improvement.

My description of the role of coach is to:

Engage people in their own thinking to enable them to gain new insights and meanings that enhance their confidence and lead to better decisions, actions, behaviour and performance.

You discover useful tips on how to coach individuals and even your whole team to be even better at what they do in the next three sections.

Taking a time out to coach

In basketball, coaches can call a time out to discuss tactics; you can do the same and you don't even have to stop the game! You can coach individual members or the whole team as part of your normal daily activities. You may think that you don't have the time to coach people every day, but you do because each opportunity may only take a few minutes.

Be on the lookout for opportunities to coach individuals and your team everyday.

Here are a few examples of the many opportunities you have to coach members of your team towards greatness:

✔ Ask a team member who brings a problem to you to also bring options with a recommendation for how to solve the problem. Talk though the proposal and praise the person if you agree with the recommendation. If you disagree, ask relevant questions to guide the person towards your preferred action. (Dip into Chapter 9 to find more on asking searching questions.)

When you've done this process a few times and are agreeing with the recommendations being put to you, help people to see that they're solving the problems, and only need to come to you if a problem is exceptional or the consequences of taking the wrong action are significant.

✔ When you notice that a task hasn't been done to the required standard, ask the relevant person to look at the task, and assess and comment on whether it meets the required standard. Ask questions to help the person spot where or how the task is sub-standard, understand the consequences of it being wrong and describe the actions to take to do the task correctly this time and in future.

✔ Catch people doing a great job by walking around and talking to them about the work they're doing. Praising people in public boosts their self-esteem and reinforces the standards that you expect people to achieve.

✔ Hold a short review of the process at the end of a team meeting to agree strengths and actions to improve how well:

 • People were prepared for the meeting.

 • Time was used.

 • Everyone was encouraged to contribute.

 • People listened to each other.

 • Decisions were made and clear actions agreed.

 • The team hold each other accountable for taking agreed actions following a meeting.

Be a great coach by regularly helping people to think things through for themselves.

Choosing the right role

I adopt and fulfil several different roles as a coach when working with chief executives, directors and other senior managers, often during each meeting with them. My clients often don't notice that I'm changing my role because my movement from one to another is subtle in response to the issues they're raising or their emotions.

I describe a few coaching roles, and situations when you need to consider using them, in Table 11-1.

Table 11-1	Coaching Roles and When to Use Them
Advisor	You've more knowledge and expertise than the people who report to you in certain aspects of their work. Advising involves guiding a person towards the correct or right way of doing a task where a best way exists.
Partner	You work together in jointly solving a problem, sharing your expertise and ideas to enhance each other's understanding of the problem and arrive at a decision that you're both committed to taking.
Reflector	You listen carefully and reflect back your interpretations to the person to check and clarify the meanings they're trying to convey, perhaps acting as a sounding board for their proposals and/or offering different interpretations. Use this approach to help people refine their thinking on an issue and acquire new insights into, for example, how to build a more productive working relationship with a colleague.
Catalyst	You prompt and probe people's thinking by asking searching questions and listening intently to notice words and phrases that seem to have significant meaning to them and, through this approach, enhance their understanding of an issue or problem and the actions that they're going to take. Useful for helping colleagues to work through what is, for them, a particularly difficult or complex problem.
Critical friend	You challenge someone about his thinking and behaviour while having a genuine interest in him as an individual, providing moral support and acting with integrity. This approach is powerful for helping people to enhance their self-awareness, acquire insights into their motives, attitudes and behaviours, and how their behaviour is impacting on others, and to increase their self-accountability.

You need to be highly skilled as a coach or have a strong relationship with a person to be a critical friend. And remember always to have critical friends yourself – they're of huge value as you go through your career.

Practising what great coaches do

Be a great coach by:

- ✔ Having a genuine interest in helping people to grow and prosper.

- ✔ Giving people your total attention when you're with them.

- ✔ Encouraging people to fulfil their potential as all times.

- ✔ Keeping your mind open to all possibilities and avoiding being judgemental.

- ✔ Asking searching and difficult questions to enhance the quality of people's thinking, explore the reasons for their actions and so on.

- ✔ Listening intently to the language people are using and noticing words and phrases that have significant meanings for them.

- ✔ Sensing whether people are showing real commitment to do what is right or necessary.

- ✔ Speaking your mind; that is, having the courage to say what needs to be said rather than ducking issues or avoiding disagreements. Be willing to challenge people's motives and behaviour.

- ✔ Reinterpreting information shared between you and individuals to create new insights and meanings about problems, and the person's self- awareness and self-knowledge.

- ✔ Being vulnerable by remaining willing to have your views questioned and challenged, and acknowledging and saying when you're wrong.

- ✔ Having humility: you're not the focus of the conversation!

Be a great coach by developing and using great skills in engaging people. (You found out about the core processes for, and how to enhance your skills in, engaging people in Chapters 8 and 9.)

Part IV
Leading People Through Change

"OK – Here's the business plan. Nigel takes charge of marketing, Tristram sales, Keith accounts and Psycho makes sure clients pay on time."

In this part . . .

You find out how to successfully lead and implement changes in your workplace in these chapters. You dive deep into uncovering workplace culture, and discover how to transform culture in your team, department or organisation. From revealing people's objections to change to finding out about the power of storytelling to reinforce a new culture, this part provides many tips on how to prevent and overcome the typical problems experienced in introducing change into a workplace.

Chapter 12

Diving into a Sea of Change

· ·

In This Chapter

▶ Understanding the difficulties of introducing change into a work group

▶ Becoming a champion and not a victim of change

▶ Acquiring insights into how people react differently to change

· ·

*L*ife in organisations is like being at sea: sometimes calm, frequently choppy and occasionally sick-making! The changes can come thick and fast as managers and company executives search for every possible improvement in performance. And the speed of that change is generally increasing.

Advances in technology, for example, are changing people's expectations and ways of working because they enable people to access information (and each other!) at speeds only dreamt about a few years ago. If knowledge is power then everyone with access to the Internet is becoming more powerful as they can now obtain instant knowledge to aid decision-making that was previously only obtainable with days of effort. Increasing competition in a worldwide market is driving many companies to strive to achieve 'more with less', and the notion of a job for life is as dead as a dodo for many employees, as the rate of mergers and acquisitions, outsourcing, restructuring and so on increase.

As a leader, you need to be competent and confident about implementing change, which is where this chapter can help. I reveal why some things about change never change, and I examine people's concerns and expectations about change being introduced into their workplace. In addition, I explore some of the dilemmas that you may encounter as a change agent who's responsible for introducing and making changes work in your department or team.

Dealing with New Changes but Perennial Problems

Although some of the causes of change may be new, such as recent advances in information technology, many of the problems of introducing change in organisations have been around for decades, because they're associated with human nature. Here are some of the most common problems or concerns that people have about changes happening in their workplace that you need to bear in mind:

- **Continuity.** Most people seem to be creatures of habit; you've probably noticed, for example, that people tend to sit in the same seats in meetings. Change, by definition, disrupts continuity in the workplace because people often have to adapt to new structures, processes and so on.

- **Control.** Many people like to have a high degree of control in their lives. Changes can cause people to feel less in control and even worry about coping with increased workloads, requiring new skills and so on.

- **Convenience.** People tend to organise themselves and their lives into routines that enable them to cope with the complexities and demands of working in a modern world. Personal routines may include start and finish times, when they take their lunch and so on.

- **Security.** People are naturally concerned about how they fulfil their financial commitments, and the consequences of not doing so for themselves and, perhaps, their family.

- **Social.** Changes can result in the loss of a person's status as well as alterations in team membership, personal friendships, reporting relationships and so on.

You may also experience two other potential problems when leading your team, which result from the introduction of advances in technology:

- **Immediate access.** Email and mobile phones enable people to keep in touch, but access to the technology is probably creating expectations among your colleagues – especially your boss – that you're always accessible regardless of where you are. I know several managers who book fictitious meetings (with themselves) in their electronic diaries to prevent their work colleagues 'stealing' all of their time by booking meetings without asking for their permission.

- **Invisibility.** Email, laptops and mobile phones are enabling more and more people to work from home for at least part of the time. Although the effective use of technology offers productivity gains due to, for example, time saved on travelling, quiet work areas and so on, you may have concerns about whether you can trust certain people who are out of sight to be as productive as you expect them to be.

Base your approach to leading people who are out of your sight on trusting them to be productive rather than mistrusting them – until they prove otherwise!

If your approach to leading them is based on mistrust, you're more likely to check up on what they're doing and ask them to justify their work. If people perceive that you mistrust them, this perception can adversely affect their attitude to doing a good job for you. A better approach is to agree the objectives or results that a person has to achieve when working out of your sight instead of talking in detail about what she's going to be doing: that way you're both clear about the work that has to completed for her to be productive while giving her the autonomy to organise and manage how she uses her time.

Appreciating what gets up people's noses

You probably have some experience of changes being introduced into your workplace within your current or previous jobs. Take a few minutes to reflect on your experiences and clarify your own expectations about how you prefer to be treated when changes are introduced that affect you and how you do your work. Doing so helps you to appreciate the concerns and potential reactions of others.

The main things that 'get up people's noses' about the introduction of change are as follows:

- **Lack of information.** People want to know:

    - The reasons why the change is being introduced, particularly the benefits of, and consequences of not, changing.

    - Why the change is being introduced now.

    - How the change is likely to affect them, especially regarding their role and responsibilities, conditions of employment, working relationships and so on.

- **Too little or no involvement.** People want to contribute to making their organisation successful, and often contribute valuable ideas and suggestions even if their suggestions adversely affect them. For example, the number of employees who volunteered to take a cut in wages or a pay freeze to help their organisations cope with the economic downturn over the last two years is unprecedented.

- **Wrong speed of change.** Change may be introduced so fast that people can't internalise the change and come to terms with it, or so slowly that it causes unnecessary worry or grief. Introduce the change as quickly as you can, complete a robust analysis of the need for a change, make the necessary decisions and formulate your plan while considering how easy or difficult the people affected will find it to come to terms with the proposed change.

- ✔ **Not being treated like adults.** Tell the truth; people can handle it and respect you for being honest with them.

- ✔ **Dithering.** Nothing's wrong with taking as much time as is required to arrive at the right decision. However, people resent persistently being told that something is 'on its way' or 'going through channels', so avoid these approaches where possible.

Swimming with sharks – and surviving!

You may sometimes be involved in introducing changes in your workplace that cause you to feel like you're swimming with sharks: everyone seems out to get you! People often get emotional when major problems are being experienced in their organisation that result in the need to make significant changes such as a reorganisation of the structure, the removal of overtime or bonuses, redundancies and so on.

When people experience such situations they often need to:

- ✔ Express their views strongly.

- ✔ Ask questions – that may be difficult to answer!

- ✔ Criticise senior managers.

Developing broad shoulders

A large company contracted me to work with the senior management team to lead a major reorganisation in which self-managed teams would be introduced and established in the company. I held several focus groups with employees from all parts of the company to obtain their views about working in the company to enable me to identify the issues that were affecting the performance of the company.

In response to my questions, I was shocked by the strength of feelings expressed by people: how critical they were of managers and the way the company was being managed. I left each meeting with an increasing sense of being overburdened by the responsibility I felt to solve the problems, and improve the working lives of employees as well as the performance of the business.

To cope with this responsibility, I reminded myself that I wasn't alone and didn't have to bear sole responsibility for solving all the problems: senior managers also had a collective responsibility to improve the business, and employees had a responsibility to contribute to improvements rather than just blame management. I would do my best and I also expected that everyone would do their best to improve the business.

If more senior managers don't make themselves available, members of your team are going to focus their attention on the person who, for them, represents the organisation and senior managers: you!

When everyone is directing their frustration and even anger at you, don't fall into the trap of taking the whole world upon your shoulders. By all means be committed to contributing to improving the situation, but don't allow yourself to be downhearted or drown in a sea of emotions.

Although taking this advice can be difficult, to help I describe how I handled an early experience of coping with employee anxiety, frustration and aggression in the following sidebar.

Riding the waves successfully

People react differently to changes being introduced into the workplace. Here are three roles that you may experience people adopting:

- ✔ **Drifters.** These people don't have any strong views about a proposed change and are willing to 'go with the flow'. They don't resist the change being introduced or proactively support it. They may experience some of the emotions described for 'wavers' (below) but only slightly.

- ✔ **Surfers.** These people see a proposed change as an opportunity; they've been watching and waiting for the change to be introduced, want to get on with it and seize the opportunity that the change presents. They're typically enthusiastic about the change and volunteer to help make the change happen successfully; all you have to do is harness their enthusiasm.

- ✔ **Wavers.** These people have concerns about the proposed change and may go through a range of emotions and experience a changing sense of self-esteem as a consequence of their views. Their responses reflect the shape of waves:

  - *No, it's not happening!* Emotions – the wave – rise as people who've become aware of a possible change propose to each other that management can't be serious about the change. People may bond closer together during this period due to their common view about the change.

  - *Crikey, they're serious!* As people realise that management are serious about the change, they may become numb – the top of the wave.

- *Oh no they're not!* Effort is put into resisting the change, probably through voicing criticisms of the change and not working hard instead of active sabotage.

- *It's not too bad in here!* People start to come to terms with and accept the change. Here their attention turns towards the future – the lull before the next wave starts to form.

- *Let's make it work!* Self-esteem – the wave – rises as people are positive about, and actively work on, making the change work.

- *Haven't we done well!* People are on the crest of the wave, feeling good about themselves due to their contribution to making the change work and getting the new way of working established.

(This description of 'wavers' is based on the stages of grief described in *On Death and Dying* by Elisabeth Kubler-Ross (Routledge).)

Be aware of, and sensitive to, the different ways in which people may react to a change being introduced into their workplace.

Being a Change Agent

Everyone occasionally finds themselves in situations that aren't of their own choosing. Some situations may be pleasant, such as an enjoyable chance meeting with a stranger that leads to a new valued relationship; others may be unpleasant, such as a painful injury resulting from an accident.

You can respond to unpleasant situations in one of two different ways:

- ✔ By being a helpless victim: feeling bad, and thinking and talking negatively about your fate.

- ✔ By being positive and making the best of a bad job!

Although you can't always control which situations you find yourself in, you can choose how you respond or react to them!

Become a successful *change agent* when leading your team, by adopting a positive attitude to change:

- ✔ Stay confident, especially in the face of adversity. (Check out Chapter 4 for all about the importance of turning negative thoughts and language into positive language, and how to learn from adversity.)

✔ Be purposeful:

- In looking for opportunities to improve processes, systems and ways of working that enhance the performance of your team.

- By explaining the reasons for the change, and the likely effects on those people affected by it.

✔ Encourage people to express their views and feelings; listen to and take notice of what they say.

✔ Sense people's commitment to the change. (You can find out how to enhance your skills in asking searching questions, listening and sensing commitment in Chapter 9.)

✔ Remain realistic; be prepared to be flexible, modify your plans and if necessary settle for a less than perfect outcome and speed of change in order to sustain people's commitment to the change.

Cruising with your crew

Engage members of your team in continuously looking for ways to improve all aspects of how the team is performing. Remember that, through this approach, you and they:

✔ Become used to making changes and also more receptive to change happening in your organisation.

✔ Have pride in the improvements you're all making.

✔ Build a stronger sense of identity and teamwork through working better together.

Turn to Chapter 15 for more on building teamwork.

Hold regular meetings with your team to ask and answer questions such as:

✔ **What's working well?** Seek to identify strengths, reinforce good practice and recognise the contributions and achievements of individuals and your whole team.

✔ **What's working poorly?** Ask people to:

- Describe what frustrates and/or annoys them in doing their work.

- Look for shortfalls regarding the targets and objectives that the team are expected to achieve.

- Identify where or how processes and systems are malfunctioning.

- Suggest actions to overcome the problems they identify.

✔ **What if we could improve . . . by 10 per cent?** Encourage team members to question and challenge current ways of working, and to think differently and even change the paradigms that constrain their views about what the team's capable of achieving.

Your team is capable of achieving significant improvements in performance if together you strive continuously to identify opportunities and solve problems, and in this way deliver small step-by-step improvements.

Implementing decisions that aren't yours

Leaders at all levels of organisations from the Managing Director or Chief Executive Officer to the Team Leader or Supervisor occasionally have to implement decisions that aren't their own. Managing Directors of many family- and public-owned businesses experience dilemmas when handling the whims of their Chairman, and Chief Executive Officers of public sector organisations have to cope with political decisions and changes in policy. So you may as well get used to handling the dilemmas caused by having to implement changes as a result of someone else's decision!

Behave like the change agent I describe earlier in this section and also:

✔ Ask your manager questions to find out:

- The reasons for the change, including the benefits of the change and the consequences of not making the change.

- Why the change has to be made now rather than at another time, because members of your team are likely to ask you.

- How much influence or control you have about how the change is to be introduced.

✔ Represent your team to your manager by conveying their suggestions, hopes and aspirations, concerns and fears about the proposed change.

✔ Attempt to address the issues raised by members of your team with your manager rather than just passing the matters over to her.

Avoid having 'slopy shoulders' and distancing yourself from someone else's decision to make a change when you're introducing the change to your team. Don't use phrases such as:

✔ 'I'm only doing what I've been told!'

✔ 'Don't shoot me I'm only the messenger!'

✔ 'It's not my fault!'

More positive alternative phrases to use are:

✔ 'We have something we must work on.'

✔ 'How can we address this most effectively?'

✔ 'We have a problem to solve.'

You now have the basis for getting everyone engaged, rather than fuelling resentment.

Leading change you disagree with

Some years ago a manager passed onto me a useful piece of wisdom: when introducing changes into the workplace, 'you can't always have the money and the applause'.

As a leader, you're going to experience occasions when you have to do what's right for the business or organisation, even though you and your staff won't like what you have to do. You're sometimes going to need to implement changes that adversely affect you and/or members of your team. (To find out the most common problems or concerns that people have about changes, turn to the earlier section 'Dealing with New Changes but Perennial Problems'.)

You're also going to be faced with implementing changes that you disagree with. Doing so is one of those situations when you need courage and expertise to discuss things with your boss to get to a position that is acceptable when explained to you, or you at least understand why you have to do it.

Behave like a change agent when introducing changes with which you disagree, and also do the following:

✔ Be willing to challenge a decision if you really believe that the decision is going to affect adversely the productivity or success of your whole organisation, as opposed to just the members of your team. Propose an alternative solution or course of action highlighting the benefits justified by facts and evidence, and any disadvantages of your proposal to demonstrate that you've been objective in your analysis of the situation. You may not get what you want but you have the right to ask!

✔ Support decisions that are right for the organisation and most employees. Sometimes difficult decisions have to be made because they're right for the overall organisation even though the decisions may adversely affect some employees.

✔ 'Keep your eye' on each person in your team to see how they're reacting to the change, and support them to cope. (You can find out how to be brilliant at building commitment in Chapter 9.)

✔ Ask your manager to help you to support members of your team to cope with changes that adversely affect them. Support activities may include:

  • Training and development to learn new skills.

  • Clarifying new roles and responsibilities.

  • Counselling to work through personal dilemmas.

You have a massive influence on how people in your team react to a change through how you react to the change: team members are always watching you and often take a lead from you in how they respond to a change being introduced into the workplace.

Leading Change, Transforming Culture

In my experience, most senior managers want changes in structures, systems, processes, procedures and so on to happen quickly, so that the benefits of the change to the organisation can be obtained as soon as possible. Although such changes can be achieved relatively quickly, transformations in culture may take much longer, especially if relatively large numbers of employees are involved.

Managers that I work with on leadership and organisational change programmes often describe the culture of an organisation as 'the way we do things around here'. I'm sure that you can see how such an attitude can inhibit the implementation of change. I prefer to be more precise in describing culture, but before reading my description of culture take a few moments to think about what culture means to you. Use the following questions as prompts:

✔ What words would you use to describe the culture of the organisation that you currently work for?

✔ What are the main differences in the cultures of organisations that you've worked in and/or schools you attended?

✔ What is different about the culture of your country compared to the national cultures of other countries?

✔ How would you describe the notion of 'culture' to a work colleague?

In the following three sections, I present my description of culture and a few key points and tips about how to transform a culture. (You can find out more about an approach to transforming culture in Chapter 13.)

Looking out for icebergs

If you ever go sailing in the North Atlantic ocean, you need to look out for icebergs if you want to survive. Similarly, I suggest you do likewise when attempting to transform the culture of your own team, a wider work group or even a whole organisation! Organisational change specialists often use the metaphor of an iceberg (see Figure 12-1) to convey the crucial aspects of culture effectively:

- ✔ You can see only the tip of a culture (like the visible tip of an iceberg): people's behaviour and the effects of their behaviour, such as the tidiness of the workplace.

- ✔ You can't see the majority of aspects of a culture: the attitudes, values and beliefs of people.

- ✔ You may find that transforming a culture is extremely difficult. The culture of an organisation is solid and well-formed, just like the frozen structure of an iceberg, and the culture of a work group or organisation can seem similarly frozen in place.

Here's my definition of a work culture: *culture* is the prevailing attitudes, values, beliefs and behaviours of a group, department and/or whole organisation that have a significant effect on the performance of that particular group.

behaviours ——————— the aspect of culture that you can see

attitudes——————— towards someone or something

values——————— what people value or deem to be important

Figure 12-1:
The iceberg
as a meta-
phor for
culture.

beliefs——————— what people see as being true or false

Be careful about trying to push through changes in work systems and so on too quickly because you may hit an iceberg: the 'out of sight' aspects of the culture that cause members of the group to passively or actively resist the change.

Diving deep to uncover culture

If you want members of the group to embrace a change in a work system, process or so on you've no option but to 'dive deep' to uncover the culture of a work group. Otherwise you won't understand the issues or factors that have to be worked through to gain the group's commitment to embrace the change.

To complete the next exercise, reflect on your experiences of changes that have been introduced into places where you've worked. This process helps you to gain practical insights into the need to uncover culture when planning to introduce your own changes into the workplace.

1. **Divide the pages of a notebook into 3 columns, as in Table 12-1.**

2. **In the first column, write a brief description of a situation in which a change was introduced into the workplace and you and/or your work colleagues actively accepted the change.** The change may involve a new or different work system, procedure, method, responsibilities and so on.

3. **In the second column, briefly describe the reasons why you and/or your work colleagues accepted the change.** Your reasons may include a description of how you (felt you) were treated during the change.

4. **In the third column, describe any actions that management took that contributed to you and/or your work colleagues accepting the change.**

5. **Repeat steps 2 to 4 for other situations in which you and/or your work colleagues accepted the change.**

6. **Repeat steps 2 to 5 for situations in which you and/or your work colleagues resisted changes that were introduced into the workplace.**

To help get you started, in the table I provide two examples of changes being introduced into a workplace, one in which the change was accepted and the other in which people were resistant towards the change.

The contents of the second column are likely to describe things that are important to people about their work; what they value and, perhaps, believe.

The contents of the last column are likely to contain examples of good and bad management practice regarding introducing changes into the workplace.

Table 12-1	Examples Where People Accepted or Resisted Changes in the Workplace	
Brief Description of the Situation	*Reasons Why I and/ or My Colleagues Accepted (or Resisted) the Change*	*Actions Management Took that Contributed to Me and/or My Work Colleagues Accepting (or Resisting) the Change:*
Introduction of a new quarterly performance appraisal process	We wanted to be clearer about what we were expected to achieve and how well we were doing our job.	Our manager clearly explained the process and benefits to us and the organisation.
Imposition of a less flexible work attendance system	Flexibility was only abused by a few people but everyone was 'punished' – this was unfair.	Our views that those abusing the flexible system should be spoken to rather than change the system were ignored.

Carry out a 'deep dive' by having conversations with individuals and/or groups affected by a potential change. Try to find out what's important to them that you need to consider when making decisions about the proposed change.

Discover more about revealing an underlying culture in Chapter 13.

Hanging onto the diver's lifeline: Stop, think, breathe!

Scuba divers have a motto: stop, think (and then) breathe! If you're diving and experience a problem with your breathing apparatus, your natural – and potentially automatic – reaction is to grab an air line from a colleague; but if you do so, you put both of you in danger.

Developing this habit of pausing before reacting is also useful for leaders. After all, people put a lot of effort into promoting or protecting the things that are important to them, including their values, and they can become emotional – anxious, frustrated, withdrawn, angry and so on – about changes in their workplace. As the leader responsible for the change, you don't want to underestimate or downplay people's responses by reacting sharply or dismissively when you meet resistance.

Don't be surprised if you find people apparently over-reacting to changes that you intend to make; they're just letting you know how important something is to them. Their reaction is also your prompt to do a 'deep dive' and discover their underlying concerns and fears about the changes you're proposing.

Use the diver's motto 'stop, think, breathe' when you experience people adversely reacting towards, or resisting, changes you propose, to ensure that you don't do or say something that you may later regret.

Chapter 13

Transforming Workplace Culture: A Leader's Approach

A s a successful leader or manager, you have to take the lead when introducing workplace changes, regardless of whether the decision to make the change is yours or you even agree with it.

In this chapter you explore why you often have to work on transforming your workplace culture when introducing changes, and I introduce a range of actions that help you. Also, you discover how to identify where to start in making a change and transforming culture, the dangers of 'initiative-itis', how to choose the right pace for change and how to handle problems that crop up along the way.

Knowing Where and How to Begin

Most changes start within organisations because someone, often a senior manager, perceives a problem that needs fixing or an opportunity to make improvements in performance or save money.

 Instead of waiting to be told to make a change, always be on the lookout for opportunities to deliver improvements in your team's performance and productivity. Encourage your team to seek out similar improvements too, and ways in which it can work more efficiently with other teams and departments.

Spotting the opportunity for change

You can utilise several starting points for making workplace changes that improve an aspect of performance: for example, get members of your team around a table to discuss how well the team is performing. (Refer to Chapter 12 to find out how to involve members in continuously seeking ways to improve performance.)

Depending on the type of work that your team does, possible starting points include the following:

✔ You recognise something unsatisfactory about your team members' attitudes, behaviours and/or the importance they place on, for example, a current standard, system, process or way of working for or with another work group or customers.

✔ You spot that a key performance indicator (KPI) that you use to measure the performance of your team isn't being achieved or can be improved. (Check out Chapter 7 for more on KPIs.)

✔ You see or hear that another team or department inside your organisation, or an external customer, is disappointed with the standard of service or products that your team is providing.

✔ You become aware of a proposed change in an information system or work process that's going to affect how your team works, and you want to ensure that your team's needs or requirements are fully considered in any such changes.

Don't assume that your staff and colleagues are automatically going to welcome and embrace your proposed workplace change. (Chapter 12 describes the most common problems or concerns that people have about changes being introduced into their workplace.) You're not going to achieve the expected improvements in performance or benefits if the people affected by the change don't fully embrace it and want to make it work.

Always think about the cultural implications regarding a proposed workplace change: consider doing a 'deep dive' to uncover the cultural effects of a making such a change by asking yourself, and better still the people involved, the following questions:

✔ What are people's attitudes towards the proposed change?

✔ How may they react or behave with regard to the proposed change?

✔ To what extent do they see the proposed change as being important or necessary?

'I'm not getting buy-in!'

One of my clients had invested many thousands of pounds and numerous hours of managers' time in learning about and introducing new systems and processes to improve the performance of his business. This Managing Director realised, however, that the improvements he'd expected from adopting the changes weren't being achieved, because managers were unable to get each other and employees to 'buy-in' to the new systems. When people don't 'buy-in' to a workplace change, they typically don't take ownership of making the change a success, often keep working the same way that they're used to working, and may overtly or covertly criticise the new system.

He asked me to work with the senior management team to discover how to engage each other and employees to build a high-performance culture. I consulted all the senior managers, as well as 10 per cent of the workforce to obtain their views about the senior management team and other issues that could be affecting the performance of the company. I then analysed all of the information I'd collected and shared the results of my analysis when working with the senior management team, individually and collectively, to build a high-performing team. I then supported senior managers to engage employees to transform the culture progressively throughout the company.

By transforming the company culture, the firm managed to bring about the expected improvements and build strong working relationships among the managers and between managers and employees.

✔ Will they believe in, and be committed to, what you're trying to do or achieve?

✔ Will they welcome or resist the proposed change?

Read the sidebar 'I'm not getting buy-in!' to find out why one Managing Director decided to invest in transforming the culture of his company.

Starting from where you are

When I have initial conversations with potential clients, I often hear senior managers say 'now is not the right time' to work on improving or building a high-performance culture – one in which everyone is striving to achieve high levels of performance. The most common reasons given include:

✔ **We have too much work.** Organisations in this situation have a healthy order or sales book, and managers think that they have to give all their attention to, and put all their efforts into, getting the work done instead of thinking about how to improve getting the work done.

✔ **We have too little work.** Managers think that they have to focus on winning more work and, perhaps, they don't have money to invest in building a high-performance culture.

✔ **We're experiencing low morale throughout the company.** Morale may be low due to the organisation underperforming, which has resulted in a ban on overtime, redundancies, a breakdown in negotiations over a wage rise and so on.

✔ **We already have poor relationships between employees and management.** Relationships may have broken down due to actions that managers or employees have taken in the past that led to mistrust between both groups. Actions may have included proposed or actual reorganisations, miscommunications, the prevailing style of management and so on.

Some managers may prefer to wait for things to be better before they invest time and effort in transforming culture, but the whole point of transforming culture is to make changes that generate improvements in productivity and performance . . . and often rebuild problematic relationships and improve staff morale!

The right time to start working on transforming culture is as soon as you notice evidence or symptoms that indicate that performance, attitudes or behaviour is below what you expect. This advice applies whether you're working within a small group, a large department or even a whole organisation.

Creating a Plan for Your Change

When you spot an opportunity for improvement and come up with an idea for a workplace change, you need to plan your approach carefully – for example, deciding on the start and end points – and take into account a number of potential problems.

Experiencing initiative fatigue!

Have you ever heard colleagues respond to finding out that management intends to introduce another change with comments such as, 'Here we go again!' or 'Oh no, not another initiative!'.

If so, your organisation is probably suffering from 'initiative-itis'.

'Initiative-itis' describes the symptom of an organisation having too many initiatives happening at the same time. As well as prompting scathing comments, 'initiative-itis' is also associated with one or more of the following characteristics:

✔ Limited resources, such as people's time, are spread too thinly across too many initiatives.

✔ Staff greet each new initiative with a degree of cynicism.

✔ Existing initiatives or projects aren't progressing as expected and several may be incomplete and have 'loose ends'.

✔ Employees see initiatives as something to be done in addition to the normal work of (managing) a team, department or organisation. Staff may even perceive that the activities associated with working on the proposed change are optional – something they have to do only when they have the time!

When faced with these attitudes, you have to think carefully about how you present and characterise the change. Be wary of being seen to treat the proposed change as just yet another initiative, or to allow others to perceive such work in that light. Staff mustn't see your proposed change as something that's optional, a low priority and only to be done after the normal work of the team or department has been completed.

Work on transforming the workplace culture on the basis of, 'This is how I am/ we are going to lead and manage the team differently'. Bed new ways of working into how the team works rather than allowing different ways of working to be seen as optional 'bolt-ons'.

Celebrating people past and present

Focusing on the future and how you want things to be when making a workplace change is quite natural. After all, you're interested in the improvements or benefits you want to achieve and your attention is likely to be on how you want your staff to behave, for example:

✔ The new things you want them to do.

✔ The skills you need them to have.

✔ How you want them to act and behave differently.

Be careful, however, that you don't focus so much on the future that you forget to think about the past and present.

Recognise the contributions that people have made in the past, and the contributions that they continue to make to the performance of the team or department, because otherwise you may unintentionally cause people to feel unappreciated or undervalued.

Clarifying the start and end points

The extent of the change you introduce into the workplace – and the accompanying transformation in culture – can be small or huge. Your change may involve a small team altering a specific work procedure or a whole organisational change involving the transformation of the entire culture of the workforce. Whatever the size of the change, however, your approach to clarifying the start and end points is roughly the same: the main variable is the number of people affected by, and potentially involved in making, the change.

In the following two lists, I suggest questions you may want to ask to clarify the start and end points for your change. Clarify the start point by conducting an analysis of the current situation by asking questions such as the following:

- ✔ **What is the current level of performance regarding this process (or system)?** Examine quantitative (numeric) and collect qualitative (anecdotal) information about the effectiveness of the relevant process or system from people using or affected by it.

- ✔ **How is this process currently being carried out?** Involve members of your team in drawing a process map that describes each step in the process, and identify any bottlenecks, failures and so on in the process, and the reasons for them.

- ✔ **What are people's attitudes towards this process (or system)? How much importance do they place on complying with it?** People may not follow a process if they don't understand the reasons for and benefits of it, or indeed the consequences of not complying with it.

- ✔ **What is it about this process (or system) that makes life easy or difficult for people?** In my experience, most people tend to follow processes that are easy rather than difficult – and take shortcuts to make life easier for them!

- ✔ **What is it that people like or dislike about the process (or system)?**

Use the responses you receive to these and other relevant questions to gather information to help you thoroughly understand the practical and cultural issues regarding the situation or problem that you and your team are experiencing.

Here are a few questions you can ask to clarify the end point of your proposed change:

✔ **What about the current process (or system) is valued and needs to be maintained?**

✔ **What are the improvements in performance or outcomes that I want to achieve with regard to this process (or system)?** (You can discover how to be 'SMART' when clarifying improvements in Chapter 11.)

✔ **What is the new process (or system) going to look like when working effectively? How is it to operate, and how is it going to change what people do or how they work?**

✔ **What, if anything, needs to be different regarding people's attitude towards, or the value or importance they place on, the process (or system)?**

✔ **What will be being achieved that's not currently being achieved by the process (or system)?**

Use the answers to the above questions to produce a specification of the new process or system and a description of the attitudes, values and behaviours that you want to establish with regard to it.

Always ask the people affected for their views, hopes and concerns when you're addressing the points in these lists. That way, they can let you know their concerns, and you can get them involved in design and implementation; and you also always get more ownership and buy-in when you do it. Such dialogue will reinforce people's perceptions of your capabilities and interest in them.

Asking and answering the above and other relevant questions helps to involve your team in making the change happen because it:

✔ Enables you to access their knowledge, experience and expertise with regard to the process you're considering changing.

✔ Makes them feel valued (you sought their views and opinions).

✔ Helps them to take ownership of, and be more committed to, making the change happen effectively (they contributed to and shaped the new process).

Bridging the gap between old and new

When you've clarified the start and end points of your proposed change (as I describe in the preceding section), you find that you've established the gap that exists between:

✔ The current process or way of working and the proposed process.

✔ The existing and the required attitudes, behaviours and values of people with regard to that process.

To bridge these gaps, you need to produce and implement an action plan that addresses the practical and cultural aspects of your change. Make sure that this action plan describes each of the actions or steps that are to be taken to bridge the gap, the deadline for each action to be completed and the name of the person to be held accountable for ensuring that the action is taken. An example of such a plan is given in Table 13-1. The last column in the table is used to capture up-to-date information of the progress made in implementing the plan.

Consider questions such as those listed below when producing your plan:

✔ **What are the various options for bridging the gap?**

✔ **What actions need to be taken, and in what order, to bridge the gap?**

✔ **What criteria am I going to use to measure or evaluate whether the change has been successful (criteria may include numeric and anecdotal evidence)?**

✔ **Which options or actions best meet the success criteria?**

✔ **How acceptable are the proposed actions going to be to the people affected?**

✔ **What can go wrong regarding making the change, and how can I recognise early signs of failure?**

✔ **How am I going to ensure that the change is maintained?**

Table 13-1	A Plan for Change		
Action	*Deadline*	*Person Accountable*	*Progress*
Brief the project team on the specification requirements of the new process.	30th May	Me	
Produce the first draft of the process flow chart describing all steps in the process.	15th June	Project Leader	

Adopting Approaches for Minimising Resistance to Change

This section takes a look at some of the problems and objections that may follow your decision to implement a workplace change. However good your preparation and planning, you can still experience problems if you don't dive deep enough to uncover people's objections.

Choosing the right pace for change

When you've decided that a new process or system needs to be introduced, make sure that you think carefully about the best pace to use to implement that change in order to gain your staff's commitment to making and sustaining it.

You can make the correct decision about the need to make a change, only to find that your staff don't embrace it (or even reject it) because you're introducing the change too quickly for their liking. They need time to come to terms with how the change affects them. On the other hand, you can also take too much time to make a decision and introduce a change, thus causing members of your team to experience unnecessary, prolonged anxiety about the possible changes that may be coming their way.

'Start! Stop!'

A company manufactures bespoke high-quality products for use in extreme environments, and the design and manufacture of its products is highly complex. One of the challenges facing the company is how best to use design expertise: whether to invest engineers' time and effort into winning contracts, and designing and manufacturing products or into research and development (R&D) activities to improve the quality of service and products offered to clients.

This dilemma was a constant one for senior managers, with engineers being asked to switch their focus from manufacturing to R&D activities, and vice versa. R&D projects were started and then paused while engineers served the needs of manufacturing. Engineers were not only confused by these changes, but they also started to question the credibility of decision-making when repeatedly being told that R&D projects were important and then to stop working on them. Morale was being affected because people were unable to progress the work they were interested in and that was important to them.

On a leadership development programme, a senior manager realised that a better approach would be to maintain the commitment, and manage the work, of engineers by planning to progress R&D projects at a pace that also allowed the manufacturing needs to be served. The analogy of shifting the gears on a car was used to maintain and yet vary momentum, instead of parking projects and picking them up again.

Avoid being inconsistent by changing your mind regarding the changes you want to make: your inconsistency may confuse people. See the sidebar 'Start, Stop!' for an example.

Uncovering people's objections

People differ in how willing they are to discuss their concerns about a proposed change. Some people are keen to let you know about their objections, whereas others are likely to be more reluctant to speak up. You need to appreciate this reluctance if you want to uncover (and therefore address) all their worries. People's reticence can be due to the following fears:

- ✔ Sharing their objections with you in a group situation, because they feel embarrassed about colleagues knowing about their objection to a proposed change.

- ✔ Revealing an objection that's particularly important to them; you may find that that some people share their most important objection last with you.

Be prepared to keep asking '. . . and what else is concerning or worrying you about the proposed change?', to uncover all the objections that a person may have regarding a proposed change.

People may object to the way a change is introduced as well as to how the change may adversely affect them. (You can read about what 'gets up people's noses' about changes being introduced into the workplace in Chapter 12.)

Getting buy-in from everyone

Few phrases are as relevant to the dilemma of introducing a workplace change as, 'You can't please all the people all the time!' Some people may find aspects of the proposed change attractive while others are concerned about those very same (or of course different) aspects.

You may find that gaining the buy-in and total commitment of everyone involved in a change is quite impossible, no matter how much time and effort you invest in explaining it and dealing with people's concerns.

Adopt slightly different approaches to getting buy-in from people, depending upon the extent to which individuals accept or resist the change:

✔ **The enthusiastic.** Harness the enthusiasm of people who want the change to happen, perhaps by making them responsible for a specific task.

✔ **The ambivalent.** Reinforce the benefits and explain the consequences of not making the proposed change to those who are neither enthusiastic nor pessimistic. Detail how progress is to be monitored and evaluated.

✔ **The resistant.** Listen carefully to, and address the concerns of, people who are resisting the proposed change. (Check out the later section 'Handling resistance to change' to find out how to work with these members of staff.)

Ask the people affected by a proposed change to describe or explain the issues that would help or hinder them when adopting the change. You can then use these factors to introduce the change in a way that helps people to adopt the change, while also addressing the hindrances.

Making change tentative

Successful leaders manage to mix a variety of characteristics. They need to be authentic as a leader (as I describe in Chapter 4) and act decisively, boldly and with conviction. They also need to gain the commitment of people to do a task by engaging them so that the task becomes meaningful, important and worthwhile to those involved.

You may think that being bold and decisive while simultaneously engaging people is a contradiction. Well, it isn't: you can say what you think, *and* listen attentively to people's views and opinions, *and* also work together to create new meanings and insights to solve problems and make changes in the workplace. If you handle a workplace change tactfully and tentatively, you can achieve all the following together:

✔ Be bold about sharing your purpose – what you're aiming to achieve; and your values – what's important to you.

✔ Engage people in helping to solve problems and shape changes.

✔ Be willing to make difficult decisions that are right for the organisation but may adversely affect some people.

To make the change tentative, implement your decision while remaining willing to modify your plan – including the actions and timing of it – in light of people's reactions. Consider modifying your plan if by doing so people embrace the change, make it happen and sustain the change more effectively.

When introducing a workplace change, avoid the following extremes:

- ✔ Being so forthright that people think or feel that you're imposing the change on them. Be aware of the implications of people making comments – especially behind your back – such as, 'It's pointless arguing with him because he (thinks he) is always right.'

- ✔ Being so tentative that you appear uncertain or unconvinced that the change is the right thing to do.

Handling resistance to change

People put a lot of effort into promoting and protecting the things that are important to them: that is why some people actively resist a change being introduced into the workplace if the change is going to affect them adversely or they feel they're being mistreated as to how the change is being introduced.

Don't be surprised if people 'dig their heels in' and push back if you attempt to force them to accept a workplace change that they're reluctant to accept.

Be positive, empathetic and support people who are reluctant or resistant towards your proposed change. Table 13-2 contains suggestions you can take to help people handle some of the factors causing them to resist, and to enable them to accept and embrace the change you intend to make.

Table 13-2	Typical Factors Causing People to Resist Changes and How You Can Work With Them
Factors Causing People to Resist Change	**Actions to Address These Factors and Encourage People to Accept the Change**
Fear of being exposed as inadequate or incompetent	Talk through any concerns and fears that people have regarding the proposed change.
	Build people's confidence by emphasising their achievements and competences, especially regarding other changes they've experienced.
	Provide training in the new system or procedure.
Fear of the unknown	Provide as much information as you can.
	Admit when you don't have all the answers, and commit to keeping people up-to-date as information becomes available.

Factors Causing People to Resist Change	Actions to Address These Factors and Encourage People to Accept the Change
Loss of status or control	Explore the reason for people holding such views, and acknowledge their concerns.
	Consider giving people extra responsibilities especially if you can use their talents in other ways.
	Be honest and frank with people if their position in the organisation is changing, including changes in reporting relationships – and clearly explain the reasons for the change.
More difficult personal circumstances such as travel arrangements, impact on home life and so on	Consider whether other arrangements can be made, at least temporarily, to offset personal difficulties and help the person make the transition to the new working arrangements.
Unreasonable attitudes and resistance or criticism of changes you want to make	Challenge people who are behaving unreasonably and explain the consequences of them continuing to behave unreasonably.

Listen attentively to people who want to share their objections to a proposed change. You may not want to hear these objections, because they present you with problems that you have to solve, but you need to know about them because they're going to affect how well people embrace, adopt and carry out your intended change.

Chapter 14

Reinforcing a New Culture: Maintaining Your Workplace Changes

*N*o doubt you've heard the saying, 'Old habits die hard.' Well, a frustrated manager may have coined this phrase, when experiencing problems with staff slipping back into old ways of working while she's trying to transform the culture of her work team. Getting people to change long-held practices is one thing, but you can also experience difficulties when working with staff to sustain the following:

✔ Changes you make to a system or process in the workplace.

✔ Positive attitudes towards, enthusiasm for and even the compliance of people with the change you've made, especially if the change isn't working as well as you expected.

In this chapter you find out how you personally have a major influence on your work colleagues' enthusiasm and commitment to maintaining a workplace change. I show you how to reinforce vital attitudes, behaviours and values — that is, the workplace culture — in order to ensure that your change continues to be a success. You also discover what you need to pay attention to, in order to provide the 'scaffolding' to help people sustain the changes you want them to make and keep everyone involved on the right track.

Walking the Talk: Leading by Example

By encouraging you to 'walk the talk', I'm not suggesting that you waste time wandering around generally chatting to staff, but that your behaviour backs up your words. When you've implemented a change, I'm asking you to do the following:

✔ Demonstrate your commitment to ensuring that the change is a success, by making sure that your actions and behaviour reinforce what you're saying about the change you've made.

✔ Be how you want others to be regarding the change, because 'being' is more than 'doing': 'being' includes how you behave and how you are — that is, your presence — and remaining aware of how you impact on people.

✔ Keep in touch with how the people involved in, and affected by, your change think, feel and are acting as regards the change.

Catch people doing things right! As well as looking out for evidence of problems, also make sure that you spot what people are doing right when adopting a change in the workplace.

You find out how to 'walk the talk' to reinforce and embed the attitudes, values and behaviours required to ensure that your change is a success in the next three sections.

Being a visible leader

Face-to-face contact is perhaps the most effective way of influencing someone (or a small group) to sustain a workplace change. In this way you can:

✔ Convey your enthusiasm and conviction to make the change a success directly to the person.

✔ Notice the effect that you're having on the person.

✔ Assess the willingness of the person to sustain the change.

✔ Listen to and address any on-going or new concerns or objections that person has about the change.

Invest in spending your time with, and giving your attention to, people directly involved in making a workplace change.

Investing in time with people

Sue is a General Practice Manager in a large medical centre. She recognised the need to change the organisational structure and reorganise the roles and responsibilities of staff in order to optimise the benefits of a new computerised information system for handling patient records. Sue realised that the introduction of the new system might adversely affect the morale and motivation of several staff, because changes were needed in established ways of working.

Sue explained the purpose of the new system to all staff during group meetings and outlined how it was intended to work. She invested time in speaking to every member of staff to find out their views, interests, skills, preferences, hopes and concerns regarding the introduction of the new system. The information she obtained proved useful during the detailed planning of the reorganisation, to help use the talents of staff and meet many of the preferences that individuals had expressed – although meeting everyone's requests was impossible.

Sue explained to all staff during further group meetings how the new system would work in detail, and then met all individuals to talk through changes in their role and responsibilities and try and fully understand their reaction to the changes. Sue was responsive to making further amendments in responsibilities if doing so was possible without undermining the structure or losing any of the benefits of the new system.

Sue regularly met every individual during the first few weeks of the new system's implementation, and spent more time with the individuals who expressed the most concerns. Although her manager thought that she was wasting time with people, Sue knew that spending time with each member of staff was a good investment. The new system was adopted in the practice without any significant problems being experienced.

To be honest, you really don't have any option, because you invest your time in ensuring the change is being adopted and maintained or spend your time finding out why the change hasn't worked, trying to correct mistakes and resolve problems that the change caused. Take a look at the true story in the sidebar 'Investing time with people', to find out how one manager successfully introduced and sustained a major change in roles and responsibilities in the workplace.

 Remain conscious of the danger of becoming 'out of sight, out of mind': convey your commitment to making the change a success by maintaining your visibility.

Using the power of story-telling

People love to relate anecdotes and tell stories in all walks of life, and the workplace is no exception. In fact, story-telling is a more natural and important part of people's daily lives than you may appreciate:

✔ Parents tell their children nursery rhymes and bedtime stories, some of which contain important meanings or messages about life.

✔ Friends and family members recount their daily experiences as stories in conversations.

✔ Friends and work colleagues tell each other jokes, many of which have a storyline.

✔ One generation hands down stories to the next in order to pass on wisdom and sustain a culture.

You can use the power of story-telling to help maintain staff support for your workplace changes.

Take a few minutes to carry out the following exercise and reflect on your own experiences of the impact that story-telling can have on an organisation's culture:

1. **Divide the page of a notebook into 3 columns, as shown in Table 14-1.**

2. **In the first column, write a brief synopsis of a story or anecdote that you heard a work colleague tell about an event or situation in an organisation in which you both worked.**

3. **In the second column, write a few words that describe the main meaning or message that the person was attempting to convey through telling the story.**

4. **In the third column, capture the effect that you think telling the story had on reinforcing or changing your own or your work colleagues' attitudes, values or behaviour towards who or what the story was about.** It may be the organisation, a group or department in the organisation, senior management and so on.

5. **Repeat steps 3 to 5 for other experiences of story-telling that were significant for you.** I provide one example in the first row to help you get started.

6. **Examine the content of the third column to see what insights you gain about the power or impact of story-telling as a means of reinforcing and/or changing culture within work groups.**

Table 14-1	Examples of How Story-telling Reinforces or Changes People's Attitudes, Values or Behaviour	
Brief Synopsis of the Story	**Main Meaning or Message being Conveyed**	**Effect that Telling the Story Had on People**
A manufacturing company was closing down part of the operation and moving to a new site, but new improved equipment and facilities would be provided at the new site. New equipment was not provided: senior managers had made several promises, including providing new equipment, but failed to deliver any of them.	Senior managers can't be trusted.	Don't trust any senior managers – even though the individuals who had made the promises had left the company.

You may be surprised by the power that some stories have had in reinforcing or changing culture in organisations where you've worked, especially stories that people who have many years of experience of being employed in the relevant organisation tell regularly. Such stories are often about significant events or people and have a particularly strong meaning for those employees and, in my experience, are often about one of the following aspects (although you can probably add to the list after completing the above exercise):

✔ How good life used to be in the organisation – as perceived by the story-teller(s).

✔ Exceptionally good or bad leaders – and how they treated employees.

✔ An event that resulted in a major improvement or breakdown in relationships between management and employees.

✔ An achievement or occasion with which the story-teller is proud to be associated, such as winning a major contract or providing exceptional service to a customer.

Use story-telling to do the following:

✔ Paint a picture of how things are going to be when your proposed workplace change is working brilliantly: describe how people will feel about their work as well as what they'll be doing and achieving. (Refer to Chapter 7 to find out about the value of visioning and being a visionary leader.)

✔ Reinforce the progress being made in making and sustaining a change in the workplace. Talk about:

• Examples of problems experienced and how people overcame them.

• Improvements in performance that people are achieving due to the change.

• Feedback from other departments or customers to whom your team is providing a service, especially anecdotes that customers have provided regarding any noticeable improvements in the attitude or behaviour of members of your team.

✔ Share and reinforce good and exceptional practice or performance by a member of your team in adopting the new process or system.

✔ Encourage members of your team to tell their own stories about difficulties and successes experienced in adopting the change in the workplace.

Spotting people straying from the path

You may find that people stray from the path — the new way of working — because they:

✔ Aren't clear about where the path is leading.

✔ Are unsure about exactly what they're expected to do.

✔ Don't have the skills or tools to keep up with the pace.

✔ Don't want to change, and/or don't want the new process or system to work.

Chapters 8 and 9 cover the importance of, and how to become skilled in, engaging people to gain their commitment to do a task. You can use these same approaches and skills to ensure that people embrace and sustain a change in the workplace. Engaging people effectively in making a change enables you to address the first three factors mentioned in the preceding list, but the last issue — spotting people who don't want to change — may be harder to detect, especially if people are unwilling to tell you what they really think about making the change work.

A person who actively undermines a workplace change, but presents the image of complying with or even embracing the change, may be particularly difficult (for you) to manage.

People can actively undermine a change by employing one or more of the following types of behaviour:

✔ Arguing to their colleagues that the change is unnecessary.

✔ Telling their colleagues that the change won't work and is 'doomed to fail'.

✔ Proposing that the change is the 'thin end of the wedge' and that work and conditions are going to become more difficult for them all.

✔ Emphasising problems experienced with the change to their colleagues.

Some of your staff may have extreme difficulty challenging a colleague who's actively undermining the change, especially if that person is a strong character.

Almost all people behave reasonably when treated fairly, but you need to be on the lookout for any evidence that a person may not be supporting, or is even undermining, your change. Look for any inconsistencies in what the person says (especially during one-to-one conversations and group meetings) and then actually does with regard to the change.

Use your skills in sensing commitment, particularly the highly developed skills of seeing 'what others may miss' and listening intensely, to notice when someone doesn't want to change. (Check out Chapter 9 for more on sensing commitment.)

Spotting people who are undermining your changes when not directly in your presence is the first step in tackling their behaviour. Chapter 11 shows you approaches that help you handle this problem, describes the golden rule of (acting) 'Now' and also details the dangers of delaying talking to a work colleague whose work or behaviour is unacceptable.

Paying Attention to the Right Things

Leading and managing people is difficult because so many things are competing for your attention, including:

✔ Ensuring that you achieve the objectives and results expected of you and your team.

✔ Organising people and work.

✔ Sticking to deadlines.

✔ Seeing to the needs and expectations of every member of your team.

✔ Solving problems and resolving disagreements or any relationship issues between members of your team.

✔ And so on, and so on . . . .

You also have to make sure that you pay enough attention to your introduced changes so that they're successful and maintained. The earlier section 'Walking the Talk: Leading by Example' describes how you personally have an impact on the enthusiasm and commitment of people to sustain a workplace change, whereas this section shows what you need to pay attention to in order to complement your personal impact.

Remembering that what gets measured gets done

Key performance indicators (KPIs) are vital in helping you to measure how effectively you're achieving your objectives. (Turn to Chapter 7 for more info on KPIs.) Well, you can also use these key performance measures to evaluate how well your workplace changes are working.

For example, if you're implementing a change in a production process to improve the quality of products coming off a production line, you may be interested in the following KPIs:

✔ Percentage of products produced within the product specification.

✔ Number of products that had to be reworked due to faulty workmanship in each team or step in the production process.

✔ Percentage, or value, of products scrapped.

✔ Number of faults, by type or cause (so that you can work on eradicating the source of the faults).

KPIs have three main uses:

✔ To inform an individual or group about the target or standard of performance that has to be achieved.

✔ To monitor progress in achieving the target or standard.

✔ To influence how people think and act regarding the specific target or standard of performance.

When implementing and sustaining a change in the workplace, you can use KPIs to reinforce important standards, attitudes and behaviour as follows:

✔ Display information about how well your team is achieving KPIs on visual display boards, using graphs to show trends in performance.

✔ Discuss KPIs with your team, highlighting achievements and focusing on aspects of performance that are below the required target or standard.

✔ Talk about good and bad examples of approaches/attitudes towards preventing or solving problems and making the change a continued success.

Keeping everyone up-to-date

From the point of view of the staff potentially affected by or involved in planned workplace changes, 'no news is bad news'. In my experience, most people prefer (and indeed expect) to be kept informed about what's happening regarding changes in their work environment.

The problem is that people tend to fill a void in information if you don't provide enough up-to-date details about a proposed change. You may find people speculating about what you or senior managers intend to do and how this is going to affect them – and people often fear the worst! Don't be surprised to discover that the 'grapevine' – the informal process by which employees pass information, views and opinions to each other – is working against you and what you're trying to achieve by your intended changes.

Generally speaking, you can't inform people too much about a proposed workplace change . . . with one exception: the sharing of information or partially formed decisions that are likely to cause unnecessary concern or worry for employees.

Use regular briefing sessions with groups of up to 20 employees, depending on the number of employees affected by the change, in order to:

✔ Inform people about proposed changes.

✔ Explain and explore how effectively changes that have been introduced are working.

✔ Encourage people to ask questions and for you to answer them.

Use your line managers to reinforce key messages and answer questions with their own, probably smaller, groups of employees who report to them. Do inform employee representatives about changes, but use the management structure to convey and reinforce key messages to employees about a change.

To the people who report to them, line managers are the organisation and represent the organisation: line managers are, potentially, the greatest single influence on an employee who reports to them.

Reacting positively to crises

As I reveal in Chapter 12, sometimes you're going to find yourself in situations that aren't of your choosing but in which you need to choose your reaction. Trying to make the best of a bad job is far better than reacting negatively and complaining about the situation. When a workplace change that you've made goes badly wrong, you may feel that you're facing a crisis:

✔ Errors or faulty products have been made.

✔ The process stops, especially if it involves, for example, an information technology or production process.

✔ You're in the spotlight: the eyes of more senior managers and everyone around you are on you!

✔ You feel intense pressure on you to solve the problem.

Hearing about problems with a change you've made can be difficult. You may be the sort of person who remains calm in a crisis but, if not, try not to overreact or do or say something that you may later regret. Here are some suggestions:

✔ Use the diving motto – 'stop, think, breathe!' – to help you keep calm. (You can find out more about this useful saying in Chapter 12.)

✔ Avoid blaming people – by all means hold people accountable, but recognise that people rarely deliberately make mistakes; recognising their good intentions helps you to deal with the problem without damaging your relationship with them.

✔ Critique a person's behaviour – what they did wrong or didn't do right – rather than criticising their personality. People can change their behaviour but not their personality.

✔ Focus on the future – on the actions to take, by when and by whom, to solve the problem.

✔ Help people to learn from their mistakes – ask searching questions to help people to think through what they could have done and, in the future, will do differently. (Refer to Chapter 9 to find out more about asking searching questions.)

Promoting good practice

Promoting good practice isn't about promoting someone who does a good job to a better position (although of course you're likely to promote people who consistently deliver high levels of performance and capability). Promoting good practice with regards to reinforcing a workplace change is about recognising and praising people who do the following:

✔ Demonstrate the most positive attitudes towards the changes being made.

✔ Place the same high level of importance as you do on the objectives, targets, standards of service and so on associated with the system, process or structure being changed.

✔ See problems experienced with the change as opportunities to make improvements and acquire knowledge and expertise about implementing changes into the workplace.

By recognising and praising good practice you can:

✔ Reinforce the attitudes, values and behaviours that you believe are important to:

  • Ensure that the specific change that has been made is maintained.

  • Sustain the success of your team.

✔ Let people know what's expected of them if they want to be recognised.

Part V
Leading Different Types of Team

'If you want to be part of our leadership team, you've got to be able to do this.'

In this part . . .

Want to know how to lead different types of teams? How to make your senior leadership team a great role model for the rest of your organisation? Step straight into this part.

Discover the characteristics that separate great teams from good teams, and how to lead project teams, virtual teams, permanent and temporary teams.

Chapter 15

Leading Your Own Team

Ask yourself the following question: can you succeed in your job without relying on other people? I suspect not, because the number of people whose work is so specialist and independent of the work going on around them is miniscule. Organisations are, by definition, collections, groups or teams of people who work together to achieve a purpose, often expressed as the organisation's goals, objectives or targets.

People don't work well as a team just because they happen to work together! Teamwork is exactly that: work. You need to work at building your team and lead team members to work at sustaining and improving teamwork, which is what this chapter is all about. You can use the team-building methods I describe in this chapter with any type of team, regardless of the context in which the team works. (For more detailed information on how to build and lead specific teams, such as project, virtual and senior management teams, check out Chapters 16, 17 and 18 respectively.)

Creating a High-Performing Team

Clearly, high-performing teams are successful teams. But what is success? In situations where teams are in direct competition with each other – such as in football where the sole measure of success is winning matches – the high-performing teams are evident: they're at the top of their league. Knowing, however, whether your work team is high-performing is difficult, because you don't have other teams against which to compare performance directly. Your team may be successful in terms of achieving the expected objectives, but how do you know whether it's performing to its full potential? This section provides several approaches that you can take to identify and adopt the characteristics of high-performing teams.

One overall aspect of a successful team is usually apparent. A high-performing team has *synergy*: that is, its members work together in ways that enable them to:

✔ Achieve and sustain exceptionally high levels of performance or output.

✔ Improve productivity, and how they work together, continuously.

Dealing with 'we're okay: leave us alone'

In this section, I show you how to tackle an obstacle to high performance: complacency. Perhaps you've been part of a work team in which people think that the team's a good one: that is, people get on well with each other, the team's doing what's expected and so on. Many teams that I meet during my work in organisations on building high-performing teams think that they're already performing well, and I sense that some people are complacently thinking, 'We're okay, leave us alone!'

You certainly don't want to disrupt or undermine teamwork by questioning or challenging team members about how good the team is, but you may want your team to be more self-critical to achieve the following:

✔ Identify the team's strengths and ensure that the team is using those strengths fully.

✔ Clarify any weaknesses and work on overcoming them.

✔ Establish a mindset or culture of continuous improvement within the team. (Chapter 12 shows you how to 'cruise with your crew' and involve team members looking for ways to improve.)

Encourage members of your team to question whether, and to what extent, they focus on improving how the team functions by examining the agenda of team meetings with them and asking questions such as:

✔ Does the agenda focus solely on progressing the work and tasks we have to do, and on solving problems we're experiencing in getting our work done?

✔ Do any agenda items focus our attention on how well we're working and interacting as a team?

✔ How often do we spend time at the end of team meetings reviewing how effectively we've worked together during the meeting?

Separating the great from the good

Some teams display most – and a few great teams, all – of the characteristics of high performance. Have you ever experienced being a member of a great team (at work or socially) that you felt was extra-special? If so, complete the following short exercise so that you can better relate to the characteristics required for work teams to be great rather than just good. If not, take a look at the list of characteristics of a great team that I include after the exercise.

1. **Divide the pages of a notebook into three columns as in Table 15-1.**

2. **Write a brief description of the team that you think was a great team.**

3. **List the characteristics in the second column that separated this team – what made it great or extra-special – from other teams that you've been in.**

4. **Describe in the third column, if you can, the contribution that each characteristic made to building or sustaining teamwork.** You may have difficulty clearly describing the contribution that each characteristic made to teamwork, because good teamwork is often the product of an amalgam of characteristics.

5. **Repeat steps 2 to 4 for any other teams that you've been part of that you think were great or outstanding.**

I give an example in Table 15-1 of an outstanding work team and two characteristics of the team to help you get started.

Table 15-1	Examining Great Teams	
Brief Description of the Team	*Characteristics of the Team*	*Contribution Each Characteristic Made to Teamwork*
Team of analysts in an industrial chemistry laboratory	Took the initiative to help colleagues to complete their work	Reinforced strong relationships or bonds among team members
	Constructively challenged any behaviour that didn't fit with the team's work ethic	Promptly raising and quickly resolving issues that may undermine teamwork became the norm

If you're yet to work as part of a great team (and even if you have), the crucial aspect is that team members are effectively engaging each other. (Check out Chapters 8 and 9 for the importance of engagement and how to become an engaging leader.) Great teams have the following characteristics:

- ✔ **Shared sense of purpose.** The purpose is so strong and meaningful that team members put more, or at least as much, emphasis on achieving this purpose as on their own needs. (You find out more about team purpose in the later section 'Harnessing the power of team purpose'.)

- ✔ **Commitment to each other.** Team members look out for and look after one another; they're sensitive to how well others are coping with, for example, demanding workloads and support each other when necessary.

- ✔ **Openness and honesty.** Every member of the team expresses their views and opinions openly and honestly, and says what's on their mind. They can to do so because of the mutual trust and respect they have for one another.

- ✔ **Willingness to challenge each other as critical friends.** Team members question and challenge each others' views, ideas, opinions and proposals regarding team decisions, and when necessary, any attitudes or behaviours that don't meet the team's standards – and members accept being challenged themselves as a natural way of how the team works together.

- ✔ **Strong sense of team identity.** Team members have such a strong sense of connection that they strongly identify with their team and each other, and feel they're part of something special.

- ✔ **Mutual accountability.** Responsibility for holding team members accountable doesn't reside solely with the team leader. Every member of the team has and uses the right to hold each other accountable for upholding team standards and so on.

- ✔ **High performance and achievement.** The team is focused on the necessary objectives, results and/or targets, has a record for achieving outstanding performance and uses the other characteristics described in this list continually to question and challenge itself to improve its productivity.

Promote these characteristics in your team by making sure that you demonstrate the attitudes and behaviours that reflect these characteristics yourself. Providing a model of appropriate behaviour when you interact with other members of your team is a great way to lead and encourage team members to think, feel and act in the same ways.

Harnessing the power of team purpose

Why should members of your team get out of bed on a freezing winter morning and trudge through deep snow to come to work? If your answer is a simplistic 'because they're getting paid to do a job', you probably don't appreciate the importance of having a clear and compelling team purpose. (You can discover the value of a leader having clarity of purpose in Chapter 7.)

People want to contribute through the work they do:

- ✔ They want their work to have meaning – to be meaningful rather than be meaningless or pointless. (Chapter 8 describes how to avoid the 'black hole' of meaningless work.)

- ✔ They want to make a positive difference, for example, to the following:

    - • The success of their organisation.

    - • The lives of other people.

The power of having a clear and compelling team purpose is that it enables team members to contribute through:

- ✔ Having a clear focus.

- ✔ Harnessing their energy.

- ✔ Enabling every individual to express themselves.

- ✔ Using their talents, wisdom and expertise.

- ✔ Experiencing a sense of fulfilment through their contribution.

Involve members of your team in considering questions such as the following, and assimilating the answers to produce a simple, clear and concise statement of your team's purpose:

- ✔ What is our *raison d'être*? Why does this team exist?

- ✔ Who do we serve – who are our customers and stakeholders – and what do they expect from us?

- ✔ What is this team's unique contribution to making our organisation successful and/or achieving our organisation's (strategic) objectives?

- ✔ Where have we been and where are we going?

- ✔ What can we extract about the purpose of this team from documents such as strategic or business plans, department objectives/plans and so on?

Share your team's purpose with your customers and stakeholders – groups who are interested in and/or are affected by the work your team does – to test whether it resonates with them.

The purpose of your team needs to contribute to your organisation's mission statement, if it has produced one. Even without such a statement, use your team's purpose to check and ensure that your expected objectives are important and worthwhile: that working on achieving these items is contributing to the team achieving its purpose in the organisation and, through this, contributing to the success of the organisation.

You may have to go over this process several times to refine your team's purpose into a simple, clear and concise statement. Try the 'lift statement' test: is the description of your team's purpose so clear and concise that you can explain it to someone in a lift in the time the lift takes to travel five floors without stopping?

Invest time in clarifying and producing the team purpose, values and behaviours that together give your team its identity and have a unifying effect on it. You want to achieve the following:

- ✔ A purpose that unites everyone because people perceive the purpose to be so irresistible that it not only grabs and holds their attention, but they also feel compelled to contribute everything they can to achieving or delivering the purpose.

- ✔ Values and behaviours that are principles and reference points to guide how team members work together in achieving the team's purpose. (You find out how to clarify and use team values in the next section.

(You can find out how to clarify the purpose of your role and the objectives you have to achieve in Chapter 7. You may use the approach described there to involve your team in clarifying the team's objectives from the team's purpose.)

Valuing team values

Many teams are hindered in becoming high-performing teams because team members haven't clarified and agreed the values that are important to them and how they expect each other to behave vis-à-vis those values. (Chapter 5 has loads more information on why values need to underpin your leadership and how to clarify your own values.)

Holding a meeting with team members to clarify the values that are important to your team enables you and them to do the following:

Hanging on and stopping back

I worked with a company's senior management team to build a high-performance culture, initially through building a high-performing management team that would be a role model for managers who reported to it and their employees. The management team held a three-hour meeting to share, explore and agree the values that were important to how members of the team worked together and how senior managers expected team members to behave to reinforce those agreed values.

Two of the team's agreed values and examples of relevant behaviour were as follows:

✔ **We value individual creativity and independence of thought.** We fully consider new ideas and concepts, and don't dismiss

or ridicule them because they challenge the norm.

✔ **We value high levels of trust among team members.** We display integrity and consistency in our discussions and actions. We don't criticise team members to other employees.

At the end of regular team meetings, the team used these values and behaviours as reference points to discuss and examine how well they were working together. They also agreed to 'hang on and stop back' after certain meetings that involved more junior managers and employees, in order to discuss how team members had reinforced or undermined the agreed values in working with those managers and employees.

✔ Get to know each other better by talking about each person's important values.

✔ Practise being open and honest with each other through revealing personal values.

✔ Experience reconciling differences by having meaningful conversations with each other.

✔ Set standards of behaviour for how team members treat each other and work together.

✔ Use the agreed values and behaviours to improve teamwork by recognising and reinforcing good behaviour, and challenging anyone whose behaviour may undermine, or is undermining, how the team performs. (You can find out in Chapter 11 how delaying tackling under-performance may cause the 'bad apple' effect: when a person's unacceptable performance or behaviour affects his work colleagues.)

Try the following exercise with your team:

1. **Organise a meeting with your team so that you're not disturbed for at least two hours.**

2. **Explain how values and behaviours are important to how team members work together.**

3. **Ask each team member to write down, without conferring, a list of the values that he thinks the team should have to enable members of the team to work effectively together.** You may need to give an example of what you mean by a value, such as 'being open and honest'. If you have a large team, form sub-groups of two to three people to produce the initial list.

4. **Share and discuss the lists identifying where values are the same or similar, and exploring the differences with the aim of agreeing the values that the team will adopt.**

5. **Take each agreed value in turn and identify and agree two or three behaviours that demonstrate that a team member is working in accord with the value.** Examples of behaviours for 'open and honest' may be:

   • All team members say what's 'on their mind'.

   • We encourage team members to express their point of view.

6. **Discuss and agree how the team are going to use the agreed list of values, and review how well every team member is acting and behaving in accord with these values.**

The following are ways of using the agreed values and behaviours:

✔ Displaying the list of values and behaviours in your team's work area.

✔ Discussing how well members of the team are working in accord with the agreed values and behaviours at the end of whole-team and sub-team meetings.

✔ Examining during one-to-one performance and capability appraisals how well each team member is putting the values into practice in working with colleagues.

Assessing the Effectiveness of Your Team

Assessing just how effectively your team is performing enables you to understand the team's strengths and the priorities to work on to improve its performance. You may have heard the adage 'what get's measured, get's done', and perhaps even already use this approach to focus team members on the team's expected targets and to know how well the team is performing. If not, consider how you can best adopt the approaches described in the following two sections to assess and improve your team's performance.

Rating your team

No doubt you have a view about how well your team's performing. This view is based on, or coloured by, a mixture of your experiences of working with individual team members and the whole team, the range of problems being encountered, the output from your team and so on.

A subjective, instinctive idea is fine, but adopting a more structured approach to considering your team's performance allows you to be more objective and thus produce a more accurate assessment to rating your team.

You can assess how effectively your team is performing against several criteria including:

✔ How well your team is achieving its objectives, targets and/or results, sometimes referred to as key performance indicators (KPIs).

✔ The extent to which team members are working in accord with the team's agreed values and behaviours. (You can discover how to clarify and agree team values and behaviours with your team in the earlier section 'Valuing team values'.)

✔ Whether the team has the characteristics that you consider are important for your team. Take a look at the earlier section 'Separating the great from the good', in which I list the key characteristics of a great team or, indeed, you identified yourself by completing the exercise.

To rate your team, book time with yourself on a regular basis and ask yourself questions such as the following:

✔ How well is my team performing against the KPIs – the objectives/targets/results – that we have to achieve? What numeric or other evidence can I use to justify my view?

✔ Has my team's performance in achieving our KPIs been steady, improved or deteriorated over the preceding one and three months? What are the reasons for any changes in performance trends?

✔ How well are team members working together? What have I noticed about how team members are behaving and treating each other that supports my view?

✔ How well do team members support each other? What evidence exists that team members are on the 'look out' for how others are coping with the workload, and are taking the initiative to help each other when they see someone struggling?

✔ Do team members hold each other accountable for doing what they expect each other to do? To what extent do team members promptly challenge their colleagues when they don't do what's expected?

✔ What evidence can I find that team members, individually and collectively, are interacting and behaving in ways that reinforce our team values? What have I done since my last review to recognise and reinforce good practice? How promptly and effectively have I intervened when I notice unacceptable behaviour and standards of work?

✔ On a scale of 1–10, what's my rating of the team atmosphere as a happy productive place to be? What is the evidence on which I have based my score? How does my score compare with previous scores? What actions am I going to take to improve the team atmosphere?

You can use any characteristics that you want your team to have in a simple questionnaire to rate your team.

Conducting a team self-assessment

No, I'm not suggesting that you buy a baton and wave your arms around maniacally like an orchestral maestro! I have something a little more collaborative in mind. Carrying out regular self-assessments of your team's performance allows you to develop an overview of how well your team's performing, especially if you hold regular reviews and look for trends in performance. Such self-assessments have the following benefits:

✔ You can reinforce KPIs, values and behaviours, and important team characteristics by using them as criteria for conducting the assessment.

✔ Team members are more likely to take ownership of the outcomes of the assessment because they've been involved in assessing their team.

✔ All team members contribute to establishing a culture of continuous improvement through regularly critiquing the team's performance. (You find out more on this subject in the later section 'Striving for Continuous Improvement'.)

Hold a team meeting to describe the reasons why you want your team to conduct a self-assessment, and the method that you're going to use, before you ask team members to assess or comment on the team's performance. Then involve team members in assessing how well their team is performing by:

✔ Examining the productivity of the team using numeric performance information, graphs showing performance trends, progress in completing projects and so on.

> ✔ Asking questions such as those described in the previous section 'Rating your team'. (Refer to Chapter 12 to find more questions that you can ask your team in order to involve them in identifying the team's strengths and priorities.)

Consider whether all team members are likely to give an honest, objective and unbiased rating of team performance during a meeting. If you think that their colleagues' views may influence how some team members rate their team in an open discussion, collect everyone's assessment anonymously first via a questionnaire and then discuss the summary of those views.

Produce a simple questionnaire containing a description of the characteristics or issues that you want members of your team to consider, together with a simple rating scheme. Table 15-2 provides examples of statements that you may want to include in a questionnaire.

Table 15-2	Examples of Statements to Use in a Team Self-assessment			
	Strongly Disagree	*Tend to Disagree*	*Tend to Agree*	*Strongly Agree*
Everyone is encouraged to express their views and opinions openly and honestly.				
Team members hold each other accountable for doing what they say they're going to do.				
Everyone strives to uphold the team's values through their actions and behaviour.				
Team members challenge colleagues whose work, attitude and/or behaviour is below the team's standards.				
We regularly question all aspects of our work to identify our strengths and focus on continuously improving the team's performance.				
I'm proud to be a member of this team.				

Striving for Continuous Improvement

If your team is already performing well, why strive to improve performance continuously? Simply, for the following reasons:

- ✔ Continuous improvement is more of a 'team mindset' or team culture – a way of working – than a set of techniques or methods.

- ✔ Teams are never standing still; their performance is improving, or deteriorating due to complacency over time.

Building your team into a high-performing team and sustaining that high performance is difficult: a large majority of your team, if not every team member, needs to be committed to the team's purpose, upholding the team's values and beliefs, and maintaining high standards in all aspects of their work and how team members work together. The task isn't easy but is worthwhile. (Refer to the characteristics of high-performing teams in the earlier section 'Separating the great from the good' to gain insights into the benefits of high-performing teams.)

The enemy of continuous improvement is thinking that you're too busy actually getting the work done to spend time on improving how members of your team work together to get the work done!

Developing a high-performance atmosphere

You've probably walked into some organisations and sensed a real 'buzz' about the place; high energy, employees really engaged in their work and enjoying themselves, an 'air' of professionalism and high productivity, and so on. You may also have experienced walking into certain shops, hotels, restaurants and so on and sensed an air of stagnation or lethargy!

The tone or mood – the atmosphere – in a workplace is partly created by the physical environment, but primarily by the people who work there. I've come across workplaces that are cathedrals of modern architecture and ergonomics but void of purposefulness and spirit.

Try to provide the best facilities, tools and equipment for your team to be productive, *and* focus most of your effort on the human aspects of work to create a high-performance atmosphere.

Work on creating a high-performance team atmosphere as follows:

✔ Share your vision of how you see your team performing as a high-performing team. (Dip into Chapter 7 to find out how to create your own vision.)

✔ Regularly reinforce the team's purpose and *raison d'être*, as well as the contribution that the team is making to the organisation's success, in team meetings and conversations with individuals and groups. (Discover how to clarify your team's purpose in the earlier section 'Harnessing the power of team purpose'.)

✔ Display the team's achievements around the workplace. Use graphs or other means of showing statistical trends in performance, feedback from customers and colleagues and so on.

✔ Catch people doing great deeds; get out of your office and walk around looking for examples of people doing a great job.

✔ Ensure that enough priority and time is given to activities focused on critically examining how well the team is performing and how well people are working together to identify strengths and agree actions to improve all aspects of team performance.

✔ Encourage people to seize opportunities to get to know each other better, such as talking about who they are, their hopes and aspirations, the challenges they face and so on.

✔ Celebrate the achievement of significant objectives and targets, passing important milestones in improving productivity and so on by organising an event for people to have fun, enjoy being together and (informally) tell stories about their achievements.

Making the un-discussable discussable

Have you ever experienced colleagues sharing their views and opinions with you after a meeting that, in your view, they should have said during the meeting? In my experience, people aren't open and honest in expressing their views in meetings for the following reasons (among others):

✔ They're concerned about appearing ignorant or foolish by expressing their views or opinions.

✔ They don't want to feel embarrassed by saying something inappropriate.

✔ They don't want to embarrass or hurt a work colleague by disagreeing with or criticising that person's view or opinion.

✔ They lack the confidence to make a statement that they can't prove or validate.

✔ They're concerned about how a colleague may react – even overreact – if that person disagrees with the view and proceeds to criticise their personality as well as their viewpoint.

Being open and honest in meetings by 'speaking your mind' is risky for many people; they have to step outside of their comfort zone to be able to take the risk. (Explore Chapter 9 to discover lots of good practice on how to have meaningful conversations with your staff, and find out more about comfort zones in Chapter 6.)

Here are some approaches to make the un-discussable discussable in team meetings:

✔ Encourage your team members to question and challenge your views, and listen attentively to their views and opinions. (Refer to Chapter 9 to find out how to invite challenge and cope with embarrassment and threat.) Adopting this approach allows you to set a great example for others to copy.

✔ Have a brief chat before a meeting with a person who you know lacks confidence to speak in meetings. Discuss agenda items that are important to that person and encourage him to express his views in the meeting: say that you'll support his viewpoint if you agree with it, especially if you expect people to have different views on the agenda item.

✔ Invite more introverted individuals to speak by using their name and ensuring that colleagues don't interrupt.

✔ Challenge (constructively) any language or behaviour that's likely to cause embarrassment, threat or undermine anyone's self-confidence.

✔ Recognise and praise individuals who ask searching questions that cause their colleagues, and even the whole team, to question existing viewpoints and lead to new insights, enhanced understanding of problems and improved decision-making. (Find out how to become more skilled in asking searching questions in Chapter 9.)

✔ Thank in private a team member who constructively challenges a colleague's unacceptable behaviour, such as regularly interrupting and 'talking over' other colleagues while they're expressing their views.

Chapter 16

Taking on a Project Team

· ·

In This Chapter

▶ Preparing your project team for action

▶ Handling team members with other priorities

▶ Encouraging team members to hold each other accountable

· ·

Some project teams form when people with a common interest join together to solve a problem or seize an opportunity. But for many project teams, employees are nominated for membership because of their knowledge and/or skills or as representatives of a department with an interest in the project. In the latter scenario, people can be thrown together and expected to work together effectively for a nominated project leader, perhaps for you!

In this chapter I lead you through the challenges that await you as a project leader and how to handle them. You explore the stages that teams go through and ways to accelerate the process of building an effective project team. You also uncover the problems of leading members who have many competing demands on their time, and how to encourage all team members to adopt a shared accountability for the success of the project.

Getting Your Team Up and Running

When initially appointed to head up a group of people who've come or been thrown together, many project leaders focus primarily on the task in hand: that is, on producing a project plan that describes the steps or actions necessary to complete the project. In my experience, however, progress in completing projects is just as much affected by how well team members work together as by the quality of the project plan.

Spend as much time on the process of how project team members are going to work together (and will continue to work together) as on planning and monitoring the project task itself.

Avoiding 'project-itis': The scourge of organisations

'Project-itis' is the term I've coined to describe the symptom of managers spawning projects in an ad hoc manner in their organisation. The features or effects of this symptom include the following:

- ✔ Competition between project sponsors and project managers for limited resources is intense.
- ✔ Projects are launched without clear specifications being agreed.
- ✔ Delays in the progress and completion of projects are common.
- ✔ Potential or expected benefits to be gained from completing projects are delayed or lost.
- ✔ Especially talented employees may be members of several project teams, and be stretched and even stressed by being pulled in different directions by their project leaders.

In severe cases an organisation may suffer from *initiative overload* (or 'initiative-itis'), a term for when people think that far too many initiatives or projects are going on in the organisation. (Flip to Chapter 13 for how to handle this problem.)

If you experience any of the above problems, encourage senior managers to conduct a review and form an overview of current projects or initiatives by taking the following actions:

1. Assemble a comprehensive list of the projects that people are working on and planning.

2. Critique the specification of each project, especially the benefits to be gained and the demand on resources.

3. Compare and prioritise projects on the basis of their contribution to the organisation's success or the return on investment with regard to costs and time consumed by each project.

4. Produce and monitor an overall organisation plan of all projects.

5. Vet all proposed major projects and consider the implications of launching more projects on existing priorities and the demand for resources.

Appreciating and using the stages of team development

Project teams and groups develop into a team as members spend time working together: people become more comfortable with each other, relationships develop and so on.

In 1965, Bruce Tuckman came up with a description of teamwork development as a group of people, even strangers, work together and become a more effective team. Tuckman's famous phrase that describes the stages of team development is *forming*, *storming*, *norming* and *performing*, and he subsequently added a fifth stage *adjourning*. In this section, I use Tuckman's model to describe my understanding of how teamwork develops and the problems that can arise; in the later section 'Accelerating through the stages' I show how you can lead your team through these stages more quickly to become a high-performing team.

Forming

The initial stage occurs when individuals come together. *Forming* is characterised by people typically being polite although individuals may be confident or anxious depending, for example, on the extent to which they need clarity about what's expected of them. Team members are highly dependent on you as project leader for direction and guidance because the team roles and responsibilities of individuals are unclear.

Storming

During this second stage, your team can experience difficulty making decisions. Perhaps team members vie for position as they attempt to establish themselves in the team, and you can find your authority as project leader being challenged. Sub-groups or cliques may form, which can lead to questioning of the team's aim or goals. Emotions running high can undermine the sense of teamwork, for example, as problems develop in the relationships between some team members.

Norming

In this stage, team members start to become more comfortable with each other. Individuals now know each other better, and roles and responsibilities become clear. Team members respect your position and authority as project leader; they grow more committed to, and make better progress towards, achieving the project objectives.

Performing

When (or if – some teams don't reach this stage of high performance because they don't develop all the characteristics of the Norming and Performing stage) your team achieves the performing stage, your job as project leader normally becomes a lot easier, because team members have discovered how to work together without much guidance from you. Team members, individually and collectively, have a high degree of autonomy and make most decisions against the measures or criteria for monitoring the success of the project that have been agreed with you. Any disagreements within the team are quickly resolved, mainly by team members themselves.

Adjourning

This final stage occurs when the team completes the project and disbands. This period can be a difficult time for individuals who've formed close relationships with other team members.

Accelerating through the stages

The developmental stages of Tuckman's teamwork model (which I describe in the preceding section) aren't distinct and separate, but you can understand how your project team is developing by noticing which of the characteristics of the team and/or behaviours of team members are most prominent.

Accelerate your project team through each of Tuckman's five stages by taking the following action:

✔ **Forming:**

- Recognise that your team is looking to you to show leadership.

- Clarify and/or enthusiastically convey the team's purpose. (You can find out more about team purpose in the later section 'Investing time in the project's purpose'.)

- Shape an overall project plan by identifying the main steps that have to be taken to complete the project and who's responsible for each step.

- Encourage team members to get to know each other better by talking about their role in the organisation, previous jobs, their own lives and so on.

✔ **Storming:**

- Facilitate a meeting to clarify and agree team members' expectations of each other in working together to complete the project. (Take a look at Chapter 15 to find out how to agree a set of team values.)

- Establish systems and processes to meet, gather and analyse data, share information and so on to enable the team to function effectively.

- Engage the relevant people in promptly addressing any tensions, conflict or disagreements between individuals and/or sub-groups. (You can discover how to become an engaging leader in Chapter 9, and how to make the un-discussable discussable to create a high-performance team atmosphere in Chapter 15.)

- Coach individuals who are anxious or struggling with their role in the team, or helping dominant individuals to be more inclusive when working with their colleagues.

✔ **Norming:**

- Take an overview of the project and how it's progressing, instead of getting involved in the details.

- Sense the commitment of individuals to drive the project forward in your occasional contact with them. (I discuss how to sense commitment in Chapter 9.)

- Organise and holding social events to enable team members to enjoy each others' company, and celebrate achieving major milestones towards completing the project.

✔ **Performing:**

- Delegate as much as you can while retaining a 'light hand on the tiller' in steering the project – remember that the buck stops with you!

- Recognise and praise individuals and groups, especially in public, for completing significant tasks.

- Promote the team's progress and achievements – rather than your own achievements – to the project sponsors.

✔ **Adjourning:**

- Celebrate achievement of the aims and objectives of the project with all the team and, perhaps, their spouses.

- Review the project with your project team to identify and share lessons learnt from being involved in the project. (Drop into Chapter 15 to discover how to conduct a team self-assessment.)

- Establish networks and make a commitment to keep in touch with individuals.

Leading Team Members with Multiple Commitments

By definition, projects have a limited life: they all have a deadline, even long-term ones. Although members of your project team may have been seconded full time to work on your project, more likely your project team consists of members who also have to do their everyday job as well as contributing to the project. Some employees, especially those recognised as having certain talents or specialist know-how – such as information technology skills – may even be members of two or more project teams.

When members of your project team have multiple commitments, you can find being a project leader challenging and difficult for the following reasons:

- ✔ People's attention is spread across many priorities.

- ✔ You're one of two or more 'managers' competing for people's time.

- ✔ Project team members' direct line managers (as opposed to you as their project leader) have more authority to manage them and more influence over what they do.

- ✔ You may have a limited amount of time yourself to spend on the project due to other work pressures.

Investing time in the project's purpose

Unless members of your project team have been seconded to your project full time, they can give you only a limited amount of their time. You and your team may feel under pressure, especially during initial meetings, due to the finite time you have together to carry out the following tasks:

- ✔ **Agreeing the project specification:**
    - The purpose, objective(s) or outcome(s) to be achieved by completing the project.
    - The criteria that you're going to use to evaluate whether the project has been successful.

- ✔ **Producing a plan to complete the project:** The later section 'Avoiding slopy shoulders' describes how to produce a project plan.

- ✔ **Monitoring progress:** Towards achieving the plan and refining the plan to keep the project on track.

Make sure that you and your project team spend enough time at the outset clarifying the purpose of the project and the roles of relevant individuals, even if people feel that they have to proceed with undue haste at the start of the project.

Ensure that you and your project team are crystal clear about the following aspects:

✔ **The purpose of – or the reasons for working on – the project.** Answer questions such as:

- What improvements and/or benefits have to be achieved by completing this project? You may have to undertake an investigation or analysis, or thoroughly question the project sponsors, to understand fully the problem or issue you need to focus on and to enable you to then clarify the expected benefits or project objectives.

- How is this project expected to contribute to the success of our organisation?

- What would be the consequences if this project wasn't undertaken?

- How confident are we that, in describing the purpose, we're focusing on the causes rather than the symptoms of problems?

✔ **The purpose of individuals being project members.** Answer questions such as:

- Why are you a member of this team?

- How important is this project to you compared with all the other work you have to do?

- What contribution do you want to make to this project?

- What's 'in it' for you; what do you want to get from being involved in this project?

Members of project teams are more committed to making a valuable contribution to the success of a project when they appreciate that the purpose of the project is important and worthwhile. (Dip into Chapter 15 to find out more about the power of a clearly defined, compelling team purpose.)

Challenging unhelpful behaviour: Sorry, wrong room, wrong team!

No doubt you've experienced the following embarrassing moment: you're in a meeting when someone barges into the room, realises that she's joined the wrong meeting, sheepishly apologises and slips back out the door! Such behaviour normally indicates that the person is:

✔ Late for her own meeting.

✔ Underprepared to make a valuable contribution to her meeting.

✔ Disorganised.

✔ All the above!

People displaying these types of behaviour may be overstretched with commitments and struggling to cope with their workload. While you're more likely to be sympathetic towards a person who's overstretched compared to someone who's just disorganised, if you experience a member of your project team displaying this type of behaviour, how you respond – and the speed with which you do so – is critical for the following reasons:

✔ Setting and maintaining your team's standard of behaviour.

✔ Preserving the performance of your team.

✔ Keeping up your credibility as project leader.

Promptly and positively challenge any member of your project team whose behaviour may undermine the team's standards or performance, and encourage that person to work to your standards. Find out about the various commitments that the person currently has, and be particularly empathetic if she's overstretched: how would you feel if you were overloaded with work commitments? Organise a joint meeting with the person and her direct line manager to discuss and resolve the problem by, perhaps, agreeing more realistic deadlines for completing relevant tasks and projects. (Chapter 11 has loads more on leading people towards maintaining your standards and the dangers of delaying taking action.)

Developing a Sense of Shared Accountability

As project leader, you're accountable for ensuring that your project is a success; the ultimate responsibility lies with you! Members of your project team probably expect you to:

✔ Hold all team members accountable for taking the actions they're expected to take.

✔ Run project meetings effectively.

✔ Sort out any disagreements or tensions between team members.

And that's just for a start!

But not every last aspect of team performance is down to you alone. Some members of your project team may think that they don't have any responsibility for how the team members work together – that is, for the team process – and expect you to be responsible and accountable for every single aspect of the project. In such a situation, a team member is likely to 'pass the buck' to you, for example, to speak to a team member who isn't completing a task as expected. You may find yourself being dragged into sorting out problems that you think you shouldn't be involved in, because team members can't sort out such problems themselves.

Avoiding slopy shoulders

The expression 'slopy shoulders' is the opposite of 'shouldering responsibility'. People with slopy shoulders don't keep their metaphorical shoulders level to take responsibility, but instead are inclined (forgive the pun!) to let it slide away, which of course means that someone else has to pick it up and take the weight!

Your starting point for encouraging team members to hold themselves and each other accountable for taking action is to ensure that all team members know what's expected of them and each other to complete the project. In other words, they need to know and shoulder their fair share of responsibility.

Involve your project team in producing and monitoring a project plan for achieving the objectives of the project as follows:

1. **List all the main tasks that have to be undertaken to complete the project.**

2. **Examine the tasks to identify which can start at anytime and which are dependent on people completing other tasks first.**

3. **Relist all the tasks so that they're in chronological order, noting task dependency – such as starting task 'F' is dependent on tasks 'A' and 'D' being completed.**

4. **Decide who's going to be held accountable for completing each task.**

5. **Estimate how long each task is going to take to complete – each task's duration time.**

6. **Use the task dependencies and duration times to set the deadline by which each task has to be completed, to complete the project on time.** Table 16-1 provides an example of the format of a project plan for starting to think about reorganising an office.

7. **Hold regular project reviews using the project plan as the basis of the meeting in order to:**

- Discuss progress and achievements.

- Identify actual and potential problems and delays, and how to overcome them to keep the project on track.

- Encourage all team members to state their expectations of other team members to enable them to complete the tasks for which they're accountable, as well as the implications and consequences of colleagues not doing what's required of them.

- Refine and update details of the project plan, focusing on how to maintain the overall project schedule and complete the project on time.

Table 16-1	Example of the Format of a Project Plan			
Description of Each Task	**Person Accountable**	**Completion Date**	**Task Dependency**	**Comments on Progress (including notes of when a task is completed)**
A) Brief staff about the pur- pose of reorganis- ing the office.	Me	23rd March	None	
B) Consult all staff about their work sta- tion needs.	Peter	7th April	'A'	
C) Produce the first draft of the proposed office layout.	Gemma	15th April	'A, B'	

We don't have time!

This real-life example shows how I involved one team in spending time on the team process.

A Managing Director of a retail business engaged me to work with his senior managers to enable them to be effective in performing a more strategic role in the business. The Managing Director had experienced difficulties in getting his managers to take onboard additional strategic responsibilities as well as manage their departments to achieve their sales targets. The managers were all equal in seniority, and took turns in 'chairing' the strategy meetings that they were expected to hold every six weeks.

I held a couple of sessions with the managers in which we examined and clarified the team's purpose – the contribution they were expected to make to the business – and the role they were expected to fulfil. All the managers expressed the same problem: finding the time to perform their strategic responsibilities as well as do their 'day jobs'.

I observed the management team in one of their strategic meetings for an hour and then intervened to explore the way in which they were working together: in other words, the team process. I explained that the productivity of the meeting wasn't solely dependent on how the managers worked together in the meeting, but that how well each and every manager prepared for the meeting also affected the team's performance. All managers were expected to submit their reports and any papers to the chairperson one week before the meeting.

I asked whether managers had submitted their reports on time and whether the reports were produced to a standard that managers expected. Several managers said they hadn't had time to do their reports correctly and had submitted their report after the deadline because achieving their sales target was more important. I made the point that the managers were, to some extent, wasting each other's time due to a lack of preparation for the meetings, and the productivity of the meetings would never improve if this situation continued.

I asked all managers how long they took to write their report properly, and was told that the time ranged between one to four hours to prepare for the meeting. I asked whether it was impossible for a manager to plan and 'ring fence' this amount of time to write their report in the fifth week after each meeting. They agreed that 'put that way' it was not unreasonable to do this.

I also enquired whether the first hour spent in the meeting had been worthwhile and everyone agreed that important decisions had been made: decisions that wouldn't be made if the managers didn't have these strategic meetings. I then asked the managers to decide whether to stop working on the strategic issues and stop meeting or improve the way they worked together.

They agreed to commit the time to doing the strategic work they were expected to do, and they also agreed to hold each other accountable if anyone failed to submit the reports on time or to the standard they expected from each other.

Remembering the team process

Most project teams, in my experience, jump straight into 'task mode' when the team members first come together: the team gets straight down to focusing on clarifying the objectives of the project and the actions that have to be taken to achieve those objectives. The result is that team members subsequently experience problems in how they work together on the project simply because they didn't invest time initially on the team process.

Your project plan (which I describe in the preceding section) describes the tasks and accountabilities of team members; the actions to be taken and who's going to take them. The team process focuses on how people are working together (now or in the future) to complete those tasks.

You can use several approaches covered elsewhere in this book to work on the team process:

- ✔ Clarify and use team values to agree how team members prefer to, and subsequently do, work together. (Check out Chapter 15 for more.)

- ✔ Conduct a team self-assessment (also described in Chapter 15).

- ✔ Work on a team member's commitment and capability to do a task. (Turn to Chapter 11 for more on this subject.)

- ✔ Identify what the team is and isn't doing well, as well as how it can improve. (Flip to Chapter 12.)

- ✔ Use the tips to speed up how your team is developing (as discussed in the earlier section 'Accelerating through the stages').

Appreciating the power of distributed leadership

Members of your project team probably expect you to take the lead in looking after the team process – how well team members work together – but in fact they need to share in this task.

Encourage team members to show leadership in contributing to sustaining and improving the team process by doing the following:

- ✔ Show a genuine interest in each other as individuals instead of only being interested in what their colleagues can do to help them complete their project work. (Explore Chapter 9 to find out how to enhance relating to people.)

✔ Step outside of their comfort zone to question and challenge any team member who's not behaving in accord with the agreed team values. Share the tips you discover in Chapter 6 about how to step outside of your own comfort zone.

✔ Develop the courage to 'speak their mind'. (Refer to Chapter 9 for guidance on how to be more courageous in having meaningful conversations.)

✔ Be able to cope with embarrassing and threatening situations. (Chapter 9 contains tips for doing so.)

✔ Approach each other directly to enquire why a task they're dependent on being completed to do their own work hasn't been done, and encouraging their colleague to complete it.

The benefits of encouraging members of your project team to show leadership in this way include:

✔ Team members promptly resolve their own problems and concerns about how other team members are working with them.

✔ You don't get bogged down in the minutiae of how the team is working, giving you more time to work on more important priorities.

✔ Your project team is able to become a high-performing team by fully using the talents and expertise of everyone and by becoming skilled at engaging each other effectively.

Chapter 17

Facilitating Virtual Teams

. . . .

. . . .

*W*ith the increasing growth of worldwide organisations and improved methods of electronic communication, virtual teams are growing in number and importance. As a team leader, you may well find yourself asked to lead a team of people who are spread across countries and continents and who rarely, if ever, meet each other in person. Clearly, leading such a team presents particular problems.

In this chapter you explore characteristics of virtual teams to help you understand the ways in which such groups differ from other teams, and the implications for you as a virtual team leader. You also find out how to establish effective ways of working with members of virtual teams and how to bring your team to a successful close.

Understanding Virtual Teams

What do you think of when you hear the term 'virtual team'? You may think that the term implies a team that isn't really a team but an illusion, perhaps because the term 'virtual reality' is often used to describe the apparent reality of a computer-generated image. Or you may think that a virtual team is one that's almost, but not quite, a team: something is missing!

Such misconceptions are dangerous to the effectiveness of a virtual team: in fact, these physically widespread groups need to be just as much of a team as ones in which the members meet face-to-face.

Naming a team

The name of a team, even a generic name such as 'senior management team', has connotations for team members. A team name:

- Gives team members an identity; a name describes a specific group of people with which team members identify.

- Provides meaning, and may even describe the purpose of the team, to team members and other people. For example, employees of an organisation generally expect 'their' senior leadership team to lead the organisation.

- Implies that the team has certain characteristics.

All sorts of different types of teams exist – project teams, senior management teams, permanent teams, temporary teams, virtual teams – and although such teams have some common characteristics, each also displays certain specific characteristics. Getting a clear understanding of a team through its name is crucial to any team's effective functioning. You discover the characteristics of virtual teams in the next three sections and some of the challenges you may experience as a virtual team leader.

Defining virtual teams

Here are some significant characteristics of a virtual team that set it apart from other types of team:

- Team members rarely, if ever, meet in person because they tend to be scattered over large geographical areas.

- Team members only have regular contact with each other via telephone, video conference or email. Such limited contact or forms of communication often have implications for how effectively members of the team work together.

- Team members are more likely to have different cultural backgrounds, values, 'first' language, preferred ways of working and so on, especially if they belong to international teams.

A virtual team can be permanent or temporary. A permanent virtual team is one with a relatively long life, perhaps existing for years rather than months, although team members rarely meet in person. A temporary virtual team is one formed to complete a specific task or project and the team disbands when it has completed the project.

The above characteristics of virtual teams can have important consequences for how team members work together.

Take a few minutes to complete the following exercise. If you've been a member of a virtual team, reflect on your experiences to identify the consequences of limited contact between (and/or restricted forms of communication on) team members, and how these consequences affected how well people worked together. If you haven't served on a virtual team yet, you can still complete the exercise by speculating about how well people may work together:

1. **Divide the pages of a notebook into three columns, as in Table 17-1.**

2. **Note one consequence of limited contact between team members in the first column.**

3. **Describe how this consequence affects the ways people work together and/or the productivity of the team in the second column.**

4. **Describe the challenge that this effect presents to you as team leader in the third column.**

5. **Repeat steps 2 to 4 for other consequences.**

I give two examples in Table 17-1 to get you started.

Table 17-1   Consequences and Effects of Limited Contact and Forms of Communication for Members of a Virtual Team

Consequence of Limited Contact and Forms of Communication	Effect of How People Worked Together and Effect on the Productivity of the Team	Challenges for You as Team Leader
Team members didn't really get to know each other well.	People didn't put themselves out to help each other due to a lack of camaraderie.	How to build good working relationships and a sense of team spirit.
Misunderstandings occurred quite often.	Misunderstandings contributed to disorganisation including duplication of effort or actions not being taken.	How to ensure that everyone clearly understands the agreed actions and responsibilities.

Comprehending the challenges of being a virtual team leader

Take a look at Table 17-2, which describes a few consequences of virtual team members rarely meeting face-to-face and the associated challenges waiting for you as team leader.

Table 17-2 Challenges Awaiting a Virtual Team Leader	
Consequences and Effects of Limited Contact and/or Forms of Communication	*Challenges Facing the Team Leader*
A clear, common and shared sense of purpose may not exist.	How to ensure that meaningful conversation occurs in which team members can explore, consider and agree the importance of the team's work to themselves, individually and collectively, and to the organisation.
Remoteness of team members restricts the formation of relationships and a strong sense of team identity.	How to build a genuine interest in each other, and a strong sense of connection and mutual interdependence in achieving success.
Team members hold back from expressing their views and saying what they really think.	How to establish mutual trust and respect that will enable team members to be open and honest with each other.
Misunderstandings due to inadequate non-verbal communication.	How to compensate for not being able to notice, appreciate and understand the significance of non-verbal cues.
Misunderstandings due to different interpretations of the meanings of words and phrases, especially between people from different countries.	How to avoid making assumptions that all team members have the same understanding of the language being used, and explore the potential for misunderstandings.
Fundamental differences in normal or preferred ways of working together.	How to work with, and minimise the negative effects of, differences in the natural ways of working of members from diverse cultural backgrounds.
Inconvenient times to arrange team meetings arising from people working in different time zones.	How to be fair and consistent in handling the effects of different time zones on individual work patterns.

Facing up to 'we're not a team because we never meet'

You may experience occasions when one or more virtual team members express the view that the team isn't really a team because the members never meet! Sometimes you may discover this view only via the organisation's grapevine unless:

✔ The people with this view are strong self-confident characters who express their views openly and honestly.

✔ You've created an environment in which team members feel safe to express potentially contentious views; that is, they feel they won't be criticised or reprimanded for expressing their opinions.

STORY

Winning people's commitment

This true story illustrates how one manager encouraged members of her virtual team to express their views, and build the commitment of team members to improve business results.

A senior manager I was coaching, Joyce, wanted to improve the commitment of agents working in different countries to promote her company's products above competitors' products that the agents also represented. Joyce recognised that she couldn't improve and sustain the commitment of agents to promote her company by just increasing commissions: it wasn't within Joyce's power to do this anyway! Joyce rarely met the agents, and it was difficult and costly to bring all the agents together.

Joyce invested time in finding out more about the expectations that agents had in working with her company, and how well their expectations were being met. She explored agents' experiences of working with the company – their hopes, aspirations, concerns, frustrations and so on – via one-to-one telephone conversations. Joyce used the information so obtained to design a questionnaire that she subsequently used to clarify how much importance agents,

individually and collectively, placed on each of the issues that she had identified that affected agents' commitment to promote her company.

Joyce analysed the results to identify the priorities to work on and quickly initiated improvements including: providing more comprehensive information on the company and its products, amending information systems and improving back-up support from the UK office. Joyce discussed the results of her survey and explained the changes she'd made in a video conference with agents. She modified the content of future telephone conferences and one-to-one telephone calls to place as much emphasis on talking about issues that agents wanted to discuss as talking about business performance, priorities and so on.

Joyce subsequently informed me that agents said that they felt they were part of the company and identified with it more strongly: they felt that the company was interested in them as people rather than them just being a representative of the company, and placed more emphasis on promoting her company's products.

State the importance of teamwork, and make sure that you challenge any team member making such a statement, because otherwise you may be seen as tacitly agreeing.

Avoid overreacting and rejecting the view so strongly that you become perceived as criticising the person expressing the viewpoint. Reacting this way may cause members of your team to keep their views to themselves, and prevent you from knowing about – and dealing with – the views, and especially the concerns, of team members. (Chapter 15 describes how to encourage all team members to speak openly and honestly, and how to make the 'undiscussable discussable'.)

Establishing Clever Ways of Working

In this section you discover how to establish a few clever ways of working, which help you to address the challenges of leading a virtual team and ensure that your team is productive.

Strive to establish clever ways of team members working together when your virtual team is formed. To do so, invest time in examining and exploring the process of how the team's going to work, as well as agreeing with members the objectives, planning and organisation of the work of the team.

Getting your 'ducks in a row'

If your virtual team is permanent, you're probably the line manager of all members; they report directly to you and so maintaining priorities is fairly straightforward. But if your virtual team is temporary, such as a project team, members may report to you for their work on your virtual team's project as well as to a line manager who expects them to do work for him. In the latter case, you may experience that you and several line managers are competing for the time and attention of your team members to complete different work priorities. Your team members can find themselves being pulled in different directions as a result of having more than one boss!

Work on 'getting your ducks in a row', which means that everyone's pulling in the same direction. Gain the commitment of team members – and for temporary teams the agreement of each member's line manager too – to spend enough time on your project to progress and complete it by doing the following:

✔ Establishing the importance of your project to your organisation or business by clarifying the benefits of completing it, and the consequences of not completing it, by its deadline. Check and agree these aspects with your project sponsor or senior managers.

✔ Explaining to your team members the importance and benefits of completing the project to your organisation, and emphasising the unique contribution you expect each team member to make to the success of the project.

✔ Explaining to relevant line managers the importance and benefits of the project to your organisation.

✔ Clarifying with all team members the time commitment required from them based on their role in the project: the amount of time, days of the week, critical dates and times such as video conferences at important project milestones and so on. Support all team members, if required, to discuss their project commitments with their line manager to gain agreement, resolve any conflicting priorities and so on.

✔ Discussing and reviewing regularly with your team members whether they're experiencing any problems in fulfilling their commitments to your project, and supporting them to resolve any tensions or conflicts over competing work priorities with their line managers.

Involve your project sponsor or relevant senior managers in resolving major disagreements about priorities with line managers only after you try to resolve these problems yourself.

Tackling 'out of sight, out of mind'

Your team members, when normally 'out of sight' of you and each other because they're dispersed over tens, hundreds or even thousands of miles, may sometimes feel that they're also out of your mind; they may think that you don't give them enough attention!

The type and amount of attention that you give to virtual team members is crucial to building and sustaining effective working relationships. Give just as much attention to showing team members that you're genuinely interested in them as individuals as you do in how they're getting on with their work.

Establish, right from the start of your virtual team, a culture of everyone having a genuine interest in each and all team members by:

✔ Inviting each person to talk about themselves: their work, personal background, what's important to them, their hopes and concerns about working in the team and so on. Carry out this activity via a video conference if your team can't meet together. Take the lead by talking about your aspirations for the team and yourself first.

✔ Encouraging individuals to connect and network with each other directly instead of insisting that contact with each other has to be via you. Facilitate good communication rather than becoming a 'bottleneck'!

✔ Taking the lead in maintaining regular contact with each team member; put dates and times into your diary system and stick to them to demonstrate that you're reliable and to set a good example.

✔ Encouraging team members to talk about the expectations they have of each other and how well those expectations are being met; including recognising how team members are helping each other and explaining any consequences of expectations not being met on each other. (Refer to the later section 'Working across different cultures' because cultural differences may affect how open and honest team members are with each other.)

✔ Surprising team members by contacting them spontaneously to enquire about how they are, instead of contacting them only when you want to talk about their work.

Appreciating differences in language

If you assume that all people attach the same meanings to the same words because they're using the English language, you do so at your peril! People from different countries may interpret words differently – even words with apparently clear meanings.

Never, not ever?

A consultant was facilitating a management group consisting of managers from countries including England and Brazil. To demonstrate that managers had to be careful to avoid unintended misunderstandings between them, he enquired how many times an employee would be late if he was never late. The English managers in the group all replied 'zero', but the Brazilian managers replied 'three or four times'. Apparently, 'never' doesn't always mean 'not ever'!

When working with people for whom English is a second language:

✔ Take care to speak clearly, concisely and more slowly than normal, using simple language where necessary.

✔ Check whether everyone has the same understanding of the meaning of language being used, especially when making important decisions and agreeing actions to be taken.

✔ Encourage team members to express their views, opinions and interpretation of discussions. Listen attentively to understand the meanings being expressed.

✔ Allow team members for whom English is their second language more time to express themselves, and avoid interrupting and completing sentences for team members even if your intention is to help them articulate their views.

✔ Don't accept the use of words and phrases with vague meanings, such as 'possibly', 'maybe', 'hopefully', 'I'll try' and so on, especially when you:

   • Must have team members' commitment to taking action.

   • Can't check individual commitment by being able to see and 'read' nonverbal cues.

Working across different cultures

In my experience, people from different cultures can have significantly different ways of working from each other. These variations can cause differing expectations among virtual team members as regards how members should work together. Some of the contrasting natural or normal ways of working, and therefore expectations, of managers from different countries in virtual teams include:

✔ Being direct and frank in expressing views and opinions.

✔ Avoiding disagreeing 'in public', and being reticent to give 'bad news' about the standard or progress of tasks.

✔ Pushing to get work completed with a strong sense of urgency.

✔ Intending to achieve, rather than really committing to, deadlines.

✔ Highly valuing relationships.

✔ Highly valuing effectiveness and efficiency.

Here are a few ways to acknowledge and work to minimise the negative effects of differences in culture:

✔ Invest time in finding out about the national cultures of members of your team (perhaps via the Internet), and use the relevant information you obtain in conversations with each team member to clarify and confirm their personal preferred ways of working.

✔ Compare and contrast the similarities and differences in how team members prefer to work. If the differences are significant, make 'expectations and preferred ways of working' an agenda item of your initial video or teleconference, to enable team members to appreciate the differences and how they may affect how team members work together. (In Chapter 15, you can read more about agreeing a shared set of values and associated behaviours in order to establish and maintain effective teamwork.)

✔ Do a cost-benefit business justification for team members to meet each other in person and accelerate building relationships if you think that the benefits will outweigh the costs. If you gain approval for your team to meet, involve team members in establishing the objectives, structure and content of the meeting to ensure that you optimise the use of the time you spend together.

Accommodating larks and owls

If members of your virtual team live in countries that span different time zones, you may have problems finding mutually convenient times for video conferences and/or teleconferences. Some team members may literally be about to get into bed as others are about to get out of bed!

Even when the differences in time zones aren't this great, you may have to take account of team members being tired as they approach the end of their work day while others are much fresher because they've recently started work.

Strive to be fair when organising video conferences and teleconferences between team members spread across different time zones, by organising these at times to minimise difficulties for all team members. If avoiding difficulties regarding timings is impossible for some of your team, vary the times of conferences to ensure that the same team members aren't always inconvenienced.

Ending Your Virtual Team

When the work of a widespread, temporary, virtual team is complete, make sure that you don't allow the group simply to dissolve. Acknowledging the work of the team and recognising that disbanding it enables members, especially those who strongly identified with the team and its work, to cope more effectively with the dissolution of the team.

Hold a video conference to celebrate the ending of your virtual project team:

- ✔ Thank your team collectively and individually for their contributions and achievements. Surprise members by organising for food to be provided at each location to symbolise sharing in a celebratory 'meal'.

- ✔ Encourage each member to state how he has benefitted from being part of the team in terms of enhanced knowledge, skills and so on.

- ✔ Share and assimilate learning to enable people who are likely to be members of future virtual teams to work together effectively with their (new) colleagues in the future.

- ✔ Reinforce the contacts and relationships that have been built, and encourage team members to continue to network with each other.

Chapter 18

Leading Your Senior Management Team

· ·

In This Chapter

▶ Building collective responsibility

▶ Coping with increasing pressure and complexity

▶ Developing a senior management team to be proud of

▶ Creating time for your strategic priorities

· ·

*Y*ou probably think that when you've made it to the top and are leading your organisation's senior management team, many of the earlier problems you experienced in leading teams are behind you. Surely, you can now expect your team to be highly committed and competent team players. After all, they have loads of experience of participating in and leading their own teams, and must have learnt from their experiences.

In fact, leading a top team can be more demanding and challenging than leading other types of team, as you discover in this chapter. You explore a range of challenges that you may experience, and find out how to build a high-performing team of responsible senior managers by using and enhancing their talents.

Developing a Collective Sense of Responsibility

This section takes a look at two common problems that you can come up against when leading a senior management team:

✔ Managers becoming too dependent on you when you exert too much control.

✔ Managers developing too narrow a viewpoint at the expense of the organisation as a whole.

Breaking the dependency cycle

Most Managing Directors (MD) and Chief Executives are, in my experience, focused on results. They expect their senior managers to achieve high results and act with a sense of urgency. Such expectations – and how an MD typically behaves as a consequence – can create a *dependency cycle* as follows:

1. The MD is impatient to see results and perceives that things are moving too slowly.

2. She therefore leaps in and instructs senior managers what to do.

3. The managers infer that the MD wants total control and so begin to wait for the intervention each time. They become dependent on the MD to make decisions.

4. The MD's frustrations grow at the lack of senior managerial input; she jumps in even earlier and the managers back off even more.

5. The dependency cycle continues.

Avoiding the dependency cycle

John was Managing Director of a large manufacturing company. When I started working with him and his senior management team, I realised quickly that John was highly results driven. For example, he expected management meetings to be productive: managers were expected to quickly get to the bottom of problems, make decisions, agree actions and deadlines for taking them, and (subsequently) hold each other accountable for taking action.

John became frustrated with what he saw as the managers' slow progress in management meetings. So he stepped in, made decisions and told managers what he wanted them to do. Managers interpreted that he wanted to make all the main decisions, and so they let John take over the meetings.

John's increasing frustration at the 'inertia' among his managers caused him to step in sooner, which caused them to wait for him to do so. Hence, the dependency cycle was established as John's managers became more dependent on him for making decisions.

I coached John to manage his frustrations and actively engage his managers in collective decision-making, while simultaneously coaching managers to encourage them and build their confidence to contribute more to meetings to break the cycle.

Constantly taking control of situations and telling people what you want them to do encourages them to stop thinking for themselves and wait, or ask, for direction: even for instructions! Just like John in the sidebar 'Avoiding the Dependency Cycle', you have to be aware that your behaviour may have unintended consequences in that you can contribute to creating what you consider to be unacceptable behaviour in others.

Effectively changing the behaviour of your managers may well need to start with you managing changes in your own behaviour. Before you can change any aspect of your behaviour regarding, for example, how you interact with your managers, you have to:

- ✔ Become aware of the behaviour.

- ✔ Recognise the effects and consequences of that behaviour on others.

- ✔ Accept that your behaviour isn't having the desired effect on your colleagues.

- ✔ Want to change your behaviour.

Continually work on developing members of your management team to contribute fully to making decisions by:

- ✔ Being aware of your behaviour and its potential effects on your managers. (Dip into Chapter 4 to find out more about how to become more aware of your behaviour and how it affects others.)

- ✔ Encouraging each of your managers to give you honest feedback about how your behaviour affects them.

- ✔ Developing and modelling the behaviour you expect from others. (You can find more about being a great role model in Chapter 11.)

- ✔ Creating space for and encouraging your managers to express themselves by not dominating or smothering them in management meetings.

Helping managers out of their silos

You've probably noticed grain silos – tall, narrow, bullet-shaped structures – in the countryside, but what are *management silos*? Well, these silos exist when managers become totally focused on their department and achieving their department objectives and targets: they develop a narrow focus – hence the notion of silos – instead of taking a broad, whole-business perspective.

As I describe in Chapter 14, 'what gets measured, gets done'! This notion is often a significant factor in creating management silos, especially because many businesses and other organisations have invested a lot of time and effort in developing *key performance indicators* (KPIs) to measure how well departments and the overall business is performing.

Robustly holding managers accountable for achieving their KPIs can have the unintended consequence of creating management silos in which your managers work independently, rather than interdependently, and rely on you to resolve issues and problems between departments.

The following actions can help managers to escape from their silos:

- ✔ Checking that the KPIs that the company is using are complementary and reinforcing the success of the whole business/organisation. Identify any departmental KPIs that may cause tensions between departments/ managers. One example is achieving sales targets and effective production efficiency in a manufacturing business: the sales department may accept orders that have to be delivered by a certain deadline to hit their sales KPIs, which causes problems for production because their schedules have to be changed in ways that lower production efficiency.

- ✔ Facilitating dialogue between managers to examine how well departments are achieving KPIs, and exploring any negative effects of any manager's actions to achieve their KPIs on other managers.

- ✔ Encouraging managers to take collective responsibility for the success of the whole organisation as well as the success of their department.

Encouraging Courageous Conversations

The work of senior management teams is, in my experience, becoming more demanding, complex and difficult, especially with regard to anticipating potential issues, understanding and solving problems, and making the right decisions. Most management teams have to wrestle with, at least some of, the following challenges:

- ✔ Customers are becoming more demanding, often wanting 'more for less'!

- ✔ Competition is increasing as businesses compete with global rather than local competitors.

- ✔ Advances in information technology are creating expectations of immediate access to people, fast responses to messages and so on.

- ✔ Organisations are becoming more complex to manage due to the increasing use of matrix structures, project and virtual teams and the advance of globalisation.

The cumulative effect of these changes may be that you and your managers experience increasing pressure to achieve results and improve performance. This pressure can result in individual managers becoming too narrowly focused and may fragment teamwork if managers become critical of other departments or colleagues who (they think) are behaving in ways that are adversely affecting the operation or performance of their own department.

An important part of your role as the most senior manager is to encourage and help your managers to engage each other effectively and build teamwork, especially when your team comprises strong characters who may hold significantly different views and opinions. Therefore, effective communication on the part of all managers is vital.

Keeping your managers' heads up

Encouraging your managers to have courageous conversations doesn't mean that they're allowed to have arguments and go into battle with each other! It does mean encouraging them to say what needs to be said to address challenges and get to the bottom of, and solve, problems. A critical factor that affects whether managers express their views is whether they fear they're going to get their head chopped off!

You – and anyone in your management team – chop colleagues' heads off when you:

- ✔ Reject their view or opinion outright without an explanation.
- ✔ Ridicule their view or opinion.
- ✔ Embarrass them in public by saying things such as, 'You should have known better.'

Encourage your managers to have courageous conversations in which they:

- ✔ Speak their mind.
- ✔ Listen attentively to each other.
- ✔ Question and challenge each others' thinking with the intention of enhancing collective understanding and making better decisions.
- ✔ Don't cut each other off when they're speaking.
- ✔ Stop intentionally ridiculing or embarrassing their colleagues.

The next section 'Critiquing each other's thoughts and ideas' contains more on challenging others' thinking. (Also, check out Chapter 8 for ways to engage colleagues effectively in meaningful conversations.)

Critiquing each other's thoughts and ideas

Have you noticed how you sometimes become attached to your thoughts? If so, you've probably felt that someone was criticising you when they questioned or challenged your idea, view, suggestion or proposal.

As senior management problems become more complex, so problem-solving becomes more complex. I suggest that the possibility of one manager knowing the best solution to a complex problem is highly unlikely. The best solution is much more likely to evolve out of a dialogue between managers, in which they enhance each others' understanding and come to a shared understanding of the problem; and, in doing so, establish a common commitment to take action.

Critiquing your colleagues' thoughts is an important aspect of enhancing understanding because:

- ✔ The validity of the individual's thought or view is tested.

- ✔ Any assumptions on which the thought or view is based can be revealed and their validity tested.

- ✔ Managers may be prompted to expand on, and even clarify, their own views as well as contribute to other people's thinking.

Help your managers to realise and accept that they're not their thoughts! By accepting this notion, your managers are more likely to:

- ✔ Keep an open mind to enable the best solution to evolve.

- ✔ Be willing to critique each other's thinking.

- ✔ Be receptive to having their colleagues question and critique their ideas, views and opinions.

Being strong by being vulnerable

Many managers that I've met seem to think that being strong means strongly articulating their views, projecting themselves in ways that have a big impact and influence on their colleagues. Such management behaviour can be perceived to be domineering by some, perhaps more introverted, managers who may find it difficult to question or challenge the views of their more outspoken colleagues.

A manager may be having an unhealthy influence on decision-making in your management team if colleagues have difficulty questioning and challenging that person's views.

Let me have it!

Neville, a Managing Director of a large engineering company, is a strong character who has a big influence on his management team. When I started working with Neville and his management team, I soon discovered that at times Neville dominated his managers.

As part of our work on improving the performance of the senior management team and the company, Neville and his team clarified the values that were important to how they worked as a team, and the associated behaviours that they expected of each other. Neville and his managers agreed to use the values and behaviours as criteria to assess informally how they were contributing to meetings, and provide feedback to each other at the end of certain meetings on how individual managers had reinforced or undermined the values through how they behaved in the meeting.

Neville noticed that managers were providing useful feedback to each other, but some seemed reluctant to give him feedback that was critical of his behaviour. He encouraged everyone to critique his behaviour by naming managers who were giving him useful feedback, even if it was in private, providing examples of the feedback, and how he valued their honesty. He explained that he was experiencing difficulty in changing aspects of his behaviour that were the habits of a lifetime, and he encouraged all his managers to continue giving him feedback about how his behaviour was reinforcing and/or undermining the team's values.

Neville still has a big influence on his team, but he now engages and empowers managers to make a greater contribution to the team.

Take the lead in encouraging everyone in your management team to question and challenge each other's thinking and/or unacceptable behaviour:

✔ Set an example through asking searching questions of your managers to clarify their thinking and express their views clearly and concisely. (Read Chapter 9 to discover how to develop your ability to ask searching questions.)

✔ Invite and encourage your managers to point out to you any aspect of your behaviour that discourages them from expressing their views and/or questioning your views. (Dip into Chapter 9 to discover how to invite your managers to challenge you, and how to cope with embarrassment.) Read the sidebar 'Let me have it!' to find out how one Managing Director encouraged his managers to challenge his unacceptable behaviour.

✔ Constructively challenge any manager whose behaviour is adversely affecting colleagues contributing to decision-making.

Sharing Accountability for Success

As head of your organisation you may sense that your managers think that the 'buck stops with you' because you're ultimately responsible and accountable for everything. The potential problem for you with this mindset is that they look to you to sort out most, if not all, things regarding the performance of your management team, instead of sharing accountability with you for how well team members work together.

One way to see whether your managers hold this unhelpful view is to test whether they share accountability with you for ensuring that management meetings are effective.

Reflect on how your managers typically act in meetings and tick one of the boxes for each of the statements listed in Table 18-1.

Table 18-1	Testing Your Managers' Accountability in Meetings			
		Never	*Rarely*	*Often*	*Always*
1.	Managers promptly point out when time is being wasted by people going off on a tangent, into too much detail and so on.				
2.	Managers promptly and constructively challenge any colleague whose behaviour is inappropriate.				
3.	Managers look to me to ensure that each meeting is productive.				
4.	Managers look to me to ensure that people work well together.				

If you ticked one of the first two columns in rows 1 and 2, and one of the last two columns in rows 3 and 4, your managers probably don't share accountability for the success of their management meetings with you. Think about any implications of your rating: if your managers don't share accountability for the effectiveness of their management meetings, what do they share accountability for?

The next three sections show you how to encourage and establish shared accountability among your managers.

Stopping the blame game

One of the most damaging things you and your managers can do is to kill a sense of shared accountability by blaming a colleague, regardless of whether that person caused the problem or not. In my experience, some managers are overly critical of colleagues in a negative, even derogatory, way; as if deliberately trying to embarrass the colleague or show the person in a 'bad light'. The intentions behind such behaviour aren't positive or constructive if the manager is:

- ✔ Projecting blame onto a colleague to keep themselves out of the spotlight when the cause of the problem is unclear.
- ✔ Promoting themselves at the expense of their colleague.
- ✔ Undermining their colleague's self-confidence or self-esteem.

Far better is to promote positive attitudes and behaviour in your team as follows:

- ✔ Promote the behaviour that you and managers expect of each other by agreeing the team's values, and associated behaviours. (You can discover how to involve team members in clarifying and agreeing team values and behaviours in Chapter 15.)
- ✔ Encourage managers to give feedback to each other at the end of team meetings on how well they're upholding the agreed values and behaviours.
- ✔ Explain the consequences of unacceptable behaviour on the performance of the team.
- ✔ Describe to a manager who behaves in an unacceptable way how you feel about her behaviour, and also describe the changes that you expect the manager to make.

Creating a healthy environment

You may be wondering what a healthy (senior management) team environment is or looks like! Such an environment is one in which:

- ✔ All managers are actively taking and sharing accountability for the success of the team and how it's performing.

✔ A real 'buzz' is present: a sense of high positive energy. (Dip into Chapter 15 to discover how to create a high-performance atmosphere.)

✔ Everyone is totally engaged, and engaging each other, in striving to achieve and improve performance.

✔ A strong sense of camaraderie is evident based on trust and mutual respect, and managers have a genuine interest in each other. (Drop into Chapter 9 to find more on having a genuine interest in others.)

✔ Occasional tension exists between team members because sharing different perspectives, views and preferences is seen as natural, and expressing and challenging differences is used constructively to improve understanding of problems and issues, and make better decisions.

✔ Managers are learning from and with each other, and developing their skills and abilities together.

Strive to establish and sustain a healthy environment in which everyone is collectively responsible and sharing accountability for optimising team performance by behaving as follows:

✔ Be enthusiastic and positive about:

- Your team's purpose; its *raison d'être*.

- The objectives and targets you want your team to achieve.

- Your vision for the organisation. (Refer to Chapter 7 to find out how to develop a sense of purpose and create your own vision.)

✔ Set high standards of behaviour and performance, and encourage your managers to meet them.

✔ Coach your managers to become skilled in engaging each other. (Find out how to become an engaging leader in Chapter 9, and discover more about coaching in Chapter 11.)

✔ Conduct team self-assessments to identify and build on your team's strengths, and involve all your team in continually improving its performance. (Flip to Chapter 15 to discover how to conduct team assessments.)

✔ Consider the value of using a highly skilled independent coach and facilitator to support you to accelerate establishing shared accountability within your team. If you're wondering what to look for in a good independent coach/facilitator and how to select one, I suggest that the person:

- Displays integrity, self-confidence and humility.

- Is skilled in quickly building trust and respect with and between all managers.

- Fully engages everyone in the team in working on improving how the team works.

- Constructively challenges and supports individuals and the whole team to be the best they can be.

- Demonstrates high personal and ethical standards.

✔ Ask a coach/facilitator for:

- Examples of how she has worked with senior management teams.

- Challenges she has faced in working with senior management teams and how she overcame them.

- References for you to contact to discuss how she works with teams and the value of her work.

Embedding the behaviours you cherish

Your senior management team should be a microcosm of the organisation you aspire to create because:

✔ Your senior management team (or, better still, your senior leadership team) is a role model for the rest of your organisation. (Chapter 11 describes how to become a great role model.)

✔ Leading a change in attitudes and behaviour – a change in culture – within your organisation starts at the top.

Old habits die hard! Managers can easily slip back into old behaviours and ways of working if you don't continually promote and reinforce the attitudes and behaviours you cherish until those attitudes and behaviours become the norm.

Here's how to embed those desired attitudes and behaviours:

✔ Be the person that you want others to become; promote through your own actions the attitude and behaviours that you expect from others.

✔ Catch your managers demonstrating the right attitudes and behaviours. Look for, recognise and praise 'in public' individuals who are demonstrating the right behaviour; noticing and talking only about what managers are doing wrong is all too easy!

✔ Tell stories of great examples of managers demonstrating the behaviours you cherish, and how those managers have contributed to the success of your organisation. (Find out about the power of story-telling in Chapter 14.)

✔ Promote managers who demonstrate the right attitudes and behaviours to reinforce to everyone that people who think and act in these ways are more likely to be promoted.

Preparing Others for Leadership

You need leaders throughout your organisation because employees' immediate line manager exerts the biggest influence on the extent to which employees are engaged in their work and committed to doing their job to the best of their ability. Some organisations adopt a structured approach to developing leaders that may include:

✔ Assessing individual competence against clearly defined leadership competences within appraisal or performance and development reviews, and planning how to develop leaders' competences.

✔ Having succession plans for key leadership positions within the organisation, and using career development to develop individuals to be ready to step into those positions.

✔ Coaching leaders to improve their performance within their current role and/or to head up business improvement projects.

✔ Secondments into a range of leadership positions in the organisation to enable individuals to:

• Develop their leadership skills through being exposed to different challenges and problems.

• Acquire knowledge and a good understanding of the organisation/ business and how it functions.

Put 'leadership' onto the agenda of your key management meetings and ensure that you and your senior management team regularly discuss the quality of leadership in your organisation and how to develop great leaders.

Spotting potential high flyers

You can adopt a structured approach to spotting and developing potential high flyers by using some of or all the methods described in the preceding section. Another approach is to get around your organisation and notice the potential high flyers doing great work. You can discover a lot about your organisation as well as your people by coming out from behind your desk and informally talking to people in their workplace. Ask people about their:

✔ Hopes and aspirations for the organisation and themselves.

✔ Frustrations and concerns about what is or isn't happening in the workplace.

✔ Ideas and suggestions about how to improve any aspect of the operation or functioning of the organisation.

Spot potential high flyers by:

✔ Wandering around your organisation and chatting to your people to get to know them and your organisation better.

✔ Being clear about the attributes, characteristics and/or competences that you're looking for in a leader so that you're better able to spot them. You may be looking for individuals who:

- Are 'standard-bearers' by promoting and achieving particularly high standards in their work area.

- Have a track record of achieving very high levels of performance.

- Are constructively critical of sub-standard work and service wherever it occurs or is produced, and take the initiative to try to influence the relevant people to take action to improve performance.

✔ Talking to employees about whether they want to be involved in making improvements that they'd like to see in the organisation. Would you see leadership potential in someone who's critical about an aspect of how the organisation's working, but doesn't want to get involved in making improvements? I wouldn't!

Working yourself out of a job

Do you – like too many MDs and other senior managers – do work that you shouldn't be doing? Do you make decisions that your managers can be making? If you plead 'guilty as charged' to these questions, be aware that managers may be working at levels below what they're being paid for throughout your organisation, because such behaviour tends to cascade down and through each management level.

You may think that I'm crazy for saying this, but I suggest that you work yourself out of your job rather than do the work of managers that report to you.

When you're doing most of the thinking and telling your managers what you want them to do, you're conditioning your managers to follow instructions: this behaviour contributes to creating the dependency that I describe in the earlier section 'Breaking the Dependency Cycle'. Engaging your managers fully in making decisions encourages them to think and learn, individually and collectively, how to solve complex and difficult problems so that they can eventually make such decisions themselves without involving you. Some individuals may eventually demonstrate that they're capable of stepping into your shoes!

Work yourself out of your job as follows:

- ✔ Hold yourself back from stepping down and making decisions for your managers. (Dip into the section 'Breaking the Dependency Cycle' earlier in this chapter for tips on how to avoid taking control.)

- ✔ Describe and show your commitment to developing your management team – and your organisation – to achieve results now and build capability to sustain success in the future.

- ✔ Encourage your managers to be collectively responsible and share accountability for the performance of your team and the results you expect them to achieve. (You can find out how to encourage your managers to share accountability in the earlier section 'Sharing Accountability for Success'.)

- ✔ Delegate tasks to your managers as they become more competent in order to free you up to concentrate on your strategic priorities.

Part VI
The Part of Tens

"It's just one meeting after another."

In this part . . .

These short chapters are packed with tips on good leadership practice. You can find inspiration here on how to take the lead, lead yourself and lead others.

Chapter 19

Ten Tips on Taking the Lead

Boundless opportunities are available for you to take the lead in all sorts of situations, if you're willing to step forward and have a positive influence and impact on the people who work for and with you. This chapter contains ten tips to help you step up and lead in ways to ensure that people accept you taking the initiative.

Making Leadership Common Sense Your Common Practice

Leadership can be challenging because you have to consider so many things when leading people in a work environment including the following:

- The business's needs.
- People's different and varying needs and expectations.
- Demands on you to deliver results.
- Your boss's, your own and work colleagues' priorities.

You may have difficulty reconciling all the different expectations that people have of you, including your own expectation of yourself.

I encourage you to use your common sense and do what you think is right in every situation, especially when you feel that you're in a dilemma. Yes, you have to be able to justify your decisions to others, but you also have to justify your decisions to yourself: you have to live with your decisions. You can't please all the people all the time and, fortunately for you and all leaders, leading people isn't a popularity contest!

All anyone, including yourself, can ask of you in any situation is to act with integrity and make the best decision you can with the information you have by using your common sense.

Believing that Everyone Wants to Make a Difference

At times you may question, and even doubt, the intentions, actions and behaviour of some people you work with, but nobody strives to be a fool. I propose that everyone wants to contribute and make a positive difference to the organisation they work for, because making a valued contribution gives people job satisfaction and a sense of fulfilment.

Encourage and help people to make important contributions to achieving the goals and objectives of your organisation by explaining why their work is important and what you expect of them. Get to know 'your' people well and find out 'what makes them tick' – for example, their hopes, needs and aspirations – and help them to fulfil their needs and use their talents in making that valuable contribution . . . and remember to thank them for doing so!

Rising to Every (Leadership) Occasion

Rise to your first formal leadership occasion – your first management position – and every promotion thereafter by setting high standards and having high expectations of yourself and everyone you work with, and challenge and support each person to meet your standards. After all, who aspires to be average?

You have many more opportunities to rise to occasions requiring leadership than only your formal leadership position: all you have to do is note them and give yourself permission to step forward and take the lead. For example, notice opportunities such as when colleagues are gossiping about the lack of leadership, when the standard of someone's work or behaviour is below par and when time is being wasted.

Every opportunity that you take enables you to practise and polish your leadership skills. Make people aware that your intention is to act in everyone's interest so that they don't perceive you to be promoting your own interests. Chapter 1 provides more details on rising to leadership occasions.

Building Up, Not Putting Down

Have you noticed that people – including managers – generally tend to notice and talk more about problems than about successes? I think that spotting problems and being critical of people is a national pastime for us Brits! You can test this notion for yourself by noticing the number of times your manager and other work colleagues initiate conversations with you about what's going wrong as against the number of times they do about what's going right.

If you mainly contact people about problems with their work, you can't be surprised to hear that they see you as critical (of them). Regularly criticising people's work lowers their self-esteem and damages their confidence.

Make sure that you often catch people doing things right, so that you build them up by recognising and praising their good work . . . while also constructively critiquing sub-standard work.

Listening Before You Leap

You're no doubt familiar with the phrase 'fools rush in'. Be aware that you can act in too much haste when you're under pressure to solve a problem that (you think) has been caused by a colleague doing a job wrong, especially when you're up against a tight deadline.

If you're not careful, you can end up making a problem worse because you act before you've obtained, and fully understand, all the relevant information. Remember that you may wrongly or overly criticise a person who you believe has done their job wrong if you take this approach.

Although you use your ears for hearing, you use your mind for listening. To really listen to what someone's saying, you have to focus your close attention on that person. Talk and listen attentively to a person who you think has caused a problem by doing their job wrong especially whenever you feel under pressure to act. (Chapter 8 guides you in how to switch on your senses.)

'Working With' People Rather Than 'Doing To' People

Many leaders take the responsibility off the people who work for them in one of two ways: they're control freaks or too helpful. I describe their behaviour as 'doing to rather than working with' people as follows:

- ✔ Control freaks keep a close eye on what people are doing and refuse to delegate because they like to ensure that everything is correct: they trust only themselves!

- ✔ Overly helpful leaders tend to give detailed instructions about how to do a task, take problems off people and solve dilemmas for them.

Both groups often don't realise the unintended consequences of their behaviour, because being overly controlling or overly helpful causes problems. People can't develop their skills and confidence when you don't give them responsibility, don't trust them to do a job or don't allow them to think for themselves.

Encourage and enable people to learn to think for themselves when you're working with them, not least because your own job becomes easier when everyone who works for you is confident and competent in their job. (You find out how to really engage people in Chapter 9.)

Being Uncomfortably Comfortable

Taking the lead often requires you to get out of your comfort zone because you have to deal with situations, problems and dilemmas that you've never encountered before, and you're probably unsure about how to deal with them. Straying out of your comfort zone is risky because you expose yourself to potential failure and embarrassment if things don't go as well as you hope.

Develop a mentality of being 'uncomfortably comfortable' and enhance your self-confidence, so that you're okay operating outside of your comfort zone and promptly tackle problems and dilemmas. See problems as opportunities for you to test out your leadership skills, and learn from your successes and failures. Chapter 4 contains information on developing your self-confidence and Chapter 6 covers expanding your comfort zone.

Speaking Up and Speaking Out!

An old Geordie saying says: 'Shy bairns get nowt!'. It literally means 'shy children get nothing', but is used to emphasise that people should speak up for themselves. I think that this saying applies to leaders.

Managers of virtually every team I've worked with have told me that they want their colleagues to speak openly and honestly in team meetings: they expect their colleagues to speak up and express their views and opinions. Speaking openly and honestly in management meetings is, however, in my experience easier said than done!

I'm not suggesting that managers are being dishonest with their colleagues; they may just be holding back from saying things that they or colleagues may find embarrassing, such as speaking up about a colleague who's behaving disrespectfully by interrupting or not listening to his peers. A management team can't improve its performance if managers are unwilling to raise issues that are affecting how they work together.

Take the lead by speaking up and expressing your views honestly and openly in your management meetings. (Turn to Chapter 8 for more information on speaking up.)

Expanding Your Sphere of Influence

Wouldn't your job be easier if you had total control over every aspect of your work! I doubt that you can achieve this desire but you can increase your influence with work colleagues who affect how well you're able to do your job. You may have to start with influencing how you think, however, before you're able to increase your influence over others.

Start to increase your influence by challenging your views about how much control you have over the people and other factors that affect your ability to do your job well: you probably have more influence than you think.

Identify the people with the biggest impact on your performance and invest time in working more closely with them to encourage and persuade them to do what you need them to do when you need it doing. (Chapter 7 provides guidance on increasing your sphere of influence.)

Keeping Your Head When Everyone Is Losing Theirs

People tend to react to a crisis in one of three unhelpful ways: by jumping in and trying to solve the problem; running away from it; or freezing.

Jumping in is risky because you may not think enough about the action you're about to take. Running away from problems rarely solves them, and you just can't think clearly when you freeze.

Stay calm when faced with a crisis and follow the advice in Chapter 12, including the diver's motto: stop, think and breathe.

Chapter 20

Ten Tips for Leading Yourself

*Y*ou may sometimes catch yourself asking, 'How do I get [this person] to change?'. Notice that your focus is on the other person rather than on you. Many leaders make the mistake of overlooking the fact that they can contribute to causing the problems they experience when leading people. You find ten tips in this chapter to help you to work on leading yourself so that you can lead others more effectively.

Leading Yourself First

You may be asking 'why do I need to think about leading myself when leadership is about leading other people?'. The reason is because you have a big impact on the people who work for and with you!

Knowing your motives and values, being aware of how you feel – your emotional state – at any time, and having a good understanding of how these things affect the way you think and act enables you to appreciate how your emotional state and behaviour can impact on colleagues. (Chapter 4 contains useful info on increasing self-knowledge through self-questioning, and obtaining feedback from people about how your behaviour is affecting them.)

Good self-knowledge and personal insight enables you to consider and choose the best approaches to working with people, approaches that have the desired effect on people and achieve your objectives.

Being Authentic

I believe that leaders have to live with themselves before they can live with anyone else. Leaders must to be true to their core values and beliefs.

Perhaps you've experienced at least one occasion when you were in a dilemma and uncertain about what to do: you made a decision only to find that you had doubts about whether it was right or not; or perhaps you even experienced those doubts gnawing away at your conscience. I suspect that these feelings indicate that the decision you made didn't fit with your values.

Be authentic and act in accord with your core values. Your colleagues appreciate when you do so and act with integrity, even if they don't always agree with your decisions. (Chapter 4 contains more on being an authentic leader.)

Looking Out! You're Always Being Watched

A lot of research has been done over the last few years into employee engagement in an attempt to improve company performance through increasing employees' commitment to their company. Two conclusions in particular are valuable for leaders:

- ✔ Line managers have the greatest impact upon the extent to which employees are committed to doing their job well.
- ✔ People take in more information through their sight than their hearing: they tend to believe what they see more than what they hear.

The people who report to you are hugely influenced by your physical behaviour. Be aware that they're watching you and are sure to notice if you have any 'double standards'. If you state verbally that a particular standard is important but then act physically in ways that undermine that same standard, employees are likely to take onboard the behaviour and not the words!

Avoiding Being a Busy Fool

Almost without exception, every manager I've worked with says that they're very busy; probably the majority also say that they're overworked! Being busy and highly productive is admirable, but being busy and misusing or wasting time because you're not spending the right time on the right priorities to be successful is not.

Spending enough time on the right priorities requires you to prioritise effectively. Your team expect you to know and share your priorities with them: they probably also expect you to give them a sense of purpose and clear direction.

Use some of your time to become absolutely clear about your own and your team's purpose, and the objectives required to optimise your contribution to the organisation's success. Share this purpose with your staff and anyone else who may benefit from being clear about your team's role. (Chapter 7 contains advice on clarifying and achieving your priorities.)

Knowing Where to Draw the Line

One problem that you may experience is ensuring that your staff and other work colleagues always meet and maintain your standards. You may even come to think that some people deliberately set out to test your boundaries: to see how far you'll let things go before you step in and 'pull them up' for not doing a good enough job – and you're probably right!

Do remember, however, that on certain occasions a colleague may well have a good reason for not doing a job to the standard you expect or completing a task on time.

Deal with each situation on its merits and be willing to make an allowance on those occasions when you think that justifiable reasons exist for doing so; but always promote and reinforce to the relevant people that maintaining your expected standards is vital.

Be clear at all times about the standards you expect from work colleagues regarding performance, quality, hitting deadlines, timekeeping and behaviour. Such clarity enables you to make decisions about where and when to draw the line, and take prompt action.

Raising Your Hand High

Have you ever sat in a project or progress review meeting when a question was asked about who caused a particular problem, and everyone looked around at each other? No one owned up to causing the problem! A lot of time can be wasted in a company searching for the cause of a problem when someone knows who caused it but doesn't raise a hand, perhaps because that person's concerned or afraid of being punished.

Hold yourself accountable and 'raise your hand high' to take responsibility for any problems you cause. In this way, you demonstrate your integrity and gain credibility with those around you as well as save time. (Chapter 18 contains a section on establishing accountability in your team.)

Being a Healthy (Self) Critic

One of the most powerful ways of becoming a better leader is to learn from your experiences. Make a point of noticing when you do something really well as a leader and store the lesson away for future use. Similarly, remember when you make a bad mistake and resolve not to do it again. Developing your leadership abilities through trial and error is a long, slow and potentially painful process.

You can accelerate the improvement of your leadership skills by optimising the way you learn from your experiences. Check out Chapter 3 for how to adopt a healthy approach to being self-critical and Chapter 4 for more on taking lessons from your experiences.

One simple way to speed up becoming the leader you aspire to be is to spend a little time every day reflecting on what you did well and what you could have done better during that day.

Talking Yourself Up

At times you may question your ability to lead people, perhaps during a particularly challenging period when certain colleagues are being difficult or a few jobs have gone wrong. You may doubt yourself especially when your boss isn't encouraging or supportive.

During such periods, encourage yourself by 'talking yourself up': positively affirm that you can and will succeed as a leader. You may want to find a private place to do this if speaking your affirmations out loud, but you can also say these affirmations 'in your mind'. (Chapter 4 has more on handling self-doubt.)

Also bring to mind times when you did a great job and had a positive influence on your work colleagues.

Modelling Yourself

Two aspects exist to modelling when you're striving to improve as a leader:

- ✔ **Looking for a role model.** Identify leaders whom you admire, notice what they do that attracts you to them and then work on adding this person's approach, style, skill, attribute and so on to your 'wardrobe'. You may, of course, have to practise developing the skill rather than expecting simply to copy it. (Chapter 2 contains an exercise to help you identify leaders you admire.)

- ✔ **Becoming a role model.** When you've developed a 'wardrobe', you're in a position to 'strut your stuff'. I don't mean strutting about like a peacock, full of your own self-importance or pride in how good you look. Remember, pride comes before a fall! I mean promoting the standards you expect from others and providing an appropriate model by demonstrating the right behaviour. (Find more on being a great role model in Chapter 11.)

Avoiding the Lonely Hearts Club

You may find that some of your friends ditch you when you step up to your first leadership position, because you've 'crossed over' into management and joined a club to which they don't belong. (Chapter 6 has more on how to be a successful leader and keep your friends.)

You may also feel lonely because you don't have anyone to discuss your problems and dilemmas with confidentially. Find someone who you respect and trust (inside or outside your organisation) to act as a 'sounding board'. In this way you can test out your thinking and proposed decisions, and receive advice. (Chapter 4 contains details on finding your own coach.)

Chapter 21

Ten Tips for Engaging People

*L*eaders lead: followers choose to follow (or choose not to)! As a leader, you need to gain the commitment of your staff. This chapter contains tips on how to engage people so that they want to work with and for you, and do their jobs to the best of their ability.

Earning People's Respect

When some managers are promoted, power goes to their head: they seem to elevate themselves to a lofty position, look down on their work colleagues and tell them what to do. This behaviour tends to upset people who in turn lose respect for their manager.

People choose to follow great leaders because they want to, not because they've been told to. You know that you're becoming a great leader when people enthusiastically do what you need them to do without you using your authority.

You can enthuse and encourage people so that they want to follow you in many different ways, and a good place to start is treating people with respect. (Chapter 3 contains more useful information on how to treat people correctly and so earn the right to lead them.)

Being Bolder

Setting relatively easy targets may give you confidence and comfort because you expect your team to achieve them, but you don't bring the best out of members of your team in this way. People apply their skills and talents more when they have to stretch themselves to achieve targets and need to get out of their comfort zone. (Turn to Chapter 6 for more on comfort zones.)

Be bold in setting and agreeing objectives and targets that stretch you and your team to make the greatest contribution you can to your organisation's success. (Chapter 7 contains lots more info in this area.)

Being bold can involve taking risks and you may, perhaps, feel uncomfortable because you're not certain of achieving demanding objectives and targets that you set yourself and your team. But playing safe means that you and your team are unlikely to perform to your full potential.

Making Things Meaningful

No doubt at times, as an employee or as a leader, you've questioned, at least in your own mind, the point or purpose of doing some tasks that you've been told to do. You know from experience that if you perceive certain work to be meaningless, you're unlikely to do it well: you may delay doing it because you have other priorities, rush through it just to get done, or simply not focus sufficiently and do a poor job. Similarly, you're unlikely fully to support a change introduced into your work area (such as a change in job roles and responsibilities, systems or procedures) when that change seems pointless.

You need to avoid your staff feeling this way. Hold conversations with work colleagues so they understand why you're asking them to do tasks or actively support a change that you intend to introduce. Better still, engage them in meaningful conversations so they can contribute their ideas and views, and question or even challenge your proposals in order to enhance your and their understanding of the issues and problems.

I propose that a better understanding of a problem is more likely to lead to a better decision being made and achieve a better outcome. (You can find much more on engaging people in meaningful conversations in Chapter 8.)

On certain occasions, such as when facing critical deadlines, you may be unable, or even not want, to involve everyone in a conversation about an issue: in such cases, you have to be decisive and instruct people to take action. But do explain your reasons for acting that way afterwards.

Striving to Gain Commitment

Employees have to comply by doing a good enough job to meet the requirements or expectations of their manager, and to avoid being disciplined. Of course most people do more than the minimum requirements, but everyone chooses whether to put in the extra effort to do outstanding work.

Ensure that all your team members choose to take ownership of their work and gain their commitment to do it to the best of their ability. Chapter 9 contains loads of great tips on being an engaging leader.

Always strive to gain the commitment of all your staff to do their work to the best of their ability, but ensure that at the very least people comply with your standards.

Getting the Most from Measurement

Many organisations invest a lot of time and effort in performance measurement/management and yet fail to achieve the best return on their investment in terms of improved performance. Reasons for not achieving the full benefits of performance measurement include the following:

- ✔ Appropriate measures haven't been identified.
- ✔ Appropriate key performance indicators (KPIs) aren't being used.
- ✔ KPIs are in conflict with each other.

Use performance measures such as KPIs effectively to ensure that they focus team members' attention on the right priorities, and create an ethos of continuous improvement in your team. Chapters 7, 14 and 18 cover measuring performance, and Chapter 15 contains a section on continuous improvement.

Avoiding Being a Victim of Change

You can't always choose the situations you find yourself in, but you can choose how you react to them. The rate of change seems to be increasing in all types of organisations due to the following:

- ✔ Advances in technology.
- ✔ Growth and globalisation of many businesses.

✔ Increasing competition.

✔ Greater customer expectations.

Such changes in your organisation can create considerable uncertainty for you and your staff.

Most of the change decisions that you're involved in or have to implement are probably made by more senior managers, and you may sometimes have to implement changes with which you disagree.

How you react in these situations is critical because your reaction has a significant impact on the people who report to you.

Avoid being a 'victim of change' and thinking that you can't do anything about these changes: you do at least choose how you communicate and introduce changes to your staff. Maintain a positive influence on how change is introduced into your workplace and look for ways in which you can increase your sphere of influence. (Flip to Chapter 12 for guidance on how to be a change agent and Chapter 7 to increase your sphere of influence.)

Celebrating People's Contributions

Quite naturally, leaders focus on the future especially during times of rapid change. Leaders have to be forward-thinking to set the direction of their company or team, and gain the commitment of everyone to go in the chosen direction. However, by focusing on the future, leaders can sometimes forget to acknowledge important aspects of the past.

One issue that many leaders overlook is the contribution that people have made to getting the organisation or team to where it is now. Employees who think that they've made an important contribution to past success can feel demoralised when their past contribution is overlooked, perhaps because the precious work was for another leader.

Celebrate the contribution that people have made and are making to the success of your team and/or organisation. (Chapters 12, 13 and 14 contain much more on leading change.)

Striking While the Iron's Hot

Some managers have good intentions to raise a team member's under-performance or unacceptable behaviour, but somehow never get round to it. Reasons for procrastinating can include the following:

- ✔ The manager is unsure how to raise the topic.
- ✔ The manager isn't assertive enough.
- ✔ The manager thinks that other priorities are more pressing.

In my experience, managerial inactivity tends to contribute to the person's behaviour or performance deteriorating further. Chapter 11 covers promoting and reinforcing your standards and working with colleagues to improve their behaviour and performance.

Act promptly – 'while the iron's hot' – when raising any instances of people not behaving or performing to your standards in order to reinforce the standards you expect.

Making a Good Team Great

I've witnessed many teams that believe they're performing pretty well and think that they're already a good team. The truth is that most teams I encounter are doing a reasonable job, but my concern is that teams that believe they're good also think that they've no need to improve. These teams tend to stop the journey towards being a great team before even starting out.

Constructively question and challenge your team, and any team you belong to for that matter, about how good it really is. Ask team members to clarify the benchmark or criteria they're using to assess how good the team is and how well it performs. (Chapter 15 describes the characteristics of great teams, and how to conduct team assessments.)

Creating Time for Coaching

Organisations are increasingly recognising that coaching is a very effective way of developing the knowledge, skills, attitude and performance of employees. Many companies are employing external coaches to work with their senior leaders to enable them to enhance their leadership ability and performance, and to become competent in coaching the people who work for them.

Invest time in developing your coaching skills, and then make time to coach each person who reports directly to you so they can enhance their skills and improve their performance. Coaching your direct reports benefits you as well as them because you can delegate some of your work and responsibilities, and free up more time to focus on other priorities.

Don't limit yourself to coaching only those people reporting directly to you: make time to informally coach your peers and even your boss! You need to be tactful as well as use current relevant evidence of unacceptable behaviour or performance when coaching people who don't report to you if you expect them to improve their performance. Chapter 11 contains useful information on making coaching part of your everyday leadership practice.

Index

Notes

FOR DUMMIES®

Making Everything Easier! ™

UK editions

BUSINESS

978-0-470-74490-1

978-0-470-74381-2

978-0-470-71382-2

REFERENCE

978-0-470-68637-9

978-0-470-68837-3

978-0-470-74535-9

HOBBIES

978-0-470-69960-7

978-0-470-68641-6

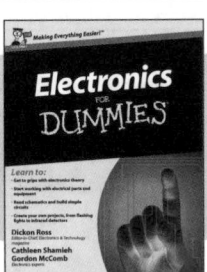

978-0-470-68178-7

Anger Management For Dummies
978-0-470-68216-6

Boosting Self-Esteem For Dummies
978-0-470-74193-1

British Sign Language
For Dummies
978-0-470-69477-0

Business NLP For Dummies
978-0-470-69757-3

Cricket For Dummies
978-0-470-03454-5

CVs For Dummies, 2nd Edition
978-0-470-74491-8

Divorce For Dummies, 2nd Edition
978-0-470-74128-3

Emotional Freedom Technique
For Dummies
978-0-470-75876-2

Emotional Healing For Dummies
978-0-470-74764-3

English Grammar For Dummies
978-0-470-05752-0

Flirting For Dummies
978-0-470-74259-4

IBS For Dummies
978-0-470-51737-6

Improving Your Relationship For
Dummies
978-0-470-68472-6

Lean Six Sigma For Dummies
978-0-470-75626-3

Life Coaching For Dummies,
2nd Edition
978-0-470-66554-1

Available wherever books are sold. For more information or to order direct go to www.wiley.com or call +44 (0) 1243 843291

14652 (p1)

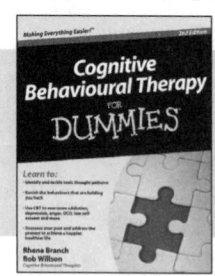

FOR DUMMIES®

A world of resources to help you grow

UK editions

SELF-HELP

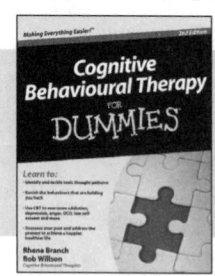

Cognitive Behavioural Therapy FOR DUMMIES

Learn to:
Rhena Branch
Rob Willson

978-0-470-66541-1

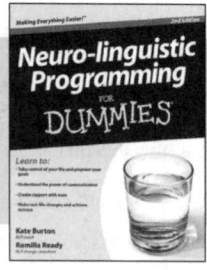

Neuro-linguistic Programming FOR DUMMIES

Learn to:
Kate Burton
Romilla Ready

978-0-470-66543-5

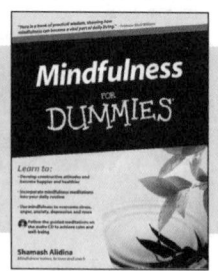

Mindfulness FOR DUMMIES

Learn to:
Shamash Alidina

978-0-470-66086-7

STUDENTS

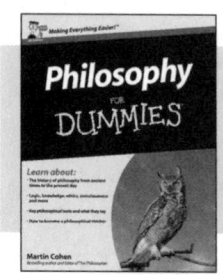

Philosophy FOR DUMMIES

Learn about:
Martin Cohen

978-0-470-68820-5

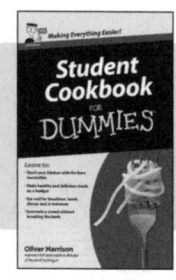

Student Cookbook FOR DUMMIES

Learn to:
Oliver Harrison

978-0-470-74711-7

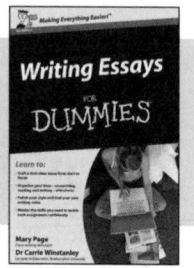

Writing Essays FOR DUMMIES

Learn to:
Mary Page
Dr Carrie Winstanley

978-0-470-74290-7

HISTORY

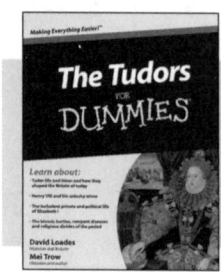

The Tudors FOR DUMMIES

Learn about:
David Loades
Mei Trow

978-0-470-68792-5

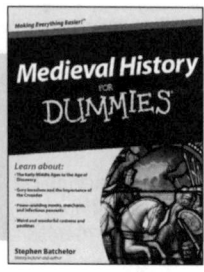

Medieval History FOR DUMMIES

Learn about:
Stephen Batchelor

978-0-470-74783-4

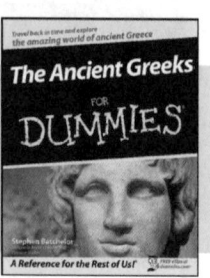

The Ancient Greeks FOR DUMMIES

Stephen Batchelor
A Reference for the Rest of Us!

978-0-470-98787-2

Origami Kit For Dummies
978-0-470-75857-1

Overcoming Depression For Dummies
978-0-470-69430-5

Positive Psychology For Dummies
978-0-470-72136-0

PRINCE2 For Dummies, 2009 Edition
978-0-470-71025-8

Psychometric Tests For Dummies
978-0-470-75366-8

Raising Happy Children
For Dummies
978-0-470-05978-4

Reading the Financial Pages
For Dummies
978-0-470-71432-4

Sage 50 Accounts For Dummies
978-0-470-71558-1

Self-Hypnosis For Dummies
978-0-470-66073-7

Starting a Business For Dummies,
2nd Edition
978-0-470-51806-9

Study Skills For Dummies
978-0-470-74047-7

Teaching English as a Foreign
Language For Dummies
978-0-470-74576-2

Teaching Skills For Dummies
978-0-470-74084-2

Time Management For Dummies
978-0-470-77765-7

Work-Life Balance For Dummies
978-0-470-71380-8